HOLY MOTHER

RAMAKRISHNA-VIVEKANANDA CENTER
OF NEW YORK
17 East 94th Street, New York, N.Y. 10028

PUBLICATIONS

By Swami Nikhilananda

HINDUISM: Its Meaning for the Liberation of the Spirit

HOLY MOTHER: Being the Life of Sri Sarada Devi, Wife of Sri Ramakrishna and Helpmate in His Mission

MAN IN SEARCH OF IMMORTALITY: Testimonials from the Hindu Scriptures

VIVEKANANDA: A BIOGRAPHY

Translated by Swami Nikhilananda

THE BHAGAVAD GITA

THE BHAGAVAD GITA (Pocket Edition)

THE GOSPEL OF SRI RAMAKRISHNA

THE GOSPEL OF SRI RAMAKRISHNA (Abridged Edition)

SELF-KNOWLEDGE (Atmabodha)

THE UPANISHADS Volumes I, II, III, and IV

By Swami Vivekananda

INSPIRED TALKS, My Master and Other Writings

JNANA-YOGA

KARMA-YOGA AND BHAKTI-YOGA

RAJA-YOGA

VIVEKANANDA: THE YOGAS AND OTHER WORKS
(Chosen and with a Biography by Swami Nikhilananda)

HOLY MOTHER

HOLY MOTHER

Being the Life of Sri Sarada Devi
Wife of Sri Ramakrishna
and Helpmate in His Mission

by

SWAMI NIKHILANANDA

RAMAKRISHNA-VIVEKANANDA CENTER
New York

HOLY MOTHER

Second Printing 1982

ISBN 0-911206-20-5

Library of Congress Catalog Card Number: 62-13423

Preface

Holy Mother was the wife of Sri Ramakrishna (1836–1886), now regarded in India and abroad as a rare manifestation of divinity in modern times. She was his constant companion during the most eventful period of his life and a witness of his spiritual experiences. Sri Ramakrishna himself moulded her life and assigned her place in the carrying out of his mission after his death.

Outwardly Holy Mother lived as an average Hindu woman, devoting herself to the faithful discharge of her household duties, often unpleasant and frustrating. Inwardly she practised total non-attachment and remained undisturbed by what happened in the physical world. Never did her mind deviate from contact with God. Thus she has become, today, a model for both householders and world-renouncing monks.

I deem it necessary to point out here two important features of her teachings and personality which may help the general reader, especially anyone unfamiliar with the background of Hindu culture, to respond sympathetically to her life. First, Holy Mother, when instructing her disciples, often asked them to regard Sri Ramakrishna as God incarnate. She accepted other Divine Incarnations, too, but looked upon Sri Ramakrishna, on account of his unceasing absorption in God, his total renunciation, and his acceptance of different faiths as valid ways to the realization of God, as the one suited to our present age. In her own experience she realized her husband's divinity. Therefore it was natural for her to speak of him as a visible symbol of the Godhead. But she was by no means dogmatic or exclusive. In teaching seekers who cherished other spiritual ideals, she always deepened their faith in these.

Second, Holy Mother is often described in this book by such epithets as the Mother of the Universe and the Divine Power. These are not mere sentimental expressions on the part of her devotees, but have a philosophical significance. According to Vedānta philosophy, Brahman, or Ultimate Reality, is inactive. It is not, Itself, involved in the activities of creation, preservation, and dissolution. These are carried on by Its inscrutable energy, called māyā or Śakti. Brahman and Śakti are inseparable, like fire and its power to burn or a gem and its lustre. The two names are given to one and the same Reality according to Its two different functions. The whole universe of the living and non-living is the projection of this divine energy, which, like an earthly mother, produces creatures from its womb and then nourishes them. This energy, again, finally withdraws the created beings into the Godhead, thus liberating them from the bondage of the world. The Hindus therefore regard it as the Mother and Saviour of all. Though this energy is present in all creatures, to a Hindu it resembles a woman more than a man. Undoubtedly all women are channels of Śakti, but a woman totally undefiled by worldliness becomes its most potent channel. Holy Mother was such a woman. Thus she too has been described as the Saviour or the Divine Mother of the Universe. She looked on all children born of a woman's womb as her own.

There are several books published in India, both in English and in local vernaculars, about the life and teachings of Holy Mother. I have freely borrowed facts and ideas from some of them, and hereby express my indebtedness to the authors. Swami Gambhirananda's book, published in English and in Bengali by the Sri Ramakrishna Math, Madras, and the Udbodhan, Calcutta, respectively, contains authenticated facts. Manadasankar Das Gupta's Bengali life analyses these facts admirably. The life of Holy Mother by Swami Tapasyananda and Swami Nikhilananda, in English, also published by the Sri Ramakrishna

Math, Madras, gives in addition a number of Holy Mother's conversations. I have included in the present book some of my own reminiscences.

In order to indicate Holy Mother's place in the history and development of Indian womanhood, I have devoted the introductory chapter to a discussion of some of the great women of India. A glossary has been added to explain terms unfamiliar in the West.

Mr. James Holsaert has edited the entire manuscript with painstaking care and given many valuable suggestions to make the book more easily understandable, especially to Western readers. Swami Atmaghanananda, besides editing the manuscript, has worked hard in looking after many mechanical details in order to prepare it for the press. Mr. Joseph Campbell, too, has revised the manuscript and made helpful suggestions. I am grateful to all of them. Though I have accepted many suggestions from the editors, I take full responsibility for the reflections and interpretations in this book. The manuscript has had to be typed several times. Mr. and Mrs. Harold Knapik, Mabel Colloredo-Mansfeld, and Dorothy Kruger cheerfully performed this chore. I am grateful to them also. The publication of this volume has been made possible through the generosity of Mr. and Mrs. Chester F. Carlson, and I express to them, as well, my deep gratitude.

Holy Mother's life and teachings have a direct bearing on the present human situation. Physical scientists, and professional philosophers influenced by the scientific method of reason and experimentation, are preoccupied to discover the laws which explain and control life and nature. They are revealing various dimensions of reality which tell us about man and the world and also how to utilize this knowledge for man's physical welfare. There is a growing number of thoughtful people who regard intellectual knowledge, unillumined by spiritual insight, as inadequate to satisfy the deep yearning of the soul. They look to religion for inner peace. But unfortunately most of the religions, as practised today, are cluttered with dogmas and creeds that conceal the truth. Men want a guide with direct experience of the true nature of the Godhead, the world, and the soul. Only thus can his words and actions become imbued with love and compassion. Moreover, this experience, if it is to transform men's lower nature and lead to the welfare of all, must be expressed in simple words. Perceptive readers may find in Holy Mother's life the fulfilment of these conditions. They will also find one who, instead of luxuriating in the enjoyment of inner peace, worked till the last moment of her life to transmit that peace to others.

This book, I believe, will be a source of inspiration to the growing number of Sri Ramakrishna's devotees and admirers among English-speaking people. Slowly Holy Mother's influence will infiltrate the general thought current of the world and give an impetus to spiritual seekers everywhere, irrespective of their religious affiliations.

NIKHILANANDA

Vivekananda Cottage
Thousand Island Park, N. Y.
July 21, 1961

Contents

Illustrations

Cover illustration:
The Temple of Holy Mother at the Belur Math

a	has the sound of				*o* in *come.*
ā	”	”	”	”	*a* in *far.*
e	”	”	”	”	*a* in *evade.*
i	”	”	”	”	*ee* in *feel.*
o	”	”	”	”	*o* in *note.*
u	”	”	”	”	*u* in *rule.*

ai, ay	has the sound of				*oy* in *boy.*
au	”	”	”	”	*o* pronounced deep in the throat.
ch	”	”	”	”	*ch* in *church.*
ḍ	”	”	”	”	hard *d* in English.
g	”	”	”	”	*g* in *god.*
jn	”	”	”	”	hard *gy* in English.
ś	”	”	”	”	*sh* in *shut.*

sh may be pronounced as in English.
t and d are pronounced as in French.
th has the sound of *t-h* in *boat-house.*

Other consonants appearing in the transliterations are pronounced as in English.

Diacritical marks have generally not been used in proper names belonging to recent times or in modern and well-known geographical names.

Introduction: Women of India

FOR ONE FULL YEAR, from December 27, 1953, to December 26, 1954, India celebrated the hundredth anniversary of the birth of Sri Sarada Devi, who is today affectionately and respectfully referred to by her devotees as Holy Mother. During that centenary countless people paid homage to her memory. Special worship was offered. There were street processions in her honour, and newspapers published articles and arranged special supplements. Meetings were addressed by Governors of Indian States, Cabinet members, men of letters, and other leaders paying tribute to her saintliness. The centenary was also observed outside India: in Ceylon, Burma, England, France, the Argentine Republic, in some of the principal cities of the United States of America, and in other parts of the world. Cutting across the barriers of colour, caste, race, creed, and nationality, the occasion evoked a spontaneous response among the devotees of Sri Ramakrishna and Holy Mother. Today there are functioning numerous public institutions—schools, hostels for students, free hospitals and dispensaries, monasteries and convents—associated with Holy Mother's name, which draw inspiration from her life and teachings. Yet of the sixty-seven years of her mortal existence, thirty-seven were spent with her relatives, out of the public gaze. And during the rest of her life she was known personally to only a few hundred disciples. Much of her life was spent in the village of her birth. Outwardly it was the ordinary life of an average Hindu woman, dedicated to back-breaking, humdrum worldly duties. This or-

1

dinariness—which is actually quite extraordinary—she maintained in her dealings with her husband, her disciples, her relatives, and her visitors. Within a few years of her death this almost illiterate woman was recognized as a rarely illumined soul, the First Lady of spiritual India. Today she receives the same respect as Sri Ramakrishna from those acquainted with their lives.

Sarada Devi[1] is a genuine product of the Indian soil. She was moulded by the tradition of the nation and influenced by its racial unconscious. The great women of India of all times have spoken to us through her. She is the fulfilment of the spiritual aspirations of millions of Hindu women of the past, and is a pointer to the women of the present and the future. In order to comprehend Sarada Devi's life, readers, especially non-Hindus, should know something of the Indian women who have helped throughout history to shape the ideal of Indian womanhood. Let us consider here, briefly, the position of women in the Hindu religion and society. Thus we shall be able to understand Sarada Devi's place in India's spiritual culture.

The Hindu religion honours womanhood, though Hindu society has sometimes deviated from this ideal. Hinduism asserts the Motherhood of God on a philosophical basis. We shall discuss this important topic in the course of the book. The deity controlling knowledge, Sarasvati, is female. The Vedas urge that women, equally with men, be given opportunities in education and the various activities of society. In Vedic times they were encouraged to cultivate the highest knowledge, the Knowledge of Brahman, though in several respects a woman's dependence upon man was acknowledged. Manu, the great Hindu lawgiver, declared that the gods are pleased where women are honoured; where they are dishonoured all works become fruitless. Conditioned by social and

---

[1] The word *Devi*, meaning goddess, is generally used by a married woman as her last name, instead of the family name of her husband.

religious traditions, Indian women have remained essentially feminine. They give and do not demand. Not assertive, but modest, they find joy through love and unselfish service. A Hindu woman gladly obeys a man if he is honourable. She often dares to face a situation even though it means suffering—something a man cannot always do. By no means is she meek or docile when challenged by injustice or wickedness.

What has been the status of women in Hindu society? With the ebb and flow of India's political and economic condition, women's status has gone up and down. When India was free women were unfettered. But when the country came under foreign subjection, society became rigid and conservative: women were denied freedom. During the Moslem rule, purdah was introduced in northern India and a general backwardness of women followed. With the attainment of India's freedom in 1947, Hindu women again came out of seclusion and took a larger part in the national life. Perhaps the darkest period of Indian culture was the last three hundred years, when the Moslem empire disintegrated and the British rule was consolidated. The latter diverted the attention of Hindu intellectuals to the Western way of life. Even then Indian women contributed to keeping the national ideals alive. Though the vast majority of them during these dark days were illiterate, and victims of social and religious injustice, yet one finds bright lights shining here and there, demonstrating the potentiality of Indian womanhood. Whatever the situation, women never lost their inner vitality.

Hinduism speaks of the wife as the *sahadharmini*, the co-partner of the husband in spiritual pursuits. Marriage does not imply the superiority of the husband or the inferiority of the wife. The one is incomplete without the other. This concept is symbolized by the Hindu deity Ardhanāriśvara, of which one half is female and the other half male. When a man regards his wife only as an object to satisfy physical desire, disaster befalls the family. A Hindu scripture says: "She is the Goddess of

Fortune for the righteous and the force of evil for the wicked."

From the Hindu standpoint, a woman may be a mother, a wife, a sister, or something else, but basically she is the mother. An unknown woman, even though she may be a beggar, is often addressed as "Mother." In a Hindu family it is the mother, and not the wife, who occupies the central position. A man marries and brings home his wife, who is regarded by his parents as a daughter. The bride obeys the mother-in-law in all family affairs. She must not stand between mother and son. The mother of her husband receives the same respect from her that she receives from her own son. Why is the mother so highly respected in a Hindu family and regarded as a veritable goddess? She is the embodiment of the Motherhood of God. Furthermore, a true mother's self-sacrificing love is without parallel. It is a love that never seeks to possess, but is content simply to give—a giving that could not wish return. The mother is nearer to the children than the father. The father chastises and the mother protects. The child can always make demands upon his mother. She is ready to forgive all his iniquities. According to a Hindu proverb, there can be a bad son, but never a bad mother.

In the building up and the preservation of Indian culture, women have played a significant and important part. Like women everywhere, as mothers, wives, and sisters, they have maintained the sweetness of the Hindu home and exerted a beneficial influence upon men. In a wider field, too, women have functioned, whenever the occasion arose, in responsible positions: as queens regent or regnant, as administrators, philosophers, mystics, scholars, and poets. Whether performing the ordinary duties of home or engaged in strenuous public work, they have exhibited calmness, patience, dignity, and other moral virtues of a high order. The literature of India—sacred or secular, written or oral—has preserved their memory since the dawn of history. Some of these characters are mythological, and some historical. Out of the thousands of women of distinction, we shall simply consider a few to show the varied nature of their character and activities.[1]

Let us first turn to the modern period. This period begins with the latter half of the nineteenth century, when the British rule was fully established. Educated people came in contact with Western culture and the national life took a new direction. In this renaissance, Indian women's inner potentialities found expression through many channels. In India's struggle for political freedom during the present century, men and women fought side by side, courted jail and persecution together. When India attained freedom, women were given, without hesitation, such positions as those of Governor of a Province, Ambassador, and Member of Parliament or Cabinet. These Indian women, like their sisters in the past, did not have to compete with men. Whenever a competent woman appeared, no attempt was made to suppress her. Since the eighties of the last century, Hindu girls have been studying in universities along with boys. After India became free, hundreds of Hindu women, often alone and sometimes with their husbands, began coming to Europe and America every year to acquire higher knowledge in science, technology, medicine, and the humanities. A few of them have secured teaching jobs in Western universities. Indian women suffer today in the estimation of the world not because of any lack of achievements on their part, but because of the world's ignorance of their achievements.

Sarojini Naidu (1879-1949) was a woman of versatile genius. A poet, idealist, and patriot, she was an effective speaker who thrilled audiences with the magic of her diction and eloquence. In 1895 Sarojini went to England for higher study and was encouraged by leading English critics to develop her poetic gift. She wrote poems about the Indian landscape, common men and women, Moghul princes and princesses, the joys and sor-

---

[1] For a fuller account of the subject, see *Great Women of India*, Mayavati, India: Advaita Āshrama, 1953.

rows of man's everyday life, and about her haunting desire for peace and tranquillity.

Sarojini Naidu flung herself into the vortex of India's political struggle. A follower of Gandhi, she pleaded for the emancipation of the depressed classes and for Hindu-Moslem unity, and went to jail. She was elected President of the Indian National Congress in 1925, and in independent India she became the first Governor of the Province of Uttara Pradesh in northern India. Mahatma Gandhi's wife Kasturbai Gandhi, too, stood always by her husband's side in his political activities. Her humility, unobtrusiveness, and motherly solicitude for the welfare of others have endeared her to millions of Indians.

The Moslem domination of India, which had preceded the British, lasted for about seven hundred and fifty years, from the eleventh century to the middle of the eighteenth. The alien rulers challenged the religious traditions, social integrity, and moral values of the country. India accepted the challenge. During that critical period women did not lag behind. They produced mystics, poets, able administrators, and military commanders.

An outstanding woman saint born probably before the twelfth century in southern India was Godāi, popularly known as Andal. Andal imbibed her father's devotional fervour and dedicated her body and soul to Vishnu, who was worshipped in her part of the country as Ranganātha. She refused to marry, and Ranganātha became the sole object of her love and devotion. She lived in her own world, created by her spiritual enthusiasm and filled with the living presence of Ranganātha and His companions. To win His love she observed vows and penances and completely detached herself from the world. Her father began to wonder how to wed his daughter to the Deity, when Ranganātha bade him in a dream to take her to the holy shrine at Srirangam. Attired in bridal garments, Andal went to the temple and fell into an ecstasy. According to tradition, she disappeared into the image. Andal composed many songs which have enriched Tamil poetry. She realized God through ecstatic love, without the practice of austerities and other spiritual disciplines.

Rudrāmbā, the ruler of Warangel, was born in southern India in the thirteenth century and was trained by her father in the art of administration. When she acceded to the throne in 1262, some of her own chieftains started a rebellion and a neighbouring king invaded the country. Evidently they belittled the power of a woman. But Rudrāmbā, who had won over the hearts of her officers by her motherly affection, suppressed the trouble-makers.

She ruled for thirty-five years, maintaining the country's peace and security, and promoted her subjects' welfare by digging tanks and canals, granting concessions to merchants in order to encourage trade and industry, and establishing centres for brāhmin scholars to foster knowledge. Marco Polo visited her kingdom and wrote about its flourishing condition with particular reference to diamond mining.

During the Moslem rule of Delhi, Rājputāna, the cradle of Hindu chivalry, nurtured many heroic women who not only fought against the alien enemies on the battlefield but, when defeated, often immolated themselves on burning pyres in order to save their honour from the invaders' lust. When the Rājput heroes came home from battle, their wives would require them to show their wounds. If the men bore marks on their backs they were regarded as deserters and told to fight again; only those who had wounds on their chests were allowed to enter the house. When the Rājput king Pritvirāj was about to give battle to his Moslem adversary, his queen, Samjuktā, armed him for the encounter and exhorted him to fight to the last, sacrificing his life if necessary. This noble spirit permeated even the common people. Pānnā, the nurse of a royal infant, was guarding her precious ward when a Moslem enemy entered the room. The nurse's own child was asleep in another bed. When the assassin asked which the prince was, she unhesitatingly pointed to her own child and witnessed his death without betraying the slightest emotion.

Padmini, queen of Rānā Ratan Singh of Mewār, has been deservedly given a high place in the epic account of Rājput chivalry. When Ālāuddin, the Moslem Emperor of Delhi, besieged the famous citadel of Chitor, the Rājputs fought against their ruthless enemies for eight months, but finally had to give way. Before the surrender of the fortress in 1303, the brave women, under the leadership of Padmini, plunged into a huge fire to escape humiliation from their conquerors. The pyre was lighted in a subterranean chamber and the male defenders of Chitor watched their wives and daughters, to the number of several thousand, marching to it in procession, Padmini bringing up the rear. The women entered the chamber and the door was closed upon them. As they could not live with honour, they died with honour.

Among the reigning queens during the Moslem period, Ahalyābāi (1735-1795) is respected for her piety and political wisdom. The daughter of a petty Mārhāttā chieftain, she was married to the ruler of Indore in central India. Her family life was rather tragic. Her indolent and irresponsible husband died at an early age and was followed by her son and daughter. Her father-in-law trained Ahalyābāi in the collection of revenue, writing of dispatches, and management of the army. She was often present on the battlefield. After her husband's death she became the ruler of the State. A contemporary English historian has said that her success in the internal administration of her domain was most wonderful and that she certainly appeared, within her limited sphere, to have been one of the finest and most extraordinary rulers that ever existed. Ahalyābāi undertook many religious and philanthropic activities and built highways, rest-houses, and temples, the most noteworthy being the road from Benares to Calcutta, and the temples at Somnath in Kathiwar, Gaya, and Benares.

We shall bring this section to a close with the story of God-intoxicated Mirā. Her name has been cherished by Hindu religious devotees for the past four hundred years and is not altogether unknown to the West. Mirābāi was born towards the end of the fifteenth or in the early part of the sixteenth century. A princess by both birth and marriage, she gave her heart and soul to her Chosen Ideal, Sri Krishna, and renounced the world at an early age in quest of her Divine Beloved. She spent many years at Mathura and Vrindavan, places associated with the memory of Sri Krishna, and died in 1546. It is said that the Emperor Ākbar visited her, attracted by her piety. Mirābāi has left behind a precious legacy in the form of devotional songs which have been sung by Hindus of all classes from Mahatma Gandhi to the humblest peasant. Imbued with simplicity of feeling and devotion to God, they have an irresistible appeal.

Mirā was not deterred from her spiritual path by the many temptations of her social position or the criticism of her contemporaries, nor by her relatives' persecution. Completely detached from the world, she always sought the company of holy men, and found solace in the repetition of God's name.

But the personages who have exerted the greatest influence upon Hindu culture have been described in the two epics: the *Rāmāyana* and the *Mahābhārata*. These epics centre, respectively, round the lives of Rāma and Krishna, who are regarded by Hindus as Divine Incarnations. The stories have a core of historic truth though they are embroidered with many poetic fancies. They have inspired many songs, plays, musical dramas, and poems, to the enrichment of Indian literature. They narrate actions, impulses, and desires of men and women of all kinds, from the most saintly to the utterly depraved. But from all this emerges one principle: the Hindu concept of dharma, or the moral order which sustains and holds together the universe and also guides upward the lives of individuals. The epics teach that in spite of the apparent and temporary triumph of wickedness, righteousness ultimately prevails.

Through the stories of the *Rāmāyana* and the *Mahābhārata*

the inner strength of Indian womanhood is revealed. The majority of these women were householders who attained to spiritual eminence through the faithful discharge of their daily duties and the display of courage and serenity in the midst of the tribulations of worldly life. We shall choose for our models three great women: Gāndhāri and Sāvitri from the *Mahābhārata,* and Sitā from the *Rāmāyana.*

Born a princess, Gāndhāri was married to the blind king Dhritarāshtra. From the day of her marriage she put a heavy bandage over her eyes so that she would not enjoy the sight of the outer world denied to her husband. She was the mother of one hundred sons, headed by Duryodhana, all of whom were greedy and wicked. She always asked them to follow the path of righteousness and warned them that the price of sin was death. Their rivals were their five cousins, known as the Pāndavas, who were noble and righteous. Gāndhāri's sons unjustly deprived the Pāndavas of their legitimate kingdom and were soon engaged in a terrible war—the war which forms the background of the Bhagavad Gitā. During the war, when Duryodhana asked Gāndhāri every morning for her blessing, she grimly reminded him of the ultimate victory of righteousness. When, inevitably, Gāndhāri's sons perished in the war, she and her husband decided to retire into the Himalayas to spend their last days in meditation on God. The final leave-taking was a touching one. Kunti, the mother of the victorious Pāndavas, led the procession. Gāndhāri, who had imposed upon herself voluntary blindness, placed her hands on Kunti's shoulders, and her blind husband placed his hands on the shoulders of the queen. The pilgrims settled in the sacred Himalayas and at last died in a forest fire, meditating on God. Though Gāndhāri's body burned slowly, she kept her eyes bandaged to the end. She was indeed a woman of great dignity and uprightness.

The story of Sāvitri shows that genuine love can nullify the decree of fate and even triumph over death. The only child of

King Aśvapati, she was brought up in royal luxury, and soon grew to be a maiden of exquisite beauty, versed in all the noble arts. No king or prince dared ask for such an accomplished girl in marriage. At the suggestion of her father, she herself set out to find a suitable husband. Sāvitri was not interested in princes or aristocrats. Entering a forest, accompanied by wise elders of the court, she met Satyavān, the son of an old blind king who, with his wife, was leading the life of an exiled hermit. The boy was completely devoted to his parents, for whom he gathered food and chopped fuel.

Sāvitri and Satyavān fell in love with each other at first sight. The princess returned to the court and told her father and mother about her choice. A sage present at once gave the warning that Satyavān would die within a year from that day and that nothing could alter his fate. Aśvapati asked his daughter to look for another man. But Sāvitri had already chosen Satyavān to be her husband and felt that she would be unchaste if she now transferred her love to someone else. She told her father that she was determined to marry Satyavān, whether he had a short or a long life, whether he was virtuous or wicked, whether he was a prince or a beggar. They were married and Sāvitri decided to live in the forest and devote herself to the service of her husband's father and mother, discarding her jewels and costly apparel. She was extremely happy in the company of Satyavān, but could not brush away from her mind the holy man's words about his death, though she did not reveal this prophecy to anyone.

Time passed and only four days were left before the arrival of the fateful moment. Sāvitri fasted and prayed day and night. On the morning of the fourth day she performed her usual household duties with a heavy heart, without betraying her emotion in the slightest degree. When Satyavān was ready to go to the forest, axe in hand, to cut fuel, she asked to accompany him. Delighted to have her by his side, he made her sit under a tree and began to chop wood. She kept an unwavering eye on him and suddenly noticed that the motion of his hands was gradually slowing down and the sound of the strokes was becoming weaker. Then he staggered towards her, saying that he was about to faint. As Satyavān lay on the ground with his head on her lap, she saw at a distance a black figure with red eyes, carrying a noose in his hand. He said to Sāvitri that he was Yama, the Lord of the nether world, the abode of the dead. Reminding her that Satyavān's days on earth were over, he drew the soul from his body, tied it with the noose, and started on his way. Sāvitri followed Yama, who at length turned round and asked her to return home and prepare her husband's funeral rites. She reminded him that an eternal law bound husband and wife together, and that she would not be parted from him. The King of Death, in order to console her, offered Sāvitri several boons which would restore her father-in-law's eyesight and kingdom and bless her own father with worthy sons to carry on the royal duties after his death. Then, because she continued to follow her husband's soul, Yama offered her one more boon—anything except Satyavān's life. This time Sāvitri prayed to him for one hundred sons, strong and wise, to perpetuate her line. Yama absent-mindedly granted the favour and asked Sāvitri to depart peacefully. Thereupon Sāvitri asked Yama how she could have children unless her husband was restored to life. She begged him to give back Satyavān to her so that his words might come true. The King of Death had no alternative but to return Satyavān to Sāvitri, and was happy to be outwitted by a woman so pure, fearless, and loyal. On account of her chaste love for her husband, Sāvitri has been raised to the position of a goddess, and even now orthodox Hindu women observe religious rites for three days, every year, in her honour.

The paragon of all the women mentioned in the epics is, of course, Sitā, whose consort, Rāma, is worshipped by the Hindus as an Incarnation of God. Her memory has been cherished by virtuous women in India for the past two thousand years. In her the virtues of her contemporaries found full expression, without any of their blemishes. Even today, when a young woman is blessed by an elder, she is asked to "be like Sitā."

According to the *Rāmāyana*, Sitā, as a newly born baby, was lying in a covered pot under the earth when she was discovered by King Janaka in the course of his ploughing a field. She was at once adopted by Janaka and brought up as a royal princess, and is therefore often referred to as the daughter of Mother Earth. In due course she was married to Prince Rāma. They were living happily when a calamity befell Rāma. His father, King Daśaratha, had arranged a day to declare him, with proper ceremony, as his heir-apparent. His second queen, however, wanted her own son to be his successor and through an evil machination managed to banish Rāma to the forest for fourteen years to lead the life of an ascetic. Sitā and Lakshmana, one of Rāma's brothers, accompanied Rāma in spite of his earnest request that his consort live at the palace performing her religious and household duties.

Rāma and his companions settled down to an austere life, often spending their time in the company of hermits. Meanwhile Rāvana, the monster[2] king of Ceylon, who was a slave of lust and greed, heard of Sitā's great beauty and wanted her as a concubine. Afraid of Rāma's power and realizing his own inability to take possession of her openly, he resorted to guile. He and his companions could assume, through their magical powers, any form they wanted. One day he sent one of his followers in the guise of a golden deer to wander about before Rāma's hut. Sitā, yielding to a woman's uncontrollable fancy, begged Rāma to capture the deer for her, and he followed the strange animal into the deep forest. Rāvana, taking this opportunity, knocked at Rāma's hut in the guise of a mendicant. As Sitā

---

[2] The monsters and monkeys described in the *Rāmāyana* most probably refer to the non-Āryans who lived in Ceylon and southern India. They had developed their own civilization and some of them possessed high moral and spiritual virtues.

came out, the monster resumed his real form, seized her, and carried her in his aerial chariot to Ceylon.

Now began a gruelling period of anguish for Sitā. Rāvana tried to seduce her with jewels, fine apparel, and other luxuries. He also threatened her with torture and destruction. Nothing could disturb her fidelity to Rāma.

In the meantime Rāma gathered an army and attacked Ceylon. In the battle that followed, Rāvana was killed and Sitā rescued. As she was brought to Rāma's presence, Rāma told her before the assembled crowd that he could not take her back because she had spent such a long time in Rāvana's palace. How would the world know what sort of life she had lived there? He further explained that he had killed Rāvana to vindicate the honour of his family and said that now she was free to live where she liked. Rāma wanted to set an example to his people. Sitā, stunned to hear these cruel words and not wishing to live, ordered a funeral pyre to be made. Pleading her innocence, she entered the fire and prayed that if she was chaste the fire might protect her. Even the hair of her body remained untouched, and Sitā walked out triumphant from the ordeal.

Rāma returned to his ancestral capital with Sitā and there was jubilation among the people. But this happiness was short-lived. A whisper went around about Rāma's having taken back his wife though she had lived long in a stranger's palace. Though himself fully convinced of her purity, he brushed aside his deep love for the queen in obedience to his duty as a king who must be a model for his subjects to follow. He banished Sitā, who was now pregnant, to the hermitage of Vālmiki, the author of the *Rāmāyana*. She understood the predicament of her husband and did not bear any ill feeling against him. In the hermitage she gave birth to twin sons.

Soon a reconciliation was brought about and Sitā returned to the palace. But the cup of her suffering was not yet full. Rāma wanted to convince sceptics of Sitā's chastity and asked her to go through a second ordeal by fire. This was too much for the proud queen. She felt, further, that the purpose of her companionship with Rāma was fulfilled; for his line was assured through the twin sons, who in due course would inherit the throne. Again proclaiming her purity before the assembled people, she prayed to Mother Earth to accept her into her bosom. The earth parted and Sitā disappeared.

As a wife who resisted torture and temptation to preserve her marriage vows, and as a royal consort who sacrificed life itself in order to uphold her husband before the world as an ideal king, Sitā is, indeed, without peer in the history of Indian womanhood.

Let us now go to the Upanishads, the philosophical section of the Vedas, which are the foundation of the different systems of Hindu philosophy systematically developed in a later period. In the *Brihadāranyaka Upanishad* we encounter a woman of great spiritual insight. Maitreyi was the second wife of Yājnavalkya, the outstanding philosopher of his time. When her husband, after the completion of his householder's duties, was about to embrace the monastic life, he wanted to divide his property between his two wives. Maitreyi asked him whether, if the whole earth, full of wealth, belonged to her, she would thereby attain to immortality. Yājnavalkya answered that she could not conquer death through wealth, but that wealth would enable her to lead a comfortable life. The wise woman lost her interest in wealth and sought to know the secret of immortality. Yājnavalkya taught her about the real nature of the soul, which alone is immortal, non-dual, and divine. The individual soul is one with the Supreme Soul, called Brahman. Realizing its true nature, the individual soul merges in Brahman. Maitreyi was frightened at the idea of losing her individuality. Her husband then explained that the individual soul is a part of the relative world, created by ignorance, where one sees another, hears another, and deals with another. But when the oneness of existence is experienced, there is found no separate object which one can see, hear, or deal with. This realization makes one truly free and immortal.[3]

The Vedic truths are regarded by the Hindus as eternal and uncreated by human intellect, but revealed to certain highly developed souls called rishis or seers. These seers gave expression to their experiences through the Vedic hymns. Among the seers one finds women. The Vedas mention twenty-seven Brahmavādinis or women seers. One of them, perhaps an exceptional one, known as Vāch, expressed in an excellent hymn the experience of her oneness with the Power behind the universe. In that hymn she declared that she was the Queen of the land, the bringer of treasure. She was the Knower and the first among the gods to be propitiated by sacrifice. She was manifold in forms and immanent in everything. By her one ate, one saw, and one breathed. They who did not know her declined. Whomsoever she loved, him she made formidable: the Creator God, the man of vision, the man of intellect. She entered and possessed the heavens and the earth. She gave birth to the Sky-god. Her birthplace was the ocean above and below the sky. She stood pervading the universe with her body. Blowing like a wind, she brought into being all the worlds. By her own greatness she transcended the heavens and the earth.[4]

In this revelation one sees the germ of the concepts of the Motherhood of God and the divinity of woman, which are special features of Hinduism.

In the foregoing pages we have pointed out some of the outstanding virtues of Indian womanhood: courage, serenity, self-control, sweetness, compassion, wisdom, and an intimate relationship with God. We have also tried to indicate how great women of India have risen to the occasion, however perilous, and with dignity suited their conduct to the demands of the time, place, and particular situation. In the pages to follow we

---

[3] *Brihadāranyaka Upanishad* II. iv. 2-3.
[4] *Rig-Veda* X. 125.

shall try to show that Sarada Devi, Holy Mother, possessed all these virtues. Though she was our contemporary, through her a Hindu can look farthest into India's past and also far into her future. Since the acquisition of the virtues found in Holy Mother is the dream of all good women, Holy Mother may aptly become a symbol of the aspiration of women everywhere.

Early Life

S ARADA DEVI WAS BORN in a poor brāhmin family at Jayrambati, a remote wayside village of Bengal. The village is situated on the southeastern border of Bankura District, about
sixty miles northwest of Calcutta. The Amodar, a perennial
small stream of transparent water which contains plentiful fish,
flows by the northern boundary of the village. Here, during
childhood, Sarada Devi bathed with her little brothers and
sister. She called it "our Ganges." After bathing they often enjoyed on its bank, before returning home, their simple refreshment of puffed rice. There are two small peninsulas formed by
the stream. One was used as a cremation ground, and the other,
on which grew banyan, mango, and other large trees, later became a favourite place of meditation for some of Sri Ramakrishna's disciples.

Compared to the rest of the district, Jayrambati is relatively
fertile. Vast fields spread on all sides. Hard-working villagers
raise paddy, potatoes, spices, and vegetables of different kinds.
In Sarada Devi's time cotton was also grown. As far as staple
foods were concerned the village was self-sufficient. But the villagers had to purchase other necessary articles, such as cloth,
salt, and oil, from neighbouring villages, where they also sold
their surplus foodstuffs. Though Bankura was notorious for
malaria and for scarcity of food, the people of Jayrambati, in
the last century, were fairly healthy and prosperous.

The village has several tanks, which supply it with water for
bathing, washing, drinking, and other purposes. At the time of

Sarada Devi's birth it was not easily accessible from the outside world. People coming from Calcutta had to walk or ride in palanquins through extensive meadows and by lonely roads often infested by highwaymen. Today one can go to Jayrambati by motor. The nearest railway station, at Vishnupur, is about twenty-six miles away. Travellers also traversed this distance in bullock carts, which took them to Koalpara or to Kotalpur. Kotalpur is about six miles from Jayrambati, and Koalpara four miles. Kamarpukur, only three miles to the east, was Sri Ramakrishna's birthplace. A hundred years ago Jayrambati had no shops. But today one can buy from its stalls cigarettes, tea, and a few other commodities hitherto unknown to the villagers. Sarada Devi loved this peaceful and simple village and respected it as if it were superior to heaven itself.

About a hundred families lived at Jayrambati, in mud huts with thatched roofs. Besides two brāhmin families, the village had families of barbers, blacksmiths, farmers, dairymen, and manual labourers. A children's school held its classes on the porch of a temple. Religious festivals, performances of religious plays, and recitals from Hindu mythology brought relief from the monotony of their daily routine. There are several small temples at Jayrambati, the chief one being dedicated to Simhavāhini, an aspect of the Divine Mother represented as riding on a lion, who is the patron deity of the village. People from neighbouring villages often worship in these temples.

It is doubtful whether any Westerners set foot in Jayrambati during Holy Mother's lifetime. Because of their association with the British rulers of India, they were regarded with awe by villagers, while orthodox Hindus, especially of the upper classes, considered their touch polluting to food and drink, and so shunned them. But now many people from abroad make pilgrimages to Jayrambati, in order to visit Sarada Devi's birthplace, and are greeted by the villagers with cordiality and affection. The inhabitants of Jayrambati, in spite of caste and economic barriers, lived happily as members of one family, the young people addressing their elders by such names as Uncle and Aunt.

The two brāhmin families of Jayrambati were the Mukherjees and the Bannerjees. The village had been their home for many generations, and they were related by ties of blood. Rāma was the family deity of the Mukherjees.

Ramachandra Mukherjee was Holy Mother's father, and Shyamasundari her mother. The father was upright, truthful, and devout. Though poor, he did not accept gifts indiscriminately. Of him Sarada Devi once remarked: "He was a very righteous man, a sincere devotee of Rāma. He had such a good heart and amiable nature that anyone passing by his house would be invited by him to share a smoke. He greatly enjoyed smoking and prepared the smoke himself." Shyamasundari was her husband's peer in every respect. About her Holy Mother said: "Mother was guileless and kind." She neatly organized every detail of the household and derived special pleasure from feeding people and helping them in various ways. Many years later Sarada Devi, speaking of her parents' virtuous nature, remarked: "How could I have been born in that family if my father and mother had not practised religious austerities?"

The birth of a saint or a godly person is often associated with supernatural phenomena, and there are two relevant legends about Sarada Devi's birth.

One day Shyamasundari was returning to Jayrambati from a visit to her father's house, when she sat under a tree in a wooded spot. Suddenly she heard jingling sounds and saw a small girl coming down from the tree. Tenderly the girl clasped Shyamasundari about the neck. At once Shyamasundari fell into a swoon. She remained unconscious for a long time, and her relatives took her home. She felt that the girl had entered into her womb.

At that time Ramachandra Mukherjee was in Calcutta. Before his departure from Jayrambati, one noon after his meal he had been asleep when he saw in a vivid dream a young girl of

A Scene in Jayrambati

The Tank at Jayrambati where Holy Mother Bathed

THE TEMPLE OF SIMHAVĀHINI AT JAYRAMBATI

THE AMODAR RIVER NEAR JAYRAMBATI

golden complexion and unusual beauty tenderly encircling his neck with her arms. Noticing her many precious ornaments, he asked her who she was. In a musical voice she replied: "You see, I have come to your family." After his return from Calcutta, Ramachandra heard from his wife about her vision, and the simple couple could not doubt the authenticity of the two experiences. They were sure that some deity would be born in the family. The husband kept away from his wife till the birth of the child.

On Thursday, December 22, 1853, the eldest daughter of Ramachandra and Shyamasundari saw the light of day.[1] In accord with the astrological calculation, she was given the name Thakurmani. But the family called her Saradamani, or Sarada for short. In the course of time the brāhmin couple had six other children: a daughter named Kadambini and five sons, named Prasanna, Umesh, Kalikumar, Barada, and Abhay. Kadambini, Umesh, and Abhay died early. The other brothers, when they had grown up, settled in their own separate homes at Jayrambati. Ramachandra had three brothers: Trailokya, Iswar, and Nilmadhav. They all lived together. Sarada was brought up in a big joint family which defrayed its expenses with difficulty through money earned from farming and the performance of priestly duties.

The poverty amidst which Sarada grew up could not, however, rob the family of love and happiness. From the time she was a little girl, she was active in helping her mother cook and in looking after her young sister and brothers, and her uncles. In later life she once remarked: "I took good care of my uncles. I wonder if modern girls would do so much!" Her father helped her lift the heavy rice-pot from the stove, and she took the children to bathe in the Amodar. She used to pick cotton in the

---

[1] On the site of her birth there now stands a white temple which was formally dedicated on April 19, 1923, by Swami Saradananda, who was Secretary of the Ramakrishna Math and Mission at that time.

field and with it made sacred threads, used by brāhmins, thus adding slightly to the family income. Sometimes Sarada would wade neck-deep into water to cut grass for the cattle, and often she carried refreshments to the field for the workers. One year the paddy crop was destroyed by locusts, and the little child gleaned grain from one field after another. From childhood she lived an active life. It was never necessary to remind her of her duties. Using her intelligence, she anticipated them and performed them cheerfully. By nature serious and reflective, she did not quarrel with her playmates. On the other hand, when they fell out with one another she acted as the pacifier. In play, it is said, she impersonated the mistress of the household. She loved her dolls, the favourite ones being of Kāli and Lakshmi, two of the Hindu goddesses, whom she devoutly worshipped with flowers and sacred leaves. One day, some years later, while watching the worship of Jagaddhātri,[2] she was absorbed in such deep concentration that a visitor mistook Sarada for the image of the Divine Mother.

It appears that at that time some sort of guardian angel kept her company. Reminiscing about her early years, she once said to a disciple: "A young girl resembling me used to move with me and help me in my work. We had great fun together. But she disappeared at other people's approach. This experience continued till I was ten or eleven years old. When I entered a pond to cut grass for the cattle, a girl of my age used to go with me. As I took one bundle to the bank and returned to the water for more grass, I found she had already made another bundle ready for me."

Now and then Sarada accompanied her brothers to school and gradually learnt the alphabet. But her relatives did not encourage her education, since at that time literacy for women was considered quite unnecessary. Sarada, however, was enthusiastic about learning to read.

---

[2] Lit., "The Support of the Universe," an aspect of the Divine Mother.

Sarada's lack of formal education did not stand in the way of her mind's development. In later years she showed unusual power of understanding while giving spiritual instruction to educated and mature devotees who sometimes spoke languages different from her own. The foundation of this understanding had been laid in childhood, outside school. First, her God-fearing parents and their life of unselfish service stimulated her mind more than formal study. Second, she became acquainted with the spiritual culture of India from the devotional songs of the many beggars and religious mendicants. She participated in the religious festivals of the village and listened to the rural dramas depicting scenes from the religious myths of the Hindus. They left such an impression on her mind that in later years she used to quote from them to her disciples. Third, the simple life of the village, the spacious fields, the open sky, the trees and the birds, gave depth and breadth to Sarada's outlook. And above all, she had, in early girlhood, the rare privilege of coming in contact with a God-man—none other than her husband —who, as we shall see, took charge of developing her mind and character.

Marriage and After

WHILE SARADA WAS GROWING UP in the rural environment of Jayrambati, there was unfolding at Dakshineshwar, near Calcutta, a drama of great spiritual significance, in whose *dénouement* Sarada later played a vital part. Sri Ramakrishna, who was born in 1836 at Kamarpukur, had shown, since early childhood, an intense longing for the realization of God.[1] In 1852 he went to Calcutta and soon accepted the duties of priest at a temple in the suburban village of Dakshineswar, where the principal deity is the Divine Mother Kāli, known as Bhavatārini, the Saviour of the World. Worship of the Divine Mother whetted his desire for direct realization, which soon became an all-consuming passion, and he was finally blessed with a vision of Her. This first experience of the Divine Mother only intensified his yearning for uninterrupted communion with God. He began to practise various disciplines to realize this ideal. Completely God-intoxicated, he became indifferent to food, sleep, and the other necessaries of life. Day and night he spent in meditation and prayer. His restless yearning for God expressed itself in agonizing cries for the Divine Mother. He shunned worldly people, and the outside world ceased to have

---

[1] Sri Ramakrishna's life has been described in a number of books. The following are especially recommended: *Life of Sri Ramakrishna* (Calcutta: Advaita Āshrama, 1955); *The Life of Ramakrishna*, by Romain Rolland (Calcutta: Advaita Āshrama, 1954); *The Gospel of Sri Ramakrishna* (New York: Ramakrishna-Vivekananda Center, 1953).

meaning for him. His conduct resembled that of a madman. During one of his visits to Kamarpukur, his mother and brother became alarmed by his abnormal behavior. They thought that Ramakrishna was suffering from a serious physical and mental ailment and arranged for various treatments, both medical and supernatural. When all this proved futile, they thought up a bold plan: they would marry him in order to bring his mind down to the normal level. Without his knowledge they began to search for a suitable bride. But they did not succeed. He, however, noticed their sadness and frustration. Instead of objecting to his marriage, he acquiesced in the proposal in a rather jovial mood and said: "Why are you fruitlessly looking for the girl hither and thither? Go to Ramachandra Mukherjee's house at Jayrambati and you will find the girl there, tied as it were with straws."[2]

According to another story, Sarada, when two years old, was taken by relatives to the neighbouring village of Sihore, the birthplace of Ramakrishna's nephew Hriday, to witness a religious festival. Ramakrishna too was present. As often happens on such an occasion, some of the women teasingly asked Sarada whom among the boys she would like to marry. With one of her tiny fingers she pointed at Sri Ramakrishna.

In May 1859 Sri Ramakrishna was married to Sarada at Jayrambati. Sri Ramakrishna was then twenty-three years old and Sarada slightly over five. Early marriage for a Hindu girl, especially one living in a village, was not then uncommon. But such a marriage was really in the nature of a betrothal. The actual marriage took place after the wife attained maturity, when she and her husband lived together. Sri Ramakrishna's marriage was, however, a strange one. Here was a bride in whom the consciousness of sex was not awakened and who remained free from it all through life. And the bridegroom

---

[2] The allusion is to a local custom. The stem of a particular fruit destined to be offered at the temple for worship is often tied with straws to set it apart from other fruits.

regarded all women as his own mother and the embodiment of the Divine Mother of the Universe—an attitude which he maintained as long as he lived. At that time, because of his absorption in spiritual practices, he was oblivious of both his body and the world, and was guided in every action by the Divine Mother Herself, with whom he had established a most intimate relationship. Therefore it may be presumed that in his marriage he was guided by the finger of God. It served no human purpose for either of them. But it fulfilled a divine mission; for Sarada was destined to continue, after his death, his unfinished work of spiritual ministration.

The day following the marriage Sri Ramakrishna returned to Kamarpukur with his bride. Sarada was warmly received by her mother-in-law, Chandra Devi. But soon a delicate situation arose. As the family was too poor to buy jewellery for the bride, Chandra Devi had borrowed some from a rich neighbour. With these Sarada was adorned at the time of the marriage. Naturally she regarded the ornaments as her own. After her coming to Kamarpukur, the ornaments had to be returned to their rightful owner. But how could Chandra tear them away from little Sarada? Sri Ramakrishna came to her rescue. When the unsuspecting child was asleep, he cleverly removed the ornaments from her body, and they were returned to the owner. But when Sarada awoke she missed them and felt upset. Her mother-in-law took her in her arms and consoled her, saying, "My son will give you more precious ornaments than these." Sarada was pacified, but one of her uncles, who happened to be present in the house, became angry and returned home with the girl. Sri Ramakrishna made light of the incident and said with a laugh: "They may take the girl back but they cannot nullify the marriage."

After his marriage Sri Ramakrishna spent about two years at Kamarpukur. During this period, in December 1860, when Sarada was seven years old, he paid a short visit to Jayrambati. Recollecting an incident of that time, Sarada said many years

Sri Ramakrishna

HOLY MOTHER AT FORTY-FIVE

later that one day, of her own accord, she washed her husband's feet and fanned him. The other girls made fun of this and teased her. She also remembered that Hriday, Sri Ramakrishna's nephew,[3] one day sought her out and to her great embarrassment worshipped her feet with flowers.

Shortly after, Sri Ramakrishna went back to Kamarpukur with Sarada. In a few days he returned to Calcutta, and, forgetting all about his marriage and his wife, plunged once more into the practice of spiritual disciplines. Sarada, on her part, returned to her parents' home and resumed her duties in the family.

In 1864, when Sarada was about ten years old, Bengal was suffering from a terrible famine, whose effect Jayrambati did not escape. People were starving, and many would come to her father's house for food. Ramachandra, a poor man himself, had stocked some rice from the previous year's surplus and he opened a free kitchen for the hungry villagers. Rice and lentils were boiled together and kept in several large pots. This preparation is called khichuri. The members of the family, together with the famine-stricken people, ate this simple meal. But Ramachandra stipulated that some especially good rice should be cooked separately for Sarada. Sometimes the hungry people came in such numbers that the khichuri would run short and a fresh supply had to be cooked. Sarada had to fan the hot stuff in order to cool it off. One day a low-class girl, with shaggy hair and bloodshot eyes, came to the house. Evidently she had been starving for some time. Seeing some powdered rice soaking in a tub for the cattle, she at once started eating it. Sarada asked her to come inside and eat khichuri. But the girl was too impatient to wait. Recalling this incident, Sarada said many years after: "Is it a joke to bear the agony of an empty stomach?"

During Sri Ramakrishna's absence at Dakshineswar, Sarada

---

[3] The son of Sri Ramakrishna's sister, and his companion and attendant for many years.

visited Kamarpukur twice. There she lived with her brother-in-
law,[4] sister-in-law, and other relatives. Her mother-in-law was
then living at Dakshineswar with Sri Ramakrishna. At Kamarpukur, Sarada learned to cook and sing, and to swim a little
with the help of an inverted jar.

About this time she wanted to improve her education and
started to read a Bengali primer with her niece Lakshmi.[5] But
Hriday snatched the book away with the remark: "Girls should
not be educated. If you learn to read you will soon be reading
novels and plays. This is not proper." But Lakshmi, a member
of the family, asserted her right and clung to her book. Sarada,
too, secretly bought a book for a few pennies and took lessons
from Lakshmi when she returned home from school. But, as
we shall see later, Sarada resumed her study seriously many
years after at Dakshineswar.

During one of the visits to Kamarpukur, Sarada had a strange
experience, which she afterwards described to her devotees: "I
was then thirteen years old, a young daughter-in-law in the
family, and would be frightened to walk alone to the village
tank to bathe. One day I came out of the house by a back door
and was worrying about the matter when there appeared, apparently from nowhere, eight young maidens. As I started for
the tank, four of them walked in front of me and four behind.
Thus guarded I walked to the water and all of us bathed together. Afterwards they brought me home."[6] This continued
as long as Sarada lived at Kamarpukur during that visit. She
could not unravel the mystery nor did she ask the girls who
they were.

In 1867 Sri Ramakrishna returned to Kamarpukur to re-
cuperate from stomach trouble. In the meantime the strenuous
period when he gave himself up completely to spiritual prac-

---

[4] Rameswar, the second brother of Sri Ramakrishna; the eldest
brother, Ramkumar, had died several years before.

[5] The daughter of Rameswar.

[6] According to Hindu mythology, the Divine Mother of the
Universe has eight maidens as attendants.

tices had come to an end. Now firmly established in God-consciousness, he appeared more natural and spontaneous.

Years later the Master described to his devotees the three stages of a man's mental evolution. During the first stage he takes the world of names and forms to be real and denies the existence of the Godhead behind it. It is a state of ignorance (ajnāna). During the second stage he negates the world as māyā and sees only Brahman, or pure spirit. This is a state of knowledge (jnāna). During the final stage he again sees the world of names and forms, but now as the manifestation of Brahman. This is a state of mature knowledge (vijnāna). The illumined soul, endowed with this mature knowledge, once more accepts the cosmic movement, seeing it as the sport (lilā) of Brahman. He remains like a child, guileless and natural. Sri Ramakrishna was now established in vijnāna.

The people of Kamarpukur were exceedingly happy to have their young Gadadhar[7] back again. They felt a strange peace in his presence and sought his company. His family had practically lost sight of him for seven long years. Now he regaled his relatives and the villagers with jokes and stories, but always reminding them of the need for spirituality. The house became a mart of joy. To make this joy complete, Sarada was brought to Kamarpukur. She was now fourteen years old. She spent six months with her husband and had her first real glimpse into his personality.

To Sarada, as to every orthodox Hindu wife, her husband was a veritable God, her sole refuge here and hereafter. Sri Ramakrishna, on his part, showed her respect and attention. Realizing his responsibility to his young wife, who was completely dependent upon him for guidance, he proceeded to instruct her, out of the infinite storehouse of his wisdom, in both spiritual and secular matters. But first of all he won her heart with a love free from any trace of worldliness.

---

[7] The name given to Sri Ramakrishna at birth; he was called Gadai, for short, by his relatives and the villagers.

Sri Ramakrishna not only held before Sarada the ideal of his own life of utter renunciation of worldly attachments, but also instructed her about the duties of a householder: how to serve guests, show respect to elders and be considerate to younger persons, and dedicate herself to the service of the family. The essence of his teaching was that one should act properly with respect to persons, time, place, and circumstances—a lesson which Sarada followed till the last day of her life in dealing with people of different tastes, temperaments, needs, character, and ages, and in different stages of moral and spiritual evolution. Often Sri Ramakrishna talked for hours before Sarada and her companions about spiritual matters and his own inner experiences. Sometimes the young wife would become tired and fall asleep on the floor. Then her companions would awaken her and say: "You were asleep! You have missed such priceless words." At that, Sri Ramakrishna would say: "No, don't wake her up. If she listens to everything I say, she will not stay on this earth; she will unfold her wings and fly away."

Sarada was impressed by her husband's ever cheerful face. She said later: "I never saw his face sad or sour. He always radiated joy—whether he was absorbed in samādhi[8] or in the company of an older person or a five-year-old child. Never did I see him gloomy." This innate joy must have impressed Sarada deeply. Speaking about her first intimate companionship with Sri Ramakrishna, she later said to her women devotees: "At that time I always felt as if a jar of bliss was set in my heart. It is impossible to describe that divine joy, which was full to the brim."

Sri Ramakrishna was by no means a stern, pain-hugging ascetic. He often joked and made fun. Narrating a lighter incident of this period, Sarada once said: "The Master[9] was suffering from stomach trouble. I was then quite young. During the

---

[8] Complete absorption in God.
[9] Refers to Sri Ramakrishna. From now on this epithet will frequently be used with reference to him.

early hours of the morning he would wake up and tell us women of the household what he would like to eat for his midday meal. I followed his directions. But one day I found I did not have a particular spice that he wanted the mixed lentil soup to be seasoned with. My sister-in-law[10] asked me to cook it without that spice. The Master heard her words and said: 'How can that be? If you do not have the spice in the house, get it from the village shop. It is not proper to cook vegetables without the proper seasoning. I left behind the rice pudding and other rich dishes of the Dakshineswar temple and came here just to enjoy the flavour of that particular spice, and you want to deprive me of it. That can't be!' My sister-in-law felt embarrassed and sent for the spice. He would say to me: 'Season your lentil soup in such a way that it will make a hog grunt!' "[11]

Soon Sri Ramakrishna grew tired of special cooking. He said to the ladies: "What a nice fix I am in! The moment I leave bed, I speak of nothing but food. Good God! Now I have lost all relish for food and shall eat whatever you cook." Constant purging due to diarrhoea made him say one day: "The body contains nothing but filth. I am sick of it." Thus he lost all interest in his body and paid no heed to it.

Sri Ramakrishna was accompanied at that time by the Bhairavi Brāhmani,[12] whom he addressed as "Mother." Sarada regarded her as her mother-in-law. But the Brāhmani was hot-tempered and often frightened her. Sarada said about her: "She was fond of chillies and cooked her own food, which she made very hot. Often she offered it to me. I silently ate it, always

[10] Sri Ramakrishna's elder brother's widow.
[11] The allusion is to a certain way of seasoning. Strong spices are thrown into boiling fat in a deep pan and then the soup or stew is poured into it. This gives out a pungent smell and makes a noise which is heard from a distance. Sri Ramakrishna liked this kind of seasoning.
[12] A nun who was Sri Ramakrishna's teacher in some of his spiritual practices.

wiping away my tears. Oh, her dishes were so hot! When she asked me how I liked them, I would say, in fear and trembling: 'Very nice indeed!' But my sister-in-law would speak the truth. The Brāhmani would be angry at such criticism of her cooking and exclaim: 'Why do you feel that way? My daughter approves my cooking. Nothing can please you. I will not give you what I cook any more.'" Sarada laughed when she narrated these incidents, much later, to her devotees.

Sri Ramakrishna was full of wit. Recalling a delightful incident, Sarada once said: "At Kamarpukur Lakshmi's mother and I prepared the meals. She was a better cook than I. One day the Master and Hriday were taking their meal. He tasted the food prepared by my sister-in-law and said in praise: 'This has been made by a real cook.' He compared her to an expert physician. Tasting what I had cooked he said: 'The one who has prepared this is a quack.' 'That may be,' said Hriday, 'but the quack will always be at your service, even ready to give you a massage. All that you have to do is to summon him. But the expert physician is very expensive; he is not always available. People first consult the quack; he is always your friend.' 'That is true,' the Master replied, smiling."

Sri Ramakrishna knew that in later years Sarada Devi would act as a spiritual teacher, and he taught her about the unsubstantial nature of the world, and its woes and sorrows. He asked her to cultivate detachment from transitory objects and develop devotion to God, who alone is real and eternal. "What good is there," he once said to her, "in giving birth, like dogs and jackals, to a whole brood of children? You have already lost a sister whom you brought up so tenderly; you have seen how deeply your parents lamented her death. You have seen all this with your own eyes. How miserable the life of the world is! Why should you bother with it? Without any such botheration, you look now like a goddess and will always remain a goddess." Hearing Sri Ramakrishna harping on death, the bashful Sarada said gently: "But do they all die?" Perhaps she had an intimation of the inner longing for motherhood which is present in all women. At once Sri Ramakrishna said to the other ladies, in a loud voice: "See! I have stepped on the tail of a real cobra. Goodness gracious! I often said to myself: 'She is such a simple soul, unaware of the ways of the world.' But see how much she keeps inside her. Did you hear what she said— 'Do they all die?' " Sarada ran away.

Whenever Sri Ramakrishna hurt Sarada's feelings, he would somehow make up for it. One day when a religious play was to be given in a neighbouring village, Sarada and the other ladies wanted to see it, but the Master refused to give permission and said that he himself would repeat it for them. Sarada was hurt. When the play was over he returned home and re-enacted the whole of it in the minutest detail. Sri Ramakrishna had a sweet musical voice and a remarkable memory, and was besides a fine actor. The ladies of the family forgot their disappointment and were charmed with his mimicry.

First Visit to Dakshineswar

SRI RAMAKRISHNA RETURNED to Dakshineswar and Sarada to Jayrambati. The Master's holy company had brought about a change, hardly noticed by others, in Sarada's conduct, her movements, and her life in general. She became quiet, thoughtful, indrawn, unselfish. She felt that she lacked nothing and was sympathetic to others in their sufferings and trials. She appeared a living image of compassion. Her outer life, however, went on as usual with her relatives at her parents' home.

Four long years passed by. Sarada naturally missed Sri Ramakrishna. An unexpressed anguish ate at her heart, but the memory of the divine bliss she had experienced at Kamarpukur enabled her somehow to endure her life from day to day. Sometimes she would say to herself: "He was very kind to me during our last meeting. How can he ever forget me? In good time he will, of his own accord, call me to his side. Let me patiently wait for that happy moment." In the meantime the report came to Jayrambati that Sri Ramakrishna was again completely insane at Dakshineswar, and that he went about naked and always shouted God's name. People mistook his God-intoxicated state for ordinary insanity. The village women, who often relished gossip more than food and drink, would point at Sarada as a "madman's wife" and add in mock sympathy: "Poor Shyamasundari has married her daughter to a lunatic. How sad!" Even at home she did not enjoy peace of mind. Shyamasundari was distressed at Sri Ramakrishna's indifference to the world. Now and then she would say in front of her daughter: "I have married my daughter to a madman; I have thrown her, as it were, into deep water with her hands and feet tied!" Sarada was stung by these remarks and avoided people as much as she could. She found relief in keeping herself busy with household duties day and night. She got some solace, however, from a village woman named Bhanu, who was addressed by all as "Aunt Bhanu." This woman, who possessed some insight, had had a glimpse into Sri Ramakrishna's personality and once said to Shyamasundari: "Your son-in-law is Śiva Himself, and Krishna too. You may not understand this now, but you will in the future. Mark my words." When stung by criticism of her husband, Sarada would often go to Aunt Bhanu's house and lie awhile on her porch. But her real relief came from her intense preoccupation with household duties. Referring to this hard time she later said: "One must always be busy. Work keeps body and mind in good shape. At Jayrambati, in my younger days, I was active day and night and did not visit anyone else's house. If I ever did, I heard people say: 'Shyama's daughter has been married to a madman!' I avoided people so that I might not hear such remarks." But the ridicule of the villagers went on unabated. At last Sarada decided to go to Dakshineswar and see things with her own eyes. Since, like the average Hindu young woman, she was too shy to speak to her father about it, a girl friend acted on her behalf. Her father agreed to accompany his daughter himself.

Soon an opportunity arrived. A number of women set out on foot for Calcutta, about sixty miles distant, for a bath in the sacred Ganges on an auspicious occasion. Sarada and her father joined the party. They started on March 25, 1872. The first two or three days they walked cheerfully. Sarada, out of her familiar surroundings for the first time, enjoyed the countryside with its paddy fields, grasslands, villages with shady trees echoing with the twittering of birds, and lakes with lilies and lotuses. But gradually her legs began to give way. Life in a malaria-stricken village had not given her robust health. At first she concealed her weariness from her father, but finally she was seized with a high fever and had to take shelter in a small wayside inn. Her mind was tortured by the fear that it might not be her fate to see her husband.

Suffering both physically and mentally, as she lay in bed almost unconscious, she saw a woman of exquisite beauty enter the room and sit by the bedside. The stranger had a very black complexion resembling that of Mother Kāli. As she stroked Sarada's body with her soft hands, Sarada's pain seemed to ooze out through the pores of her skin. She asked the visitor where she came from.

Visitor: "From Dakshineswar."

Sarada (with surprise): "Indeed! I wanted to go to Dakshineswar myself, see him there, and serve him. Perhaps ill luck will prevent my desire's being fulfilled."

Visitor: "Don't say that. You will surely go to Dakshineswar. You will get well and see him. It is for your sake that I am keeping him there."

Sarada: "Is that true? Who are you? Any relation of ours?"

Visitor: "I am your sister."

Sarada: "Is that so? Perhaps that is why you have come."

Sarada noticed that the stranger's feet were covered with dust, as if from a long walk, and inquired why no one had given her water to wash them. The stranger said that she would be leaving immediately, and disappeared.[1]

Soon Sarada fell into a deep sleep. Next morning her temperature was normal. She felt refreshed and the vision brought back her lost enthusiasm. Her father said that it would not be wise to stay alone very long in an unknown place, and proposed to start immediately. Sarada cheerfully agreed. After they walked some distance a palanquin was found. On the road she had another attack of fever, but it was a mild one and she kept it secret from her father. At last they reached their journey's

---

[1] It was evidently none other than the Goddess Kāli who had appeared to her in this vision.

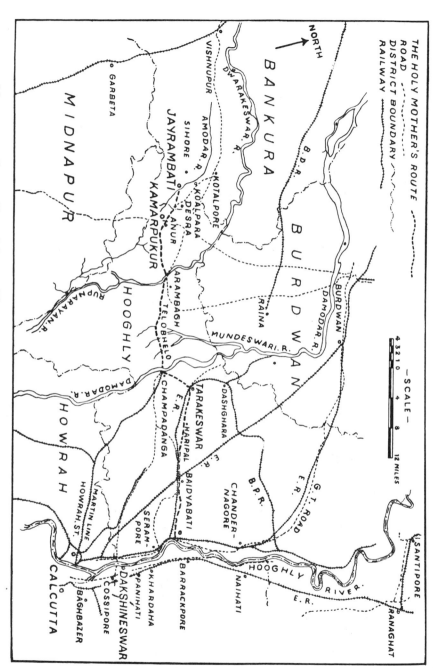

MAP OF THE ROUTE HOLY MOTHER TRAVELLED BETWEEN DAKSHINESWAR AND JAYRAMBATI

SRI RAMAKRISHNA'S PARENTAL HOME AT KAMARPUKUR

THE TEMPLE ON THE SITE OF SRI RAMAKRISHNA'S BIRTH (right),
SRI RAMAKRISHNA'S HOUSE (middle), THE FAMILY SHRINE (left)

end. The last part of the trip was made on the Ganges in a country boat.

The party arrived at Dakshineswar at nine o'clock in the evening. As Sarada was alighting from the boat, she heard Sri Ramakrishna saying to Hriday from his porch on the river: "This is her first visit. I hope the hour is auspicious." These first words of the Master, laden with tenderness, encouraged Sarada to go straight into her husband's room. Her companions went to their respective lodgings.

As soon as Sri Ramakrishna saw Sarada, he said: "So you have come. I am very happy." He asked someone to spread a straw mat on the floor. They sat on it and began to talk. Hearing of her illness on the way, he expressed concern. Eager to provide for her treatment and physical comfort, he said again and again: "You have come so late. Alas, my Mathur[2] is no longer alive to look after you. With his death I feel as if I have lost my right arm." Sarada wanted to go to the Nahabat,[3] where her old mother-in-law was living. Sri Ramakrishna said: "Oh no, stay in my room. It will be inconvenient for the physician to see you there." A separate bed was made for Sarada in the Master's room and it was arranged that one of her companions should spend the night with her. As it was past meal time, Hriday gave the visitors a large basket of puffed rice for supper. Next day the physician came, and within three or four days Sarada was completely well. She then went to the Nahabat to be near her mother-in-law.

Sarada always cherished great affection and respect for the members of her husband's family. Her father-in-law had died long before. About him she once remarked with great pride:

_____

[2] The wealthy custodian of the Kāli temple at Dakshineswar and grateful provider of Sri Ramakrishna's personal needs. He had died a few months earlier.

[3] A small building to the north of the Master's room, originally intended for the playing of music at certain hours of the day and night to entertain the deities. There was a similar structure on the south side of the temple grounds.

"He was a brāhmin of great spirit. Orthodox to the bone, he never accepted gifts from non-brāhmins, nor would he allow anyone in the family to receive such gifts. If a villager gave the poor family a present of vegetables, my mother-in-law would cook them and make an offering of them to the family deity. This made my father-in-law very angry. He had a burning love for God. Because of this love, God Himself was born as his son." An affectionate daughter-in-law, she was devoted to her mother-in-law and learnt from her about the many joys and sorrows of the family. Much impressed with its orthodoxy, she said later to a devotee: "Though he was born in such an ortho-dox family, the Master had to accept the work of a priest in a temple owned by a fisherman!"[4]

Her direct meeting with Sri Ramakrishna at once convinced Sarada of the falseness of the villagers' gossip about his insanity. Whatever slight misgiving might have cast a shadow upon her mind on account of persistent rumours was dissipated during that first visit. She found him as kindly, loving, and tender as before, if not more so. In no time she found out what her present duties were, and devoted herself completely to the service of her husband and her mother-in-law. Her father, im-pressed by his son-in-law's thoughtfulness and assured of Sarada's happiness at Dakshineswar, left for Jayrambati with a cheerful mind.

Sri Ramakrishna now set himself to the task of testing the depth and genuineness of his knowledge of Brahman. But he also wanted to discharge the unfinished duties towards his wife which he had begun at Kamarpukur and which had been inter-rupted by his attention to spiritual practices at Dakshineswar. His teacher in monastic life, Totapuri, when he had learnt of his marriage had said: "He alone is established in the realiza-tion of Brahman who sees the same Self in both men and

---

[4] Rāni Rashmani and her son-in-law belonged to the fisherman caste, considered low in Hindu society. A high-caste brāhmin does not work under a member of a lower caste.

women. He who sees a difference between the sexes may be an aspirant, but he is far from having experienced Brahman." Totapuri had also said that an illumined seer like Sri Ramakrishna, firm in Self-knowledge, could discharge his duties towards his' wife without in any way harming his spiritual life. Sri Ramakrishna began to teach Sarada about the householder's duties. For instance, in regard to such practical matters as travelling, he asked her always to be the first to get into a boat or a railway compartment so that she could occupy a good seat, and to be the last to come out so that she might not, in her hurry, forget her luggage. He taught her that in arranging objects of domestic use one must think out beforehand where particular articles were to be kept. What was frequently required must be kept near at hand and other things at a distance. When an article was temporarily removed from its place, it should be put back in exactly the same place so that one might not fail to find it even in the dark. He taught her how to roll the wick of an oil lamp, dress vegetables, and prepare betel leaves.[5] He repeatedly told her to fit her conduct to the time, place, and circumstances, and the nature of the people she had to deal with. He asked her not to hurt anyone's feelings. "If you see a lame person," he taught her, "do not directly ask him how he became lame. You may ask him why he walks that way." He emphasized that she should have friendly feelings for all. Once when she was going to Kamarpukur he said to her: "Be nice to your neighbours. If anyone falls ill, inquire about his health from time to time." On another occasion, years later, the wife of Balaram Bose, a householder devotee of Sri Ramakrishna, was ill in Calcutta. The Master asked Sarada to visit her. Unaccustomed to walking in the public streets of the city, she wanted to know how she should go, since there was no carriage or other conveyance. "Go on foot," Sri Ramakrishna said forcefully. "My Balaram may lose his wife and you will not see her? Go on foot."

---

[5] Betel leaves are chewed with spices after meals as a digestive.

Sri Ramakrishna also taught Sarada about meditation, prayer, samādhi, and the knowledge of Brahman. He never missed an opportunity to impress upon her that the realization of God was the sole aim of human life. He not only gave her instructions in spiritual discipline but also closely watched whether the instructions were carried out. One day, when she asked him about God, Sri Ramakrishna said to Sarada: "As the moon is the 'Uncle' of all children, so God is everyone's very own. All have an equal right to call on Him. He who prays to God will surely be blessed by His vision. Pray to God and you will certainly see Him."

Sri Ramakrishna often put Sarada's spiritual yearning to test. Though she spent the whole day at the Nahabat, she returned at night to the Master's room to sleep. One night, finding her alone, he asked her: "Tell me if you have come here to drag me down the road leading to the worldly life." "Certainly not," she replied without a moment's hesitation. "Why should I drag you to the world? I am here to help you to realize your spiritual ideal." Sarada, too, one day asked Sri Ramakrishna, as she was stroking his feet: "How do you regard me?" He replied: "The Mother who is worshipped in the temple, and the mother who gave birth to this [pointing to his body] and is now living in the Nahabat—the same mother is now stroking my feet. Really and truly I always regard you as the embodiment of the blissful Mother of the Universe."

But Sri Ramakrishna, wanting to test his complete spiritual integrity, asked Sarada to sleep in the same bed with him. He often passed the night in samādhi, unconscious of his body. But one night, while in a normal mood, he cast his eyes on the body of his youthful wife, sleeping by his side, and said to himself: "O mind, this is a woman's body. People regard it as a most covetable object and are ever eager to enjoy it. But if a man embraces this body, he becomes entangled in the world and cannot realize God. Now, O mind, don't be a hypocrite. Your tongue must not say what you do not feel at heart. Be truthful and tell me what you want: this body or God. If you want the body, it is right here in front of you. Take it." Discriminating in this way, as he stretched his hand to touch Sarada, it shrank back and he entered into samādhi. That night he did not regain the normal mood. The next day, after repeated efforts, he was brought back to consciousness of the physical world.

For eight long months Sri Ramakrishna and Sarada spent their nights together. Her mind, too, like her husband's, constantly soared to a higher plane. Neither had the slightest desire for physical enjoyment. Many days later, referring to his wife's innate purity, Sri Ramakrishna said to his disciples: "If she had not been completely pure, if she had forgotten herself and made physical demands on me, then would not I, too, have lost self-control and brought my mind down to the physical level? Who can tell? After my marriage, I eagerly prayed to the Divine Mother: 'O Mother, please remove even a trace of lust from my wife's mind.' That my prayer was literally fulfilled I came to know when I lived with her."

Years after, certain critics said that Sri Ramakrishna virtually forced Sarada to lead the life of a virgin or a widow. When such a criticism was once made to Max Müller by a leader of the Brāhmo Samāj, a Westernized liberal Hindu religious movement, he said: "Why do you talk that way? Did his wife ever make a complaint against Ramakrishna?" "Sri Ramakrishna," Romain Rolland writes, "has at times been blamed, and very coarsely blamed, for having sacrificed her. She herself never showed any trace of it. She showered peace and serenity throughout her life on all who came in contact with her. . . . It was by the consent of his wife that he was free to follow the life of his choice. Magnanimously she renounced the wife's binding right over her husband and encouraged him in his mission."

Awakening of Divinity

SRI RAMAKRISHNA WAS EAGER to awaken completely the innate divinity in Sarada. After repeated tests he had become convinced of her unsullied purity and of her being now fully prepared to become aware of her divine nature. The following event not only accomplished this but also revealed his own spiritual relationship with his wife and the rôle she was to play in the future.

It was the fifth of June, 1872. Sarada was eighteen years old and Sri Ramakrishna thirty-six. The day was especially auspicious for worship of the Divine Mother. The Master made a special arrangement for the Shoḍashi Pujā.¹ Public worship performed with music and great pomp was going on in the Kāli temple. But Sri Ramakrishna arranged a private ceremony in his room. Flowers, sacred bel leaves, food offerings, and other necessary articles were gathered. A seat was arranged for the image of the Goddess in its proper place. Sri Ramakrishna had asked Sarada to be present at the worship, which began at 9 P.M. After the preliminaries, the Master signed to her to take the seat reserved for the image. Already in a semi-conscious spiritual mood, she carried out his order as if under a spell. He invoked the Deity by uttering the following prayer:

"O Divine Mother! O Eternal Virgin, possessor of all power! Please open the gate of perfection. Purify her body and mind, and manifest Thyself through her for the welfare of all."

¹ The term refers to the worship of the Divine Mother in one of Her ten aspects, namely Shoḍashi, a woman as beautiful as a sixteen-year-old virgin.

42

Through the prescribed rituals, he identified Sarada with the Deity and worshipped her according to the scriptural rules. All through the ceremony she was in a semi-conscious state, watching everything but powerless to move or utter a single word. Very soon Sri Ramakrishna and Sarada lost all awareness of the outer world. Both worshipper and worshipped were united on a transcendental plane. Some time passed in this way. It was long after midnight when Sri Ramakrishna regained partial consciousness of the world. Then he offered himself completely to the Divine Mother manifest in the person of Sarada, and surrendered at her feet his rosary, himself, and everything that was his, reciting the following sacred text:

"O most auspicious of all auspicious beings, O Consort of Śiva, Fulfiller of all desires, O Refuge of all, O three-eyed[2] Goddess of golden complexion, O Power of Nārāyana, I salute Thee again and again."

The worship was completed. The simple girl brought up in a wayside village now became conscious of a new power, and through her the womanhood of the world was sanctified. Sarada Devi quietly left for her room in the Nahabat after mentally saluting Sri Ramakrishna.

The above-mentioned ceremony is most significant. For Sri Ramakrishna it signified the final destruction of lust and the complete triumph of the spirit over matter, the total suppression of the animal in man. He recognized divinity where ordinary men are least disposed to see it.

Sri Ramakrishna, through this worship, gave a special status to his wife, rare in the spiritual history of the world. Some of the higher religions, such as Buddhism, Hinduism, and Roman Catholicism, stress the monastic ideal. Highly advanced seekers are taught to regard the enjoyment of carnal desires as an obstacle to spiritual progress. Many among the prophets and saints have remained unmarried or, if married, renounced their wives. Sri Ramakrishna not only was married but kept his wife

---

[2] The third eye, placed on the forehead between the eyebrows, denotes the eye of wisdom.

with him till the last moment of his life, neither of them allowing the mind to come down to the physical level. Through
Sarada Devi, Sri Ramakrishna taught that all earnest women
could reveal their divinity and obtain respect and homage from
members of the opposite sex.

For Sarada Devi, too, the worship was highly meaningful.
From her very birth she had been pure. Even as a child she
used to pray, looking at a tuberose: "O Lord, make my character as white and fragrant as this flower." No shadow was
ever cast upon her purity. Now, at the end of the ceremony,
when Sri Ramakrishna surrendered at her feet the fruit of his
austerities and spiritual endeavours, he recognized her as a real
partner in life, well matched with him in every respect. Further,
by this act he made her the full sharer of his spiritual glory. As
we shall see later, she attained the exalted position of a teacher
without going through the usual disciplines practised by saints.
Whatever spiritual disciplines she practised were not so much
for her own illumination as for setting an example to other
aspirants or helping weak-minded disciples. Finally, Sri Ramakrishna from now on began to hint to Sarada Devi about her
future rôle as a teacher to complete the task he had begun.

For about six months after this special worship, Sarada Devi
spent her nights, as usual, in Sri Ramakrishna's room. The company of her husband was, no doubt, a source of great joy to her.
But she frequently had to spend sleepless nights on account of
his constant ecstasies, which at that time she did not know how
to cope with. Reminiscing about this period, Sarada Devi subsequently said to her devotees: "It is impossible to describe his
spiritual moods in those days. In the God-intoxicated state he
would sometimes say words incomprehensible to me, sometimes
laugh, sometimes weep, and sometimes remain motionless in
samādhi, like a corpse. The whole night would pass that way.
My body trembled in fear and I eagerly awaited the break of
day. At that time I knew almost nothing about samādhi. One
night his mind did not come down to the ordinary plane of

consciousness for a long time. I was frightened and sent for Hriday. He came and for a while repeated the Lord's name into the Master's ear. Only then did the Master regain the normal mood. After that the Master taught me various mantras[3] and also told me how to use them for different kinds of samādhi. Thus I gradually got rid of my fear and also succeeded in bringing his mind down from samādhi. But as I did not know when he would go into samādhi, I kept awake all night. Coming to realize my plight, he asked me to sleep at the Nahabat."

Sarada Devi, while living at Dakshineswar, made service to the Master and his mother the sole preoccupation of her life. The old lady was so infirm that she could hardly move about, and she depended upon her daughter-in-law for everything. Her room was on the second floor of the Nahabat and Sarada's was on the ground floor, which meant that Sarada often had to run up the stairs at the summons of her mother-in-law. Whatever time Sarada could spend with her husband was of inestimable spiritual significance. That she was able to bear the spiritual radiance of the Master shows her own spiritual depth and maturity.

During this first visit Sarada Devi spent a year and eight months at Dakshineswar. In October 1873 she returned to Kamarpukur and also saw her relatives at Jayrambati.

At Dakshineswar she spent in all about ten years with her husband. Once a disciple asked her how long she lived at Dakshineswar. "Oh, a long time," she said. "I first came when I was sixteen,[4] and after that I continued to live there until the Master's death. Every two or three years I visited Kamarpukur and Jayrambati." Sarada Devi visited Kamarpukur eight times from Dakshineswar, her last visit having been in October 1885, when Sri Ramakrishna was suffering from cancer. Needless to

---

[3] Sacred words associated with the various names of God or of a deity.

[4] As Holy Mother was born in December 1853 and paid her first visit to Dakshineswar in March 1872, she was evidently eighteen years old at the time.

say, during those visits she always made short trips to Jayrambati. All this time the chrysalis was being slowly transformed
into a butterfly.

There were several important events during this period.
Sarada's brother-in-law Rameswar died when she was at Kamarpukur, and on March 26, 1874, her magnanimous father, the
devout worshipper of Rāma, breathed his last. The widow
Shyamasundari now faced dire poverty, for with her husband's
death the regular income from his priestly duties was stopped.
Fortunately she had a good physique and strong will-power,
and she took up the work of husking paddy in the family of a
well-to-do neighbour. This hard work gave her a small income,
which was, however, inadequate to bring up her children, and
her sons later found shelter with different relatives.

Shortly after her return to Dakshineswar in April 1874,
Sarada Devi took up her residence at the Nahabat. As the room
was very small, Sambhu Mallick[5] built a rather spacious house
for her near the temple garden, where she lived with a maidservant. There she cooked the Master's meals and took them to
his room. Sri Ramakrishna kept her company now and then.
One evening when he was with Sarada Devi a heavy rain
started which lasted till midnight. He was compelled to spend
the night at her house. Joking about this incident, he said to
her: "The priests of the Kāli temple spend the night with their
families after working the whole day at the temple. The same
thing has happened tonight with me."[6]

The house, however, was damp. After staying in it for a year,
Sarada Devi was stricken with a serious attack of dysentery.
Sambhu arranged for her treatment. She returned to Jayrambati
in September 1875, when she felt a little better. But soon the
ailment came back in a rather serious form and there was fear
for her life. At the news of her illness Sri Ramakrishna became

---

[5] A householder devotee of Sri Ramakrishna, and one of the
suppliers of his personal needs.
[6] Sri Ramakrishna was himself, at first, a priest in the Kāli
temple.

very sad and said to Hriday: "What is going to happen? If she just comes to the world and departs, when will she fulfil the purpose of her human embodiment?" Sarada Devi became a mere skeleton. Looking at her reflection in the water of a pond, she once said to herself: "How disgusting! Such is the body! Let me give it up here and now. Why keep it alive any more?" Recounting this illness, she said later: "My body at one time was swollen all over. My nose, eyes, and ears were running profusely. My brother said that I should lie down before the image of Simhavāhini without food or drink till the Goddess revealed a suitable medicine.[7] I agreed and he supported me as I walked to the temple. There I lay down. At last in a vision I was asked to put on my nearly blind eyes, drop by drop, the juice of the flower of the bottle-gourd pressed with salt, and was assured of my cure. I applied the medicine and almost immediately my eyes cleared up. Gradually the swelling of the body disappeared and I recovered. I told people about the medicine I had received from Simhavāhini. My uncle, too, once had lain down in the temple for a similar purpose. But he was so hotly pursued by big ants that he had to run away. The Goddess appeared to my mother in a dream and said: 'I am sleeping now. Why is he disturbing me? He is a brāhmin. Doesn't he know the rules? Go at once and take him home.' My mother said to me: 'Why, if the Goddess could say all this, didn't she take the trouble to name the medicine?' " From that time on the power of the Goddess became known far and near, and people in large numbers began to visit her. Sarada Devi always kept with her a little earth from the temple grounds and used to eat one or two grains of it daily.

Sarada Devi was unfortunate in her health. Hardly had she recovered from dysentery when she was attacked with malaria, accompanied by an enlargement of the spleen. The customary treatment was bizarre and very painful. The patient, after a

---

[7] A custom often followed by people in order to recover from a difficult illness.

bath, was made to lie down on the floor of a certain Śiva temple near Jayrambati. Three or four people tightly held his hands and feet to the ground so that he might not get away. Then his abdomen was branded with the lighted branch of a plum tree. This burnt the skin and tortured the patient. Sarada went to this temple to be cured of her ailment. She watched patients undergoing the cruel treatment and heard their piteous cries. When her turn came she did not allow anyone to touch her, but lay down on the ground and was branded. Silently she bore the excruciating pain, and her spleen again became normal.

We come across numerous events like this in the life of both Sarada Devi and Sri Ramakrishna. In such matters they simply followed the local belief. There was a similar acceptance on their part of the various myths, rituals, and religious ceremonies followed by the Hindus. However incomprehensible that may be to the rational mind, such things are found in all religious traditions.

While Sarada Devi was still at Jayrambati, Sri Ramakrishna's mother died at Dakshineswar. Chandra Devi was eighty-five years old. Sarada now became worried about the Master and returned to Dakshineswar on March 17, 1876, accompanied by two companions, and took up her abode in the house built by Sambhu Mallick. Soon Sri Ramakrishna was stricken with a severe attack of dysentery. An elderly lady from Benares began to nurse him. At her insistence, Sarada Devi went to live in the Nahabat in order to remain near her husband. After Sri Ramakrishna's recovery the elderly lady went away and was not seen again. Sarada Devi said later: "Strangers came to Dakshineswar whenever the Master needed them, and afterwards disappeared." It was this lady from Benares who persuaded Sarada Devi to uncover her face before the Master. She had always kept her face veiled in his presence. One night the old lady took Sarada to Sri Ramakrishna's room and removed her veil. The Master started to talk to them about God and they listened spellbound. They were so absorbed that they did not notice the sunrise.

While returning to Dakshineswar from her fourth visit, in February 1877, Sarada encountered a highwayman. On this occasion she showed exceptional courage, intelligence, and self-control. She was going on foot, as she usually did during these trips, accompanied by several companions, including Lakshmi and Sivaram.[8] Part of the way lay through a long and lonesome meadow infested by highwaymen, who not only robbed helpless travellers but also occasionally killed them. People did not dare to cross this dangerous place at night or alone. Sarada Devi arrived there with her companions some time before sundown and resolved to cross it while it was still light. Tired and footsore, she could hardly keep up with her friends, and asked the others to walk fast, as they were afraid of the approaching night and the fearsome robbers. It was her nature never to inconvenience others for her own sake. So they moved on, asking her to hurry. Sarada was trudging on alone[9] when the sun went below the horizon and twilight fell over the earth. Naturally she was worried. Suddenly she saw a tall, uncouth figure, with a shock of thick hair, coming towards her in the dusk. Observing that he carried a long and stout stick on his shoulder, Sarada Devi realized what he was and stood still. The man wanted to frighten her and said in a stern voice: "Who is standing there all alone at this hour of the night? Where are you going?" She said timidly: "I am going towards the east." The robber said: "You have missed your direction. You must go the other way." Sarada Devi still stood motionless and the man came nearer. As he looked at her face something strange happened within him, and he said gently: "Don't be afraid. There is a woman with me. She will be here presently." Sarada felt reassured as she saw the figure of a woman at a distance. She said to the robber: "Father, my companions have left me behind. Perhaps I am going in the wrong direction. Your son-

---

[8] Son of Rameswar, Sri Ramakrishna's elder brother; his pet name was Sibu.

[9] According to some reports she was accompanied by two women, but this appears unlikely.

in-law[10] lives at the Kāli temple at Dakshineswar. I am going to him. Please accompany me there. He will certainly appreciate your kindness and show you proper courtesy." No sooner had Sarada said these words than the woman came up. She was the robber's wife. Trustfully Sarada clasped her hand and said: "Mother, I am your child Sarada. My companions have left me behind. I am terribly frightened. It is by sheer luck that you and Father have come; otherwise I do not know what I would have done."

These simple and straightforward words melted the hearts of the low-caste robber and his wife, who at once adopted her as their daughter and bid her be of good cheer. Finding her tired, they stopped at the nearest village and spent the night in a small inn. The man bought some simple food from a shop and the wife improvised a bed with her clothes. Gently she was put to sleep, and the robber kept watch all night, sitting outside with his stick near by. Early next morning they set out for the village of Tarakeswar, where Sarada Devi had planned to spend the night with her companions. On the way, the robber's wife picked some tender peas for Sarada from the fields. She ate them with relish. Soon after their arrival at Tarakeswar they took shelter at an inn. The woman said to her husband: "My daughter practically fasted last night. Quickly finish the worship at the Śiva temple and buy some fish and vegetables. I would like to feed her well." In a short while Sarada Devi's companions found her. They were relieved to see her safe and sound. She said to them, referring to the robber and his wife: "I don't know what I would have done last evening if they hadn't taken me under their wing." All of them ate together and had a happy time. Soon the party set out for Dakshineswar. They walked together for some distance, and when the moment of parting came, Sarada Devi and her new parents began to weep. The robber's wife again picked some green peas from the roadside, tied them in a corner of Sarada Devi's sāri, and said

---

[10] Referring to Sri Ramakrishna.

affectionately: "Child, when you eat puffed rice tonight, please take these peas with it." Sarada Devi reached Dakshineswar and told the Master of her experiences of the previous night.

Afterwards the robber and his wife visited Sri Ramakrishna several times with suitable gifts, and he, too, treated them kindly, as if they were his relatives. Describing the story to her devotees later, Sarada Devi said: "Though my adopted father was so honest and good, yet I believe he had been a highwayman before." One can only conjecture how she made such a deep impression on his mind. Did he and his wife get a glimpse of her real nature? At one time she asked them: "Why do you show me such kindness and affection?" They replied: "But you are not an ordinary human being. We saw you as Mother Kāli." "How is that?" she interrupted. "What did you see?" They replied firmly: "No, child, we have really seen you as Kāli. You hide that form from us because we are sinners." "You may say so," Sarada Devi said in an indifferent tone, "but really I know nothing about it." Many years after, a disciple of Holy Mother asked her: "What did the robber see in you?"

Mother: "He said later that he saw Kāli."

Disciple: "Then you appeared before him as Mother Kāli. Please don't hide anything from us. Please tell us frankly what happened."

Mother: "Why should I have shown him the form of Kāli? It was he who said that he had seen that form."

During Sarada Devi's visit to Jayrambati, some time in the early part of 1877, Shyamasundari was bidden in a dream by the Goddess Jagaddhātri, a manifestation of the Divine Mother of the Universe, to introduce Her worship in the family. From then on it became an annual affair, and Sarada Devi gave whatever assistance she could for the performance of the worship.

When Sarada Devi returned to Dakshineswar in March 1881 from her fifth visit to her native village, she stayed there only a day. She was accompanied by her mother, Lakshmi, and several neighbours. The moment they arrived, Hriday, for some unknown reason, treated them very rudely. Sri Ramakrishna, afraid to annoy him, kept silent. Shyamasundari said: "With whom shall I leave my daughter here? Let us all return home." Sarada Devi, as she took her leave, said, addressing Mother Kāli: "Mother, if you bring me here again, I shall come."

Hriday used to treat Sarada Devi rudely now and then. Once Sri Ramakrishna gave him a warning and said: "Look here. You may insult me, but don't hurt her feelings. If He who dwells in this[11] hisses, you may somehow get by; but if He who dwells in her[12] hisses, no one—not even Brahmā, Vishnu, or Śiva—will be able to protect you." Soon after, Hriday lost his job in the Kāli temple because of an indiscreet action and was forbidden to enter its compound.

Ramlal[13] now became Kāli's priest. Puffed up with pride, he began to neglect Sri Ramakrishna, who often remained unconscious on account of his deep spiritual moods. The Master's food would dry up on the plate and no one would look after him. He repeatedly wrote to Sarada Devi to come to Dakshineswar. "I am experiencing great difficulty here," he sent word to her. "Ramlal pays no heed to me. Please come, by all means, whatever may be the cost, and I shall see to it. Come any way you like—in a palanquin or in anything else." She returned to Dakshineswar in the early part of 1882.

Next year she again visited Kamarpukur and Jayrambati— this being her seventh visit—and returned to Dakshineswar after seven or eight months. After depositing her bundles in the Nahabat, she went to Sri Ramakrishna's room. Some time before, in a state of samādhi, the Master had fallen and dislocated a bone in his left arm. Sri Ramakrishna asked her when she had left home, and learnt that it was at an inauspicious hour according to the tradition in Bengal. Bowing before tradition, he said: "This is why I have broken my arm. Return home

---

[11] Meaning his own body.
[12] Meaning Sarada Devi.
[13] A son of Rameswar, Sri Ramakrishna's elder brother.

at once and start again at an auspicious hour." Sarada Devi was
ready to leave then and there, but was requested by her husband to spend the night. The following day she left for Jayrambati and came back to Dakshineswar within a few days.

In 1884 she went to Kamarpukur to attend the marriage
ceremony of her nephew Ramlal and also visited Jayrambati,
returning to Dakshineswar in March 1885. This was her last
visit to Kamarpukur and Jayrambati during Sri Ramakrishna's
lifetime.

Sri Ramakrishna, too, went to Kamarpukur many times during this period of his life, his last visit being in 1880. The damp
climate of Dakshineswar in the rainy season often told on his
health, and he visited his native village almost yearly for a
change of air. He also went to Jayrambati and to Sihore,
Hriday's birthplace. Everywhere he mixed freely with the villagers and many times regaled them with his songs and conversation. But people in Jayrambati often ridiculed him as the
"mad son-in-law." Now and then he would jump up from his
seat and exclaim: "This time everyone will be liberated, including the Mussalmāns and the untouchables. None will be left
behind." At this the villagers would say: "What a madman!"
When village women came to see him he would make witty
remarks, sometimes off-colour, which would convulse them with
laughter and cause many of them to run away in embarrassment. Sri Ramakrishna would say to those who remained: "The
weeds have been removed. Now be seated and I shall talk to
you."

We have already mentioned Aunt Bhanu, a neighbour of
Sarada Devi's, who had had a glimpse of Sri Ramakrishna's
spiritual mood and had become very fond of him. She told the
present writer that once she made a garland and wanted to put
it on Sri Ramakrishna's neck. Hiding it under her sāri, she went
to the Master but felt shy about offering it to him in the
presence of other women. The Master somehow came to know
about her intention and told a naughty joke which made the

women laugh and leave the room. When Bhanu was alone with him he asked her to offer the garland. As soon as it was put on his neck he went into deep samādhi. Unfamiliar with this mood, Bhanu was frightened, thinking he might have been stung by a poisonous insect hidden in the flowers. Presently Hriday arrived and brought the Master back to the normal state of mind with the help of certain mystical words. After that incident, Shyamasundari tried to keep women away from his presence.

Shyamasundari, deep in her heart, felt an anguish for her daughter. Often she said: "I have married my daughter to such a madman that she will never know the happiness of a house-holder's life. She will not have any children and feel the joy of being addressed as 'Mother.'" Sri Ramakrishna once heard these words and said: "Mother, please do not worry about that. Your daughter will have so many children that her ears will burn from her constantly being called 'Mother.'" It will be seen later how literally this prophecy was fulfilled.

In the March of Events

DURING THE TEN YEARS Sarada Devi spent at Dakshineswar, she lived most of the time in the Nahabat, a two-storey brick structure about seventy-five feet north of the Master's room. Situated on the bank of the Ganges, it commands a beautiful view of the sacred river and the spacious temple garden. On the upper storey Sarada's mother-in-law lived till her death. Sarada Devi's own room on the ground floor, about twenty inches above the ground level, was octagonal, each wall measuring inside a little more than three feet, the maximum distance between the walls across the floor being a little less than eight feet. The height from floor to ceiling was a little more than nine feet, and the floor space about fifty square feet. All around the room was a narrow verandah, about four feet wide, with only one door leading to the room. There were two ventilators but no windows. The door, about four feet by two feet, was so low that Sarada Devi hurt her head many times before getting used to passing through it without knocking it. Once she cut her head. For the sake of privacy, the verandah was screened with plaited bamboo mats, which cut off the sun and fresh air. On the east side of the verandah was the staircase leading upstairs. Under the stairs she had her kitchen.

In her small, stuffy room Sarada Devi kept her supplies and necessary belongings. She also worshipped, meditated, and slept here. Two or three of the Master's women devotees often spent the night with Sarada Devi in her room. From the ceiling hung a pot in a sling containing live fish, used for Sri Ramakrishna's meals. They splashed water all night. Often fat ladies from rich families of Calcutta visited the Kāli temple. Some of them, out of curiosity, peeped into Sarada Devi's room. Standing at the door and holding the jambs, they would lean forward and say: "Ah, what a tiny room for our good child! She is in exile, as it were, like Sitā."[1]

Sarada Devi often referred to the time she spent in the Nahabat as the best period of her life. Speaking about it years after, she would often forget herself in joy. "How happy I was then!" she said again and again. Few people, indeed, could stand such a cramped life. The holy atmosphere of the Ganges and the temples, service to the devotees, attendance on her husband, and her own spiritual practices and experiences lifted her mind above the physical hardship. Her days were filled with unceasing activity alternating with the stillness of prayer.

Sarada Devi's day began between three and four in the morning, before other people were awake. Here is a picture of her life on an average day. She went to the Ganges for her bath. Her companions were fishwives, who also bathed at that time, leaving their baskets on the steps of the Nahabat. Sarada Devi talked to them. After their bath they returned home, taking their baskets with them, and Sarada Devi hurried to her room to avoid being seen by others. At night the fishermen sang as they caught fish. Sarada Devi listened to their songs. One morning, while going into the water in the darkness, she almost stepped on a crocodile lying near the bank. When the Master heard about it, he asked her not to go to the river without a light. She spent about an hour and a half in prayer and meditation. Then she started cooking, which was a complicated affair. Afterwards she would rub Sri Ramakrishna's body with oil before his bath. This, however, did not happen every day, especially when his male disciples were present. Next she took his

---

[1] An allusion to the story of Sitā and Rāma described in the *Rāmāyana*. Sitā was imprisoned in a small room in the palace grounds of Rāvana, the monster-king of Ceylon.

The Nahabat

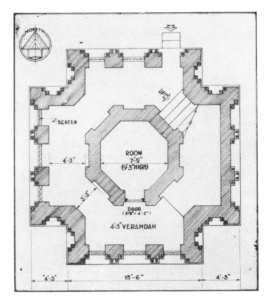

Ground Plan of the Nahabat

THE TEMPLE AT DAKSHINESWAR

VIEW OF THE TEMPLE FROM THE NAHABAT

midday meal to his room and personally watched over his eating. She often diverted his mind with light talk so that he might not fall into samādhi, which frequently happened without any warning. It was she alone who could make him take his meals without such spiritual disturbances. After he finished his meal, Sarada Devi returned to her room and took a little refreshment. Then she prepared rolls of betel leaf for the Master and the devotees. At that time she would often sing in a voice so low that people outside the room did not know she was singing. She had a musical voice and Sri Ramakrishna encouraged her and his niece Lakshmi to sing. The latter afterwards became an expert singer. At one o'clock a near-by factory blew its whistle, which Ramakrishna's mother called Krishna's flute played at Vaikuntha,[2] and Sarada Devi sat down to her own midday meal. After taking a short rest, she would sit on the steps of the Nahabat, when the sun's light fell there for a while and nobody was around, to sun her hair. By that time it would be three o'clock. She would then trim the lamps for the evening, burn incense before her altar, and meditate. Sri Ramakrishna always insisted on daily meditation, morning and evening. Then came the cooking of the evening meal. After feeding Sri Ramakrishna, and his mother as long as she was alive, Sarada took her own supper and then retired to bed about eleven o'clock. Her greatest difficulty was to answer the call of nature. No latrine was provided for her. She used the jungle on the bank of the Ganges for the purpose. It was a real problem during the daytime when people were around. If she felt the urge at that time, she would control it till evening and pray to the Lord to spare her the embarrassment. She thus developed intestinal trouble.

Sri Ramakrishna used to say: "Women must be active. They should not sit idle, otherwise useless and injurious thoughts will fill their minds." He kept a close watch on Sarada Devi so that

---

[2] The celestial abode of Vishnu. Krishna is His human embodiment.

she might not spend any time in idleness. Besides her arduous regular duties she had to do many odd jobs. One day, for instance, the Master gave her some jute fibre and asked her to plait it into strings which could be used for slings to hang pots of sweets in his room for his young disciples. With the rejected fibres she stuffed her pillow. She slept on a hard mat under which she spread some hessian. Referring to this kind of austere bed, she said later on to her devotees: "Now I use a soft pillow and a mattress. How different from the hard bed I slept on at Dakshineswar! But I slept then as well as I do now. I don't feel any difference."

Cooking consumed a great deal of Sarada Devi's time and energy. Now and then she received help from a maidservant. During the first part of her life at Dakshineswar she cooked for only a few people: the Master, his mother, and from time to time relatives and occasional guests. But from 1880 the number of Sri Ramakrishna's devotees increased and she often had to cook for them. Three kitchens were set up. She had to cook for herself, for the Master, and for the devotees. Sometimes special food had to be prepared for Gopāler-Mā, an orthodox widow and devotee of the Master, who was a strict vegetarian. Before her meal was cooked the oven had to be washed with Ganges water in order to remove all pollution from the touch of fish or flesh. For male devotees different dishes had to be prepared to suit their taste. On the occasion of the Master's birthday Sarada Devi had to cook for as many as fifty or sixty people. She often made chāpātis, the Indian bread, from seven or eight pounds of flour. One disciple, the elder Gopal,[3] did the marketing for her, and later another disciple, Latu,[4] kneaded the flour and washed the dishes. Suresh, a householder disciple, gave ten

---

[3] After the Master's death, Gopal renounced the world and received the name of Advaitananda.

[4] When he became a monk he received the name of Adbhutananda. He was among the first disciples of Sri Ramakrishna to embrace the monastic life.

rupees a month to meet the expenses for devotees' meals. The brunt of managing the household fell upon ungrudging Sarada Devi.

But her most pleasant and responsible duty was to cook for Sri Ramakrishna, who, on account of his weak stomach, had to be given special food. The sight of a large quantity of rice on the plate would often make him nervous, and he would refuse to take it for fear of upsetting his digestion. Sarada Devi would therefore play a trick: she pressed the rice down hard into a small heap. In the same way she would boil down his milk to make the quantity appear small. Once he was taking a special treatment which forbade his taking even a drop of water. She boiled for him about three quarts of milk down to less than a quart. But the Master had his suspicions and asked about the real amount. Sarada Devi said that it was about a quart. One day Golap-Mā, a woman disciple, was asked the exact quantity and she told the truth. The Master became nervous and said that the excessive milk caused him indigestion. When Sarada Devi was sent for, she pacified him by saying that Golap-Mā did not know the size of the pot in which the milk was measured. Another day he again inquired of Golap-Mā about the milk and she told him the exact quantity. He sent for Sarada Devi and asked her in detail about how many quarts and pints the pot held. She replied: "I don't know about quarts and pints. Please drink the milk. Why all these calculations?" He was not satisfied and said he might get indigestion. And that day his stomach was upset. Golap-Mā felt very sorry about the whole incident and said to Sarada Devi: "You should have told me your secret beforehand. How was I to know? I have spoiled his whole meal." Sarada Devi replied: "There is no harm in telling fibs about food. This is how I coax him to eat." It was only thus that Sri Ramakrishna improved his health, became almost cured of stomach trouble, and gained some weight. Many years later Sarada Devi, asked by an American devotee, Mrs. Ole Bull, about her attitude towards Sri Ramakrishna, said: "In spiritual matters absolute obedience; in other things I used my own common sense."

It will be of interest to describe briefly some of Sri Rama-krishna's women disciples who were frequent visitors at Dak-shineswar and who spent a great deal of time with Sarada Devi. Years later two of them lived with her permanently.[5]

Yogindra Mohini Devi, known as Yogin-Mā,[6] was regal in appearance and dignified in deportment. She hailed from an aristocratic family of Calcutta. At an early age she was given in marriage to a handsome youth of a well-known wealthy family who soon gave himself up to excesses, became a moral wreck, and squandered his fortune. Yogin-Mā's married life was a tragic one. Her first son died within six months of his birth. In the course of time her daughter was married. Soon after, this daughter left her husband's home to live with her widowed mother. The romantic picture of a happy and peaceful family life being shattered, Yogin-Mā was desolate and turned her mind to religion. At this time she visited Sri Ramakrishna at Dakshineswar and saw the Master, who was in a state of ecstasy, reeling like a drunkard. The bitter memory of her tipsy husband made her shudder, but she soon realized the true nature of the Master's spiritual emotion. When he learnt that she had come without taking food, he sent her at once to the Nahabat, where Sarada Devi with great affection fed her. Soon an intimate relationship grew up between them, and Sarada Devi often referred to her new companion as "my Jayā."[7] Speaking of Sarada Devi, Yogin-Mā said: "Whenever I went to

---

[5] For a fuller account of the women devotees of Sri Ramakrishna see *Great Women of India*, Calcutta, Advaita Ashrama, 1953.

[6] Yogin-Mā, often called "Yogin" by Sarada Devi, should be distinguished from Yogen, an intimate male devotee of Sri Rama-krishna, who later renounced the world and assumed the monastic name of Swami Yogananda. Sarada Devi also addressed Yogin-Mā as "Daughter Yogen," and Yogen as "Son Yogen."

[7] One of the attendants of Durgā, the Divine Mother; the other is Vijayā.

Mother, she took me into her confidence and unbosomed all her secrets. She often sought my advice. Even a moment's separation from her caused me great pain. I used to visit Dakshineswar almost every week, and sometimes spent the night there. On those occasions Mother would not allow me to sleep separately. She dragged me to her side, on her own bed. Once, a short while after my first becoming acquainted with her, Mother got into a boat to make a trip to Kamarpukur. I watched her departure with tears in my eyes and as the boat went out of sight I wept bitterly. The Master consoled me by recounting some of his spiritual experiences. When Mother returned after a year and a half, he said to her: 'That girl with big, beautiful eyes loves you dearly. She was upset when you left for Kamarpukur, and wept.' Mother said: 'Yes, I know her quite well. Her name is Yogin.' " Yogin-Mā used to braid Holy Mother's hair. Holy Mother liked so much the way she braided it that she often waited three or four days till Yogin-Mā's return to have it done again.

Golap Sundari Devi, addressed afterwards by the Master's devotees as Golap-Mā, was born in an orthodox brāhmin family, though she herself cherished liberal ideas. Her married life was not a happy one. Her husband died young, leaving her a son and a daughter. The son soon followed the father and her daughter expired shortly after her marriage. Weighed down by these misfortunes, Golap-Mā turned her attention to the inner life. While seeking spiritual solace she met Yogin-Mā, who lived in the neighbourhood, and she took her to Sri Ramakrishna. Golap-Mā unburdened herself to the Master and burst into tears. Introducing her to Sarada Devi, he said: "Give her a lot of food to fill her stomach. That will assuage her grief." He told Golap-Mā about the transitoriness of worldly happiness and exhorted her to love God alone. One day he said to Sarada Devi: "Keep your eyes on this brāhmin woman. She will live with you permanently." Golap-Mā loved orderliness, but she possessed a sharp tongue. Sarada Devi once said of her:

"Golāp's mind is very pure; it is never ruffled. She does not know what pride or vanity is."

Lakshmimani, affectionately called by the Master's devotees Lakshmi-Didi, who has already been mentioned several times, was Sri Ramakrishna's niece, the daughter of Rameswar. Exceptionally intelligent and possessed of a prodigious memory, she was reserved even at an early age and spoke only to her near relatives. Though her formal education did not go far, she could read in Bengali the *Rāmāyana*, the *Mahābhārata*, and other books of Hindu mythology. At the age of twelve she was married, but Sri Ramakrishna prophesied her early widowhood. One day, soon after marriage, her husband left the house in search of a job and was never seen again. After twelve years, according to Hindu tradition, Lakshmi considered herself a widow. At the age of fourteen she came to Dakshineswar and began to live with Sarada Devi in the latter's small room in the Nahabat. Lakshmi was initiated by Sri Ramakrishna. She later developed something of a masculine nature, with which the Master did not interfere. Sarada Devi once remarked: "Lakshmi used to sing and dance before the Master, imitating professional musicians. He said to me: 'That is her nature, but you must not imitate her and lose your womanly modesty.'"

Gauri-Mā was twenty-five years old when she first visited Sri Ramakrishna. At that time Sarada Devi was twenty-nine. Born in 1857, near Calcutta, she showed a strong desire for the spiritual life and a great attachment to the Hindu gods and goddesses even when very young. She entered a Christian missionary school but was repelled by the anti-Hindu attitude of the authorities. In the meantime she learnt by heart many Sanskrit hymns and came to know the Sanskrit language well, with a smattering of English and Persian. At the age of ten Gauri-Mā was initiated into spiritual life by a brāhmin and accepted as her spiritual ideal Sri Krishna, whom she worshipped in a stone emblem called Dāmodar. This emblem remained her lifelong companion and object of worship. Her widowed mother, alarmed at her detachment from the world, arranged her marriage. When Gauri-Mā came to know about it she remarked: "I will marry only Him who is immortal"—evidently meaning that she would marry Sri Krishna. On the eve of her marriage she ran away. Inflamed by her passion to realize God, Gauri-Mā left home at the age of eighteen and travelled in the company of religious mendicants to various holy places, her sole possessions being a few sacred books and the stone emblem of Krishna hanging from her neck in a small bag. When, after seven years, she came to Sri Ramakrishna, he at once accepted her as one of his disciples. During her second visit the Master introduced her to Sarada Devi. From that time on she lived now and then with Sarada Devi at the Nahabat and frequently visited the Master, whom she regarded as her father and mother. She prepared various delicacies for the Master and fed him with great devotion. In the Nahabat she often sang devotional songs in her melodious voice, which made Sri Ramakrishna go into samādhi. One day Sri Ramakrishna saw Gauri-Mā gathering flowers from the garden and said: "Well, Gauri, I am pouring water on the earth; you knead the clay." Explaining this cryptic remark, he asked her to work for the welfare of Indian women, who were in a sad plight. When she told him that she would like to train some girls in the solitude of the Himalayas, he replied: "No, no! You must work in this very town. You have had enough of spiritual practice. Now dedicate your life to the service of women. They are suffering dreadfully." Eventually she fulfilled the Master's wish.

Though a disciple of Sri Ramakrishna, Gauri-Mā often manifested greater love for Sarada Devi. One day the Master asked her jokingly, in Sarada Devi's presence, whom she loved more, himself or her. She rose to the occasion and answered in a song:

"O Krishna, player of the flute, surely You are not greater than Rādhā:[8]

---

[8] The divine Consort of Sri Krishna.

Those who are in distress may pray to You,
But when You are distressed, it is Rādhā You call upon
  with Your flute."

Sarada Devi was naturally embarrassed and pressed Gauri's
hand. The Master laughed and went away. Gauri-Mā often experienced spiritual moods at Dakshineswar.

Another woman, Aghoremani by name, visited Sri Ramakrishna now and then. Later she came to be known as Gopāler-
Mā, or Gopāla's Mother, on account of her intimate relationship
with Gopāla, the Baby Krishna. Born in 1822, Gopāler-Mā
was given in marriage at the age of nine but became a widow
immediately after. Soon she moved to a temple near Calcutta
where she was provided with her own room for spiritual exercises. In the words of Sister Nivedita:[9] "Her room was absolutely without comforts. Her bed was of stone, and her floor of
stone, and the piece of matting she offered her guests to sit on
had to be taken down from a shelf and unrolled. The handful
of parched rice and sugar candy that formed her only store, and
were all she could give in hospitality, were taken from an
earthen pot that hung from the roof by a few cords. But the
place was spotlessly clean, washed by the Ganges water of her
own sturdy carrying. And in a niche near her hand, lay an old
copy of the *Rāmāyana*, and her great horn spectacles, and a
little white bag containing the rosary. On these Gopāler-Mā
became a saint. Hour after hour, day after day, for how many
years, she had sat, day and night, absorbed in them." Gopāler-
Mā had many exalted spiritual experiences and often saw the
manifestation of Gopāla, her spiritual ideal, in Sri Ramakrishna.
At Dakshineswar she frequently took her meals with Sarada
Devi, whom she loved as her daughter-in-law.

These women devotees were tied to Sarada Devi by bonds of
indissoluble love. They were her friends and companions, and

---

[9] An Irish disciple of Swami Vivekananda, formerly known as
Margaret E. Noble.

while at Dakshineswar they helped her with the cooking and other household duties. This relationship continued throughout their lives.

To resume the narrative of Sarada Devi's life at Dakshineswar. The boy Latu used to knead the flour for bread, wash the dishes, and do the errands of a house-boy. One day Sarada Devi had been kneading a large quantity of flour while Latu was meditating by the bank of the Ganges. The Master happened to pass by and said to him: "Look here, Latu, the one on whom you are meditating is here now sweating over the flour."[10] He took Latu to the Nahabat and said to Sarada Devi: "He is a pure-souled boy. Whenever you need any help, please ask him." Latu became a member of Sarada Devi's household.

Sri Ramakrishna depended entirely upon Sarada Devi for his physical comforts, especially for his meals. According to social custom among orthodox Hindus, a Hindu woman is considered unclean for three days during her monthly period and is debarred from cooking and performing other household duties. When Sarada Devi for that reason could not cook for the Master, he used to get his food from the kitchen of the Kāli temple. That food invariably disagreed with him. One day when his stomach was upset, he sent for Sarada Devi and asked her the reason for her not preparing his meals. When she explained, he said: "Who told you that a woman cannot cook for those three days? You must cook for me as usual. There is nothing wrong about it. Please tell me what is impure in a person—the skin, the flesh, the bones, the marrow? It is the mind that makes one pure or impure. There is no impurity outside the mind."

On the occasion of one of her periodical visits to Kamarpukur, Sarada Devi had taken leave of the Master. At his midday meal Sri Ramakrishna said to some of his disciples: "She

---

[10] Evidently Sri Ramakrishna meant Sarada Devi, whom he regarded as identical with the Divine Mother Kāli. Latu had been meditating on Kāli.

left today—I mean Ramlal's aunt.[11] Ramlal is going to be married. That is why she is going to Kamarpukur. I watched her departure and didn't feel anything about it. Honestly I thought of her as a stranger. But the next moment I was worried about my meals. I said to myself: 'Who will cook for me?' You know I cannot digest every sort of food. Further, while I am eating I do not always retain normal consciousness. She knows what suits my stomach; so she cooks different vegetables. Now I am frankly worried about my meals." After a few months he wrote to her to return as soon as possible. One day he humorously asked a disciple: "Well, what does a wife signify in the case of one like me?" He himself gave the reply with a smile: "Don't you see? But for her, who would prepare the food just the way that agrees with my stomach?"

Though every Hindu woman is taught to regard her husband almost as God and serve him with body, heart, and soul, Sarada Devi looked upon Sri Ramakrishna as "God eternal and absolute," to use her own words—both as her husband and also in his own right. To serve him, she felt, was to worship God. This attitude enabled her to face her daily tasks joyfully. She said later: "When I thought that I was serving him, no physical discomfort bothered me. The days passed in unmixed bliss." But often, when she did not have the privilege of being near him or serving his meals, she had to forgo this bliss. This happened especially when the number of the Master's men disciples increased and they used to attend him. Sarada Devi was too shy to appear before them, and Sri Ramakrishna did not approve of it. "Sometimes," she once remarked, "I could not see him even once in two months. Naturally I felt depressed. At that time I used to say to myself: 'O mind, why should you think yourself so fortunate as to be able to see him every day?' I would stand for hours behind a small hole in the screen of my porch and listen to his singing. On account of standing long hours on my feet, I got rheumatism." Sarada

[11] Referring to Sarada Devi.

Devi watched him and the devotees singing day and night in his room and often said to herself: "Ah, if only I were one of those devotees! Then I could hear him and witness his ecstasies." Regarding Sarada Devi's natural bashfulness and retiring habits, the manager of the temple garden once remarked: "Yes, we have heard about her living there, but never seen her."

When Golap-Mā first visited the Master he asked her one day to bring his food. From that time she carried it every day. This prevented Sarada Devi from seeing her husband at meal times. Golap-Mā often spent long hours in the evening in the Master's room and would not have returned to Sarada Devi even by ten o'clock. Sarada Devi had to wait for a long while with Golap-Mā's meal. This annoyed her and one day the Master heard her remark: "Let this food be eaten by a dog or a cat. I cannot look after it any more." The next day the Master said to Golap-Mā: "You spend a long time here. This inconveniences her. She has to keep her eyes on your food." "No, no," Golap-Mā said. "Mother loves me very much and regards me as her own daughter. She calls me by my first name."

Though Sri Ramakrishna and Sarada Devi sometimes did not see each other for a long period of time, in spite of their living within seventy-five feet of each other, and though because of his constantly dwelling on a higher plane of consciousness he was forgetful of the world and his body, yet he was not indifferent about her welfare. On the contrary, he kept a close watch on her health and comfort. One day, coming to know about her having a headache, he repeatedly asked Ramlal: "Why has she a headache?"

Sri Ramakrishna called Sarada Devi's room, with its porch covered by bamboo mats, a "cage." Often Lakshmi shared the room with her. The Master jokingly called them a pair of parakeets. When the food-offering from the Kāli temple was brought to his room he would say to Ramlal: "The birdies are in the cage. Give them some fruit and grain." Sometimes even his intimate disciples—not having seen the Mother—took his joke literally.

Sarada Devi had developed a touch of rheumatism, which in later years became rather painful. She also often lived alone at the Nahabat. This worried the Master. He said to her: "A wild bird becomes rheumatic if it is kept in a cage day and night. Walk to the village now and then." He saw to it that after luncheon, when most people were resting, she went out of the temple compound through a back door and visited her neighbours.

Sri Ramakrishna, who never had any money, worried from time to time about Sarada's support after his death. One day he asked her how much money she needed for her monthly expenses. She told him that five or six rupees should be enough. But this evidently did not satisfy him. "How many pieces of bread do you eat at night?" Sri Ramakrishna asked. The shy wife blushed at the mention of her eating. When he pressed the point repeatedly she said: "Five or six pieces." "Then," the Master said, "five or six rupees should be enough." He deposited with Balaram Bose, a householder disciple, sufficient money to yield that much in interest.

Though a girl brought up in a backward village and scarcely able to read or write, Sarada Devi possessed keen intelligence and unusual circumspection. Once a wealthy devotee noticed that Sri Ramakrishna's bed-sheet was soiled and wanted to give him ten thousand rupees to provide for his necessary comforts. The embodiment of renunciation, he felt extreme pain, as if someone was cutting his head with a saw. "O Mother," he prayed to Kāli tearfully, "why are you tempting me again at this stage of my life?" He refused to accept the gift. But the devotee insisted. Sri Ramakrishna, wanting to test Sarada Devi, sent for her and said: "Look here, the devotee wants me to accept this money. This is utterly impossible for me. Now he wants to leave the gift with you. Why should you not accept it?" Much to his relief, Sarada Devi immediately replied:

"What are you saying? How can that be? The money must never be accepted. If I take it, it will be the same as your taking it, because even if it is kept with me the money will be spent for you. People show you respect for your renunciation. So you must refuse the gift."

Sarada Devi was thoroughly aware of Sri Ramakrishna's renunciation, both in spirit and in practice. She had seen many instances of it. She knew very well how even his nervous system recoiled at the idea of hoarding. Here is an example. The Master was fond of chewing certain spices now and then, especially after meals. One day after he had taken his meal at her room Sarada Devi gave him some spices in a packet of paper and asked him to take them to his room. The Master started for his room but felt confused. He walked straight to the embankment and was about to fall into the river. Sarada Devi did not know what to do. She was too bashful to come out in public and restrain him. Suddenly she saw a priest of the temple and asked him to call Hriday, who saved the Master from the imminent catastrophe. Evidently, to Sri Ramakrishna, the carrying of a small packet of spices was an act of hoarding.

It may be remembered that at the time of Sri Ramakrishna's marriage, his mother had borrowed some ornaments for Sarada Devi which had to be returned soon after. At that time the mother-in-law promised that the Master would give her more precious ornaments. At Dakshineswar he did in fact provide her with these. He said to Hriday that she was an incarnation of the Goddess Sarasvati,[12] who loves ornaments, and asked him to procure some for her. One day garrulous Golap-Mā said to Sarada Devi, "Manomohan's[13] mother asked me the other

---

[12] The Goddess of Wisdom and Music. She is a manifestation of the Divine Mother. One of the hymns used by devotees in saluting her is the following: "Hail to Thee, Goddess, the essence of all beings, moving and unmoving. A pearl necklace hangs on Thy bosom; Thou holdest in Thy hands a vinā and a book. Hail Mother, I salute Thee."

[13] Manomohan was a householder devotee of Sri Ramakrishna.

day whether, since the Master was a perfect example of renunciation, it looked well that you should adorn your body with so
much gold." At once Sarada Devi removed practically all the
ornaments.

Watching the actions and movements of Sri Ramakrishna
for a long time, Sarada Devi learnt to divine his thoughts and
feelings easily. One day the Master was returning from the Kāli
temple when she was sweeping his room and making his bed.
As he walked through the paved courtyard, his eyes were bloodshot and his legs unsteady. He looked like a drunkard. He
entered the room and touching Sarada Devi asked her if he was
really drunk. She looked at him and said: "No, no, why should
you be drunk?" "Then," the Master asked, "why am I reeling?
I cannot talk. Am I intoxicated?" "No, no," she said again.
"Why should you be intoxicated like an ordinary drunkard?
You are drunk with love of the Divine Mother." Sri Ramakrishna was delighted and said: "You are right."

For several years Sri Ramakrishna attended a religious festival at Panihati, a few miles north of Dakshineswar, in which
thousands of people took part. In 1885 he wanted to participate
in the function and invited some of his devotees, both men and
women, to join him. Sarada Devi requested a woman devotee
to ask the Master if she should accompany them. The Master
told her: "She may go if she wishes." Sarada thought for a
while and said she would not go because of the great crowd.
The Master and the devotees went to the festival. After his return at night he said to a devotee: "What a crowd of people!
On account of my spiritual moods I became the centre of attraction of all. It was wise that she [referring to Sarada Devi]
did not accompany me. If people had seen her with me they
would have made fun of us and teasingly said: 'There go the
hamsa and the hamsi.'[14] She is very intelligent."

[14] The Sanskrit word for gander is *hamsa,* and for goose, *hamsi.*
Hamsa also signifies God or Soul. Sri Ramakrishna was often called
the Paramahamsa (Great Soul), the title of one belonging to the
highest order of monks.

When Sarada Devi was told what the Master had said, she remarked: "I realized he was not wholeheartedly giving me permission to go. Instead of saying: 'Yes, of course she will go,' he merely said: 'She may go if she wishes.' He left the decision to me. So I gave up the idea of going."

Though Sarada Devi obeyed Sri Ramakrishna absolutely in most things, nevertheless in certain matters she exercised her own judgement. During her earlier days at Dakshineswar she lived practically alone in the Nahabat. A maidservant occasionally helped her with her domestic duties, and a certain old woman visited her now and then. This woman had not led a moral life in her younger days, but in later years she turned to religion. One day the Master said to Sarada Devi: "Why do you allow her in your room?" He told her of the woman's past. Sarada Devi said: "That may be, but now she talks only about God and spiritual matters." "But," the Master insisted, "whatever she may say now, she was once a prostitute. Why should you speak to her? Goodness gracious!" Sarada Devi remained unmoved. She could not let a person down who was repentant and sought her grace. As we shall see later, she never deviated from this attitude.

The Master's devotees used to bring offerings of fruit and sweets for him. Sarada Devi distributed these freely among the devotees and neighbours, sometimes forgetting to keep a share for her husband. Expressing his disapproval, the Master said to her one day: "If you give things away in this manner, how will you run the house?" Abruptly Sarada Devi left the room. Greatly distressed, Sri Ramakrishna said to his nephew Ramlal: "Go at once and pacify your aunt. If she gets angry then all my spirituality will come to naught."

Sarada Devi's liberality and compassion were the result of the awakening of motherhood in her. She felt that she was mother to all who came to Sri Ramakrishna, and acted accordingly. In this particular area of her life, she permitted no outside interference. She could not turn away anybody who addressed her as "Mother." To give an instance, one day, as was her habit, she was carrying Sri Ramakrishna's food to his room when a woman said to her: "Mother, please let me carry the plate." Sarada agreed and the woman took the plate to the Master's room, placed it before him, and went away. Sarada Devi sat near Sri Ramakrishna in order to watch him eat. But he could not even touch the food. Looking at Sarada Devi, he said: "What have you done? Why did you allow her to touch the plate? Don't you know she leads an immoral life? How can I eat food she has touched?" Sarada said: "I know all about it; please eat the food today." But still the Master could not touch the plate. At her repeated request he said: "Please promise not to allow that woman to carry my food again." Sarada Devi said firmly, with folded hands: "Master, I cannot give any such promise, but I shall try to bring your food myself. If someone addresses me as 'Mother' and wishes to carry the plate, I shall not be able to refuse. You must not forget that you are not only my Lord; you are the Lord of all." Sri Ramakrishna was satisfied and ate his meal.

Sarada Devi never hesitated to fulfil the demands of motherhood, which, as we shall see later, were based on a profound spiritual insight. To Sri Ramakrishna's devotees she was at that time like an earthly mother, though afterwards they regarded her as the veritable incarnation of the Divine Mother of the Universe. At Dakshineswar she was always solicitous about their physical welfare. Sri Ramakrishna kept a close watch on the daily habits of the young disciples destined to be monks. He warned them against eating too much at night lest they should become lazy and neglect their meditation in the early hours of the morning. But Sarada Devi, who cooked for them, saw to it that they had plenty to eat. Once Sri Ramakrishna came to know that a disciple had taken two or three extra pieces of bread beyond what he approved of, and that Sarada Devi's motherly solicitude was responsible for this excess. He was annoyed and forbade her to do so in the future. But she was not a person to be ordered around concerning such matters and said to the Master sharply: "Why are you worrying just because he has eaten two extra pieces of bread? I am looking after these children. I do not want you to criticize them about food." Reminiscing about such incidents at Dakshineswar, Sarada Devi once said to Yogin-Mā: "Can a person obey every word of another human being?" She did not hesitate to speak the blunt truth to her husband when the occasion demanded it. At one time the kitchen at Kamarpukur badly needed repair and the Master was asked to pay the expense. He said: "We do not live there; let them somehow manage it." "How selfish!" Sarada Devi said at once. Thereupon the Master gave her a discourse on selfishness.

Though Sarada Devi always obeyed her husband implicitly, the Master never failed to show her respect and courtesy. Describing this attitude on his part, she said: "I was married to such a husband that he never addressed me as *tui*.[15] He never struck me even with a flower." One night she brought him his meal. Finding him absorbed in meditation, she put it in its usual place and was about to leave the room. Suddenly the Master came down from his spiritual state and said: "Shut the door as you go out," using *tui*. He thought it was Lakshmi, his niece, who had brought the food. "All right," Sarada Devi said, "I am closing the door." Recognizing her voice, he said repentantly: "Is it you? I thought it was Lakshmi. Please forgive me for addressing you as *tui*." That unkind word he had addressed to Sarada Devi disturbed the Master so much that he went to her room the next day and again apologized. "You see, I couldn't sleep the whole night. I felt very badly for addressing you so disrespectfully."

---

[15] A pronoun generally used in Bengali in addressing a servant, a junior, or an inferior.

Spiritual Practices

THE TENDER PLANT of Sarada Devi's spiritual life which later grew into a mighty tree, giving shelter to many a seeker of God, developed silently in the holy atmosphere of Dakshineswar. About this significant period of her life Sarada Devi gave only a few hints to her devotees, which we shall narrate in this chapter.

Sri Ramakrishna began to train Sarada Devi in the practice of spiritual disciplines. To her he was teacher, father, mother, companion, husband, and God Himself. He revealed himself to her in two different ways: as the demonstration of the eternal principles of all religions, and also as her Ishta-devatā, her Chosen Ideal, or the Personal God. God no doubt pervades the whole creation as Satchidānanda, Existence-Consciousness-Bliss. But He is manifest more through animate beings than through inanimate nature. Among animate beings He is manifest more through man than through subhuman beings, more through saints than through ordinary worldly persons. But He manifests Himself in the highest measure through a God-man, who, though living in the world, is completely detached from it, who is constantly absorbed in God-consciousness, and who, to quote Sri Ramakrishna's words, "sings, dances, and forgets himself in divine ecstasy."

Sarada Devi observed with her own eyes all the signs of divinity in Sri Ramakrishna. She witnessed his complete conquest of lust and greed. Every woman, to him, was a manifestation of the Divine Mother. He never thought of her in any other way, even in dreams. Money and worldly possessions never tempted him in the slightest degree. If he touched a coin he felt as if his body had been—as he would say—"stung by a horned fish." She said later that complete renunciation was his special message to this age. Sarada Devi watched his frequent samādhis, in which he was totally absorbed in God. She loved to hear devotional music. When Sri Ramakrishna sang and danced with the devotees in ecstasy in his room, he would ask Ramlal to keep open the door of his room facing the Nahabat, saying: "In this room intense feeling and love of God will be expressed. She must witness it; otherwise, how will she learn?"

Sarada Devi and Lakshmi had been initiated by a monk while they were living at Kamarpukur. The Master again initiated them at Dakshineswar. Sarada Devi, though occupied with many household duties, spent a long time in repeating the sacred word. She said that she used to repeat it daily one hundred thousand times.[1] Recalling an incident of that time, Sarada Devi said: "At Dakshineswar I used to get up at three o'clock in the morning and sit in meditation. Often I totally forgot my body and the world. Once, during the early hours of the morning, as I was meditating, a gentle breeze blew my red-bordered cloth off my back, but I did not know it. The Master saw me in that condition, though I was unaware of it. On moonlit nights I would look at the moon and pray: 'May my mind be pure as the rays of the moon!' or 'O Lord, there are stains even on the moon, but let my mind be absolutely stainless.' If a person is steady in meditation, he will clearly see the Lord in his heart and hear His voice. The moment an idea flashes in his mind, it will at once be fulfilled and he will be bathed in peace. Ah, what a state of mind I was in at that time! One day the maidservant dropped a metal plate in front of me with a bang. The sound hit me and penetrated, as it were, into my heart."

Sarada Devi experienced great joy at Dakshineswar. She lived

---

[1] It appears that through rigorous discipline she formed the habit of repeating the mantra mentally, even while performing domestic and other work.

with one who was the embodiment of bliss. Referring to Sri Ramakrishna's blissful state she said:

"What a unique man he was! How many minds he illumined! What unceasing bliss he radiated! Day and night his room echoed and re-echoed with laughter, stories, talk, and music.

"The Master sang, and I would listen hour after hour, standing behind the screen of the Nahabat. When the singing was over I saluted him with folded hands. What joyous days we passed through! People poured in day and night, and there was no end of spiritual talk.

"I never saw him sad. He made merry with all—a boy of five or an old man."

Sri Ramakrishna closely watched Sarada Devi's spiritual practices and saw to it that she meditated regularly. At three o'clock in the morning he would go to the door of the Nahabat and say to Lakshmi: "Get up and wake up your aunt. How long will you sleep? It is going to be dawn. Begin your meditation." In wintertime Sarada Devi wanted Lakshmi to sleep a little longer. When she knew that the Master was outside, she would whisper in Lakshmi's ear: "Don't answer him. He cannot sleep. It is not yet time to get up. Even the crows and cuckoos are asleep. Don't move from your bed." Hearing no response from inside, and thinking they were still asleep, the Master would sometimes tease them by pouring water under the door. The ladies had to get up quickly for fear of the bed's getting wet. Sometimes the bed actually got wet. Thus Lakshmi acquired the habit of early rising.

One morning Sarada Devi felt unwell and did not leave her bed at three o'clock. This happened on several successive days. At once she understood it was a trick of the mind and forced herself to get up at the usual time. She often taught her disciples that one does not succeed in spiritual life without firmness and determination.

Whenever the opportunity arose Sri Ramakrishna gave Sarada Devi spiritual instruction. One evening he spoke at length to her and Lakshmi about love of God. As they were about to take leave of him he said to his niece: "Discuss what you have heard from me with your aunt tonight. You have seen the cows eating grass in the field during the daytime; at night they chew the cud. Therefore go over with your aunt what you have learnt now. Then you will not forget my words." Many years later, when someone read to Sarada Devi from *The Gospel of Sri Ramakrishna,* she said: "He used to give me such fine instruction. If I had only known how to write, I would have noted down his words."

Sarada Devi never allowed her meditation and other spiritual practices to interfere with her daily duties. She pursued both work and worship. During her spare time she now and then made garlands for the image in the Kāli temple. But she never made work an excuse for neglecting worship.

As we have already noted, Sarada Devi kept away from male outsiders. She was bashful and modest. Sri Ramakrishna approved of this and forbade even Ramlal to frequent her room. One day he sharply reprimanded Hriday for spending a long time at the Nahabat indulging in jokes and laughter.

One night she and Lakshmi were singing in a low voice. The Master heard it from outside. The next day he said to Sarada Devi: "Last night I heard you singing, and you seemed to be absorbed. That's very good."

She was reticent about her spiritual experiences. Though she had many visions, she did not stress their value very much. About the essence of spiritual realization she once said to her devotees: "Through realization the mind becomes pure, and through that pure mind one obtains enlightenment."

When Sarada Devi first came to Dakshineswar she had most probably not experienced samādhi, though later she attained even to nirvikalpa samādhi.[2] But she frequently witnessed Sri

---

[2] The highest spiritual experience, in which a man realizes his complete oneness with God and the universe.

Ramakrishna's deep ecstasies and also the spiritual moods of his devotees. Watching Gauri-Mā's ecstasies, Sarada Devi, too, wanted to experience them and, through Lakshmi, requested the Master to fulfil her desire. The Master said in reply: "Why does she wish to have ecstasies? Gauri has a masculine nature. But she [referring to Sarada Devi] should suppress her spiritual emotions." Then quoting a proverb he said: "A helpless woman develops her strength by remaining helpless. That way alone she succeeds. A woman should lead a self-effacing life. Bashfulness is her religion. If she loses it people speak ill of her."

Another day Sarada Devi, through Yogin-Mā, conveyed her request to the Master for samādhi. "Please tell him," she said, "that I would like to experience it. I do not find him alone to speak about the matter myself." Next day Yogin-Mā informed the Master of Sarada Devi's wish. He listened to it but remained silent and grave. Yogin-Mā felt nervous and returned at once to the Nahabat. Sarada Devi was then meditating in her room, with the door ajar. Yogin-Mā peeped in and saw a strange sight. Sarada Devi was now weeping and now laughing. Tears streamed from her eyes. After a while she became still, immobile as a stone. Yogin-Mā shut the door and went away. After a long while she came back, and Sarada Devi asked her when she had returned from the Master's room. "Go on, Mother!" Yogin-Mā said. "So you do not experience samādhi!" Sarada Devi laughed.

One night Yogin-Mā was sleeping in the same bed with Sarada Devi when someone began to play on the flute. Sarada Devi fell into samādhi. Every now and then she laughed. Yogin-Mā woke up and saw the whole thing. Being nervous about touching her at that time, she sat in a corner for a long time before Sarada Devi regained her normal mood.

As we have seen, Sri Ramakrishna did not much encourage outer manifestations of spiritual feeling in Sarada Devi. One day when she complained to the Master that she had not experienced much of such feeling, he said: "What will happen if you fall into ecstasy? You will drop your clothes and cut capers. Who will look after your clothes?" Sri Ramakrishna, himself, often became unconscious in samādhi and his clothes dropped to the ground as he danced.

Sarada Devi did not outwardly practise austerities or observe rituals to the extent Sri Ramakrishna did. Her life was one of quiet prayer and meditation, and she never neglected the performance of her daily duties. She appeared to others more like a householder than a recluse or ascetic. Yet the ocean of her spiritual experience was as bottomless as his. This shows that she was not just a saint or a mystic, but, like her husband, a manifestation of Divinity.

Sri Ramakrishna was fully aware of Sarada Devi's future. Referring to her one day, he said to a woman disciple: "She is Sarasvati. She has assumed a human body to impart wisdom to men; but she has hidden her celestial beauty lest people, by looking at her, should befoul their minds with sinful thoughts." Both before and after his death the Master often reminded her of her future rôle. He gave her detailed instructions about awakening the spiritual power of her future disciples.

Sri Ramakrishna trained Sarada Devi to fulfil a special mission, namely, demonstration of the Motherhood of God. From an early age she expressed the motherhood innate in women in many ways: by taking care of her brothers, by feeding the poor, and afterwards by looking after Sri Ramakrishna's young disciples at Dakshineswar. As is natural with women, she occasionally wished she had children. In Hindu society a woman without children is considered unlucky and unfit to participate in certain religious observances. At Kamarpukur she had heard the jibes of her neighbours on account of her not having any children, and she felt sad at heart. Several times she thought about it at Dakshineswar. We have already spoken of her mother's grief for having married her daughter to an insane man and thus depriving her of the joy of being addressed as "Mother." One day Sri Ramakrishna read Sarada Devi's thought and said: "Why should you worry? I shall leave you many children, all pure as gold, the like of whom women do not get even through the prayers and austerities of millions of lives. So many people will call you mother that you will find it hard to look after them all." Perhaps this assurance did not completely satisfy Sarada Devi. Still she wanted to hear the sweet word "mother." Sri Ramakrishna again read her thought and instructed some of his disciples from Calcutta to stop in front of the Nahabat, before coming to his room, and say loudly: "Mother, here we are!"

How well she fulfilled the demands of motherhood! Once an insane woman acted immodestly before Sri Ramakrishna, who became angry and scolded her sharply. Sarada Devi, when she learnt of it, said to Golap-Mā in a distressed voice: "See what he has done. If the girl acted foolishly, why didn't he send her to me? Why did he scold her?" Then she sent for the woman and said to her: "My child, if he is annoyed by your presence, don't go to him. Why don't you come to me?"

The normal woman feels the urge of motherhood, which God has planted in her heart for the perpetuation of the creation, and also for the gradual sublimation of carnal desires. Women who are creative in body satisfy this urge through physical offspring; but a rare few, creative in spirit, satisfy the same urge through children of the spirit. Sarada Devi belongs to the latter category and is therefore affectionately called Holy Mother by her disciples and by the devotees of Sri Ramakrishna. One day she said to a disciple: "The Master regarded all creatures as manifestations of the Divine Mother. He left me behind to give expression to this Motherhood."

The concept of the Motherhood of God, and the worship of God as the Divine Mother, form a special feature of Hinduism. Sri Ramakrishna, who had his first communion with God through worship of the Divine Mother and who cherished a life-long devotion to Her, said that to worship God as Mother is the final stage in spiritual evolution. A Hindu, to be sure, worships God as Father, Friend, and Beloved, but the idea of God as Mother draws him nearest to God. According to Vedānta, Ultimate Reality, which is known as Brahman, is a nameless, formless, attributeless, and transcendental neutral entity. In the final non-dual experience, Brahman alone exists. The soul and the universe become one with It. It is Śakti, also called māyā, the inscrutable potency of Brahman, that projects and preserves the universe and animate and inanimate beings. At the end of a cycle all names and forms return to Her[3] and remain in seed state, and at the beginning of the new cycle they all reappear in their tangible gross forms. Śakti is the totality of creation, with all its pairs of opposites: good and evil, pain and pleasure, life and death. She functions through both knowledge and ignorance. Both are necessary to perpetuate the creation. Through Her aspect of ignorance, avidyā-māyā, She deludes creatures, binding them to the world and lengthening their phenomenal existence. Through Her aspect of knowledge, vidyā-māyā, She gives insight to spiritual aspirants, removing their chains and finally liberating them. This Śakti controls both bondage and liberation. Sri Ramakrishna worshipped Her as Kālī, the Mother, and often affectionately called Her "my Mother." Brahman and Kālī, the Godhead and Its potency, are inseparable, like fire and its power to burn, like a gem and its lustre, like a word and its meaning. All creatures—gods and angels, prophets and saints, the worldly and the wicked—are manifestations or offspring of Her. She resembles an earthly mother in that created beings come out of Her, and after they are born are preserved by Her. At the time of final liberation they enter Brahman through the portal of Her grace.

God's love for man—unselfish, unsolicited, and undeserved—has been stressed by the mystics and prophets of all religions. The nearest example of this love in human experience is the love of a mother for her children. A mother's love and sacrifice qualify her spiritually to stand above all other relatives. A wife's

---

[3] Śakti, regarded as the Divine Mother, is feminine.

love may fluctuate with the sweetness bestowed upon her. But the mother's affection, by its very nature, grows deeper as the need grows and follows the beloved child even to hell. A yearning love that can never refuse us, a benediction that for ever abides with us, a presence from which we cannot grow away, a heart in which we are always safe, a sweetness unfathomed, a bond unbreakable, holiness without a shadow—all these indeed, and more, constitute motherhood.

Sri Ramakrishna made Sarada Devi a symbol of God's Motherhood because through her immaculate body and mind the divine Śakti manifested Herself to the fullest degree in modern times. His action served two important purposes. By worshipping God as the omnipotent, compassionate, and all-forgiving Mother, an aspirant develops fearlessness and comes closer to reality. By seeing God in a woman he gradually sublimates his carnal desires. Carnality, which seeks fulfilment through physical relationship with a member of the opposite sex, is one of the deadly enemies with which spiritual seekers, both men and women, have to wrestle. A woman can easily conquer it by regarding a man as her child. She is, in essence, the mother of all men, no matter what other relationships society may sanction or speak of. A man, too, easily subdues his lust by seeing in a woman the symbol of motherhood. But alas, an ignorant person regards woman as an object to satisfy his physical appetite. He craves her body and pushes away the Divinity in her. Thus he becomes entangled in the coils of the world. If he worships the Divinity in her, he is blessed with the nectar of immortality.

Once Sri Ramakrishna asked a young disciple how he looked upon women. He said: "I hate them. They are obstacles to spiritual life. I shun them as impurity itself. There is a lion in me which roars in the presence of women." "My child," the Master said, "you cannot get over the infatuation of sex by hating women. That way you will be more entangled in their snares. Regard a woman as your mother, and she will not hurt you but help you to overcome your passion." Sri Ramakrishna showed the easier way of overcoming the sex instinct. He left behind Sarada Devi, whose body always remained pure, whose character was pure, and who was the embodiment of purity, so that by contemplating her men could overcome the last traces of impurity.

It may also be mentioned here that Hinduism asks a wife to regard her husband as God. By associating him with Divinity she can gradually sublimate her physical desire. Blessed indeed is the family where husband and wife regard each other as manifestations of God, and children look upon their parents as His earthly symbols.

In concluding this chapter it will be appropriate to discuss the necessity for the practice of spiritual disciplines by Sarada Devi, who was a manifestation of Divinity.

All the major religions, as well as saints, prophets, and mystics, emphasize the need of spiritual discipline for spiritual aspirants for the purification of their hearts. But what about Incarnations of God, who are born free and who remain unstained by the blemishes of the world? Why should they practise spiritual disciplines like ordinary human beings? The mystery of the Divine Incarnation seems to lie in the fact that though God is eternally pure, enlightened, free; though, in essence, He is Existence-Consciousness-Bliss Absolute; and though He is incorporeal, nameless, and formless Spirit, yet through His own inscrutable potency He assumes a human form without any compulsion from outside or any desire to fulfil a selfish purpose. The entire meaning of the embodiment of the Divine is to show man the way out of the labyrinth of the world. God becomes man so that man may become God. When, in course of time, righteousness declines and wickedness prevails, God becomes incarnated to restore spiritual values.

An Incarnation is a God-man, a blending of Divinity and humanity. He descends on earth, covering Himself with a thin veil of māyā or cosmic ignorance, through which He now and then gets a glimpse of His divine nature and mission. Of His own accord He assumes some of the imperfections of humanity and acts like a man with regard to hunger, thirst, sickness, and the other characteristics of bodily existence. Like a man, again, He prays, meditates, worships, and observes spiritual disciplines so as to rend the self-imposed veil of māyā. His spiritual struggle resembles that of a man because He Himself has assumed a human form. Otherwise there would seem to be no purpose in His being incarnated. A man cannot understand transcendental truth unless it is expressed through human actions. Once the veil is pierced, the Incarnation becomes fully aware of Himself. Yet even then He practises disciplines to set an example for others. His meditation and worship before He is conscious of His divinity serve the same purpose, for He does not need them for His own liberation.

A God-man practises disciplines most intensely, condensing the efforts of many ordinary lives into one, because it is His mission to bring about the liberation of many and to arouse the spiritual consciousness of humanity. We know what a protracted struggle is necessary for an ordinary man to develop even a small amount of God-consciousness. This explains the superhuman renunciation, austerity, yearning, purity, and self-control manifested in the short life of a God-man. His ecstasies and intimate communion with the Godhead make Him appear almost abnormal. To be sure, He is abnormal: if He were normal like us, he would not be a God-man, an awakener of the spiritual consciousness of humanity.

The Divine Power becomes incarnated in the flesh to fulfil a cosmic spiritual necessity. Hinduism does not limit the Incarnation of God to a particular person or time. Sri Ramakrishna is now regarded as a God-man for our age, and the same Divinity which was manifested through Sri Ramakrishna was also manifested through Sarada Devi. The purpose of this dual manifestation, through what society calls the husband-and-wife relationship, will be revealed as the drama of Sarada Devi's life unfolds itself through these pages.

Sri Ramakrishna once said to Sarada Devi: "I know who you are, but I shall not reveal it now." He characterized her as a cat hidden in ashes. When the ashes are shaken off, one can see the cat.

The Master's Death and After

A T Dakshineswar Sarada Devi was happy in every way. But in this impermanent world nothing lasts forever. The happy days at Dakshineswar were soon to be over. In April 1885 Sri Ramakrishna felt a soreness in his throat. As simple treatment brought him no relief, a specialist was called for, and the illness was diagnosed as cancer. Sarada Devi and the young disciples took charge of the nursing, and Sarada Devi prepared his special diet. The physician warned the Master against conversation and ecstasies, but he did not pay much heed. The disease became aggravated.

One day in September the Master's throat bled. Some of the older disciples thought it prudent to remove him to Calcutta for facility of treatment and nursing. Accordingly a house was rented at Shyampukur, in the northern part of the city, where he took up his residence in October. Sarada Devi continued to live at Dakshineswar. There she led a quiet life without realizing the real significance of the Master's illness. She was then thirty-two years old. She utilized her leisure time in brushing up on her reading, which had been interrupted after she left Kamarpukur. A girl from the neighbourhood visited her every now and then and gave her lessons. Sarada Devi rewarded her with vegetables and fruits from the garden. Thus she learnt to read in Bengali the *Rāmāyana*, the *Mahābhārata*, and similar books. But she could not write. Once, many years after, pressed by a disciple for an autograph, she made great efforts to scrawl her name but did not succeed.

While she was thus passing melancholy days at Dakshineswar, a cruel remark made unwittingly by tactless Golap-Mā hurt her feelings deeply. Golap-Mā said to Yogin-Mā that the Master had probably left Dakshineswar because he was annoyed with Sarada Devi. Greatly troubled in mind, she went at once to Shyampukur and asked him with tears in her eyes if she had really offended him. Sri Ramakrishna denied the whole thing and sent her back to the Nahabat in a peaceful mood. Later he scolded Golap-Mā severely for her stupid chatter and asked her to beg Sarada Devi's forgiveness. Golap-Mā walked on foot all the way to Dakshineswar and, weeping, implored Sarada Devi to forgive her. Sarada Devi, who could never bear ill feeling against anyone, laughed and gently patted her on her back three times.

The preparation of Sri Ramakrishna's diet became a real problem, and the devotees discussed the idea of bringing Sarada Devi to Shyampukur. But the house had no quarters where she could have privacy. When Sri Ramakrishna was told of the situation, he reminded the disciples of Sarada Devi's natural bashfulness and said: "Will she be able to live here? You had better ask her about it. If, after knowing all the facts, she is willing to come, let her do so." Remembering her husband's precept to suit one's conduct and action to the time and circumstances, she brushed aside the inconvenience of living in a cramped space and arrived at Shyampukur. Immediately she devoted herself to Sri Ramakrishna's service.

At Shyampukur Sarada Devi had to live with the Master's disciples. With the exception of Latu and the senior Gopal, she had never exchanged a word with them. Sri Ramakrishna occupied a large drawing-room on the second floor, and Sarada Devi was given a small adjoining room. The kitchen was situated in a small covered space on the way to the roof. Before three o'clock in the morning, when the other inmates were still asleep, she finished her bath in the only bathroom in the house and went to the kitchen. Her sleep at night lasted about three hours. There she meditated, cooked for the Master and his attendants, and carried out her other household duties. When the Master's meal was ready, she sent word to the devotees. Whenever convenient, they left Sri Ramakrishna's room so that she could herself bring down his food and supervise his eating. Thus she lived practically invisible to the devotees, except Latu and the senior Gopal. Golap-Mā and Lakshmi rendered her occasional help. The inmates of the house were hardly aware of her presence. Four or five disciples, including Narendranath,[1] regularly spent the night there attending Sri Ramakrishna. About two months passed but the Master's illness only became worse. At last, on December 11, 1885, he was removed to a garden house at Cossipore, a northern suburb of Calcutta, where he could breathe fresh air and enjoy sunlight.

At the Cossipore garden house Sarada Devi felt relieved, since she could move about more freely. The garden comprised about five acres of land with trees, flowering plants, and shrubs. The two-storey house was away from the noises of the street. Sri Ramakrishna occupied a fairly large room on the second floor, and Sarada Devi, a small one on the ground floor. Lakshmi lived with her as her helper and companion. A few women devotees visited Sarada Devi from time to time and spent the night with her. Narendranath and several young disciples took up residence there in order to be available for the Master's service. Sometimes as many as twelve of them lived there in the two other rooms on the ground floor. Three different kinds of meals had to be cooked daily: one for Sri Ramakrishna, one for Narendranath and the other young disciples, and the third for the rest of the inmates. The expenses were met from donations by the elderly householder devotees.

The senior Gopal and Latu conveyed to Sarada Devi the doctor's directions about Sri Ramakrishna's special diet, and she prepared it herself. The doctor prescribed a variety of food,

---

[1] Narendranath Datta, the foremost monastic disciple of Sri Ramakrishna, subsequently world-famous as Swami Vivekananda.

such as boiled cream of wheat, which had to be strained, rice gruel, and meat and clam stew. When asked to prepare the clam stew, Sarada Devi objected, remarking that clams were living creatures and that she had seen them moving in the water. How could she kill them? Thereupon Sri Ramakrishna said: "How is that? I shall eat the stew and you can't prepare it?" She made up her mind to carry out his wish. She was relieved, however, by a revelation in which she saw that God alone is both the killer and the killed.

Though things were better organized at Cossipore than at Dakshineswar or Shyampukur, Sarada Devi had little respite from hard work. She had to do a great deal of cooking and had to supervise the Master's midday and evening meals. One day she was carrying a heavy vessel of milk up the stairs when she became dizzy and fainted. One of her legs was badly sprained and for a few days she was confined to her room. The Master humorously asked Baburam, a young disciple,[2] by a sign of the hand, as he could hardly talk on account of the ailment in his throat, to bring her to the room at meal time, if necessary, in a basket. In order to identify her he made a circle with a finger suggesting her nose-ring. Sri Ramakrishna felt slightly better at Cossipore for about a fortnight. Then his condition began to deteriorate. His tall, stout body was reduced to a mere skeleton. Sarada Devi used to clean the sore with a wick and remove the pus.

Five years earlier Sri Ramakrishna had made some remarks foretelling his death. He said that when he could no longer discriminate about people's touching his food, when he would spend nights in Calcutta, when he would allow others to eat a part of his food before he himself took it, and finally when large numbers of people would respect him and worship him as God, he would give up the body. Sarada Devi noticed that all the conditions but the last one had been fulfilled before he left

---

[2] A foremost monastic disciple of Sri Ramakrishna who was later known as Swami Premananda.

Dakshineswar. Now that one, too, was satisfied at Cossipore. One day some householder devotees went to Dakshineswar to visit the Master with offerings of sweets and fruit. Learning that he was at Cossipore, they offered the food before his picture. When Sri Ramakrishna heard about it he said: "Why did they make the offering to my picture instead of to Goddess Kāli in the temple?" Sarada Devi was frightened, remembering what he had foretold about his end. Sri Ramakrishna said to her: "Don't be worried. You will see later that people will worship my picture in their homes. I mean it. I swear it."

In spite of his excruciating pain and emaciated physical condition, Sri Ramakrishna unceasingly ministered to the spiritual needs of his disciples and devotees. He talked to them by signs or in whispers. On the first of January he felt a little better and about three in the afternoon went downstairs accompanied by an attendant and slowly walked to the garden. There he saw a number of householder devotees, some seated under the trees and some strolling about. Suddenly as they gathered around him and saluted him by touching his feet, he entered into an ecstatic mood and touched their heads or chests, saying: "May your spiritual consciousness be awakened." The devotees were beside themselves with joy and each one was blessed with a spiritual experience.

At Cossipore Sri Ramakrishna took special care to mould the spiritual life of Narendranath, who was to broadcast his message in India and carry it across the ocean. It was here that Narendranath experienced nirvikalpa samādhi. Sri Ramakrishna told him repeatedly to look after the spiritual welfare of his young brother disciples and to see that they did not return home. Here, too, he gave some of these disciples ochre robes in preparation for the monastic life and asked them to beg their food like mendicant friars. Thus he himself laid the foundation of the order of monks which later became associated with his name. All this happened before Sarada Devi's eyes, and perhaps she intuitively felt that she would have to play a prominent part in the future propagation of the Master's message. At the Cossipore garden, shortly before his death, Sri Ramakrishna was one day gazing intently at her when she said: "Tell me what is in your mind." He replied in a tone of complaint: "Look here, won't you do anything? Must this [pointing to his body] do everything?" "But," she protested, "what can I do? I am a mere woman." "No, no," Sri Ramakrishna insisted. "You will have to do many things."

On another occasion Sarada Devi carried the Master's food to his room and found him lying in bed with his eyes closed. She said aloud: "Please get up; this is your meal time." Sri Ramakrishna appeared to have returned from a trip to a far-away realm and said to her, in an abstracted mood: "Look at the people of Calcutta; they are like worms squirming in darkness. You must bring light to them." Sarada Devi replied: "We shall think of it later. Now take your meal."

Now and then the Master sang in the presence of Sarada Devi:

"What a burden I am bearing! Whom shall I explain it
    to?
Only the bearer knows his burden: how can others know?"

Then he would say to her: "This is not my burden alone. You, too, shall have to share it."

Sri Ramakrishna's physical condition deteriorated greatly. Finding medical treatment ineffective, Sarada Devi resolved to seek divine help. With that end in view she went to the famous Śiva temple at Tarakeswar, on the other side of the Ganges, determined to fast and keep vigil until she obtained the remedy through intercession with Śiva. After passing two days without food or sleep, on the third night she suddenly saw, in a vision, a heap of baked earthen pots, which were soon reduced to powder with a resounding crash, as if struck by a heavy cudgel. A voice rang out in her mind: "Who is one's husband? Who are one's relatives? For whose sake am I about to commit suicide here?" At once she felt a vast detachment and resigned herself to God. After quenching her thirst with a handful of water she returned to Dakshineswar. The moment the Master saw her he asked: "Well, did you get anything? Nothing is real—isn't that so?"

Did Sarada Devi, at Tarakeswar, have a glimpse of what was decided in the foreordaining mind of God? It is said that through sincere prayer we may not always obtain the fulfilment of our immediate objective, but we can come to know about the Divine Will and also get the strength to accept it with calmness.

Sarada Devi had other indications of the Master's approaching end. One day he told her of a dream he had had. An elephant was digging the earth for his medicine, when suddenly Gopāla woke him up.[3] The Master asked Sarada Devi if she had had any dream. She replied: "I saw Mother Kāli with her neck tilted on one side. I asked Her why She stood that way. She replied: 'Because of his having that trouble, I too am ill.'" Sarada Devi now realized that the Master's illness was beyond remedy; for otherwise, why should the Divine Mother, fully conscious of his suffering, not cure him? She felt inwardly calm when the Master said: "I am going through all this suffering. You have escaped it. I have taken upon myself the suffering of the world." Suddenly the purpose of his illness was revealed to her, and she felt an indescribable compassion for humanity.

Only a few days of the Master's life on earth were left. He was thinking of Sarada Devi's future and one day said to her: "Let me tell you something. Do not stretch out your hand to anyone even for a penny. You will not lack simple food and clothes. If you hold your hand out to anyone, remember, you will sell him your head also. If absolutely necessary, you may beg your food, but never live in anyone else's house. The devotees may welcome you in their houses with great respect and

---

[3] Gopāla is the name of the Baby Krishna. Evidently the Master was not to get the medicine for his illness.

affection, but never allow your own hut in Kamarpukur to fall into disrepair."

One day, shortly after, he was seated leaning against the pillow, without uttering a word. Sarada Devi was sent for. He said to her in a whisper: "I do not know why my mind nowadays remains constantly absorbed in Brahman." She understood and shed a few silent tears.

The final day arrived. It was August 16, 1886. Looking at Sarada Devi, who entered the room with Lakshmi, he said: "I am glad you are here. I feel as if I am going to a far-away country across the water—very far away." Sarada Devi burst into tears. "Why should you feel troubled?" Sri Ramakrishna consoled her. "You will live as you are living now," he said. "They [referring to Narendra and the other disciples] will do for you what they are doing for me. Look after Lakshmi and keep her with you." These were his last words to Sarada Devi in his physical body.

At six minutes past one, after midnight, Sri Ramakrishna thrice repeated in a clear voice the name of Kāli, his beloved Deity, and entered into a deep samādhi from which his soul did not again return to the body. Sarada Devi stood by the bedside and cried like a bereaved child. She said as she wept: "Mother! O Kāli! What have I done that you have departed, leaving me alone in the world?"[4] But immediately she restrained herself, returned to her room, and fell into a solemn silence.

Next day the Master's body was cremated and his ashes were brought to the garden house in an urn. In the evening Sarada Devi began to discard her ornaments, following the custom of Hindu widows. As she was about to take off her bracelets, Sri Ramakrishna appeared before her, looking as he did before he was stricken with cancer. Pressing her hand, he said: "Am I dead, that you are acting like a widow? I have just moved from

---

[4] Many years after, Sarada Devi said to a disciple that she always looked upon the Master as Mother Kāli.

one room to another." She did not take off the bracelets, and wore them as long as she lived.

Balaram Bose, a beloved householder disciple of Sri Ramakrishna, gave Golap-Mā a white, borderless sāri for Sarada Devi, the sort that orthodox widows wear. Golap-Mā shuddered at the very sight of it and said: "Good God! Who can give her this white cloth?" When she came to Sarada Devi she saw that the latter herself had torn off a great part of the wide red borders of her sāri. From that day on she always wore a sāri with a narrow red border. Three or four days later Sarada Devi, accompanied by Golap-Mā, Lakshmi, and Latu, paid a visit to Dakshineswar and returned the same evening to Cossipore.

Soon a problem arose about the feasibility of maintaining the garden house and the disposal of the Master's relics and ashes. Narendra and the other young disciples wanted to keep the house a little longer, but many of the older householder disciples who bore the expenses advised that Sarada Devi should move elsewhere. They further said that the ashes should be preserved at the garden house of Ramchandra Datta, one of Sri Ramakrishna's foremost householder disciples, and that the young disciples should go back to their homes. But the disciples had a different idea. They wanted to buy a plot of land on the bank of the Ganges and take the ashes there in a copper vessel. They had, however, no money with which to buy the land. After a great deal of argument it was decided that some of the ashes should be buried at Ramchandra's place and the rest kept, for the time being, at Balaram's house and regularly worshipped. Sarada Devi heard of the heated controversy between the older and the young disciples, but did not take sides. She only gave a long sigh and said to Golap-Mā: "Such a golden person has left us, and now, Golap, they are quarrelling over his ashes!"

About a week after the cremation of Sri Ramakrishna's body, Holy Mother,[5] at the earnest invitation of Balaram Bose, left

[5] From now on it will be appropriate to refer to Sarada Devi as Holy Mother, an epithet by which she has ever since been cherished by her devotees and disciples and by those of Sri Ramakrishna as well.

the Cossipore garden house and went to his residence. The vessel containing the Master's ashes was also carried there and daily worshipped as his visible presence. Naturally Holy Mother's grief was boundless. Referring to her state of mind at that time, she remarked later: "After his passing away my sorrow became unbearable. Again and again I said to myself: 'Such a golden man has gone away; why should I stay behind?' I did not relish anything and shunned people's company."

In order to restore her inner peace, Balaram planned to send her on a pilgrimage. Two weeks after the Master's death, Holy Mother left for Vrindavan, a sacred place associated with the life of Sri Krishna, in the company of Golap-Mā, Lakshmi, the wife of Mahendranath Gupta,[6] Yogen, Latu, and Kali.[7]

Soon after her departure for Vrindavan, in the autumn of 1886, most of the young disciples of the Master destined to be monks renounced the world and moved to a small dilapidated house at Baranagore, a northern suburb of Calcutta. There they established a monastery, practised austerities, spent their days in meditation and study, and worshipped the relics of Sri Ramakrishna. The remaining monastic disciples joined them in a short time. From here they set out, from time to time, to lead the life of wandering monks. This monastery gradually developed into the Belur Math, which, as we shall see, was established in 1898 as the permanent headquarters of the monks of the Ramakrishna Order.

On the way to Vrindavan, Holy Mother and her party stopped at Deoghar, in Bihar, and worshipped in its famous Śiva temple. The next day they left for Benares, where they spent over a week. In Benares Holy Mother offered worship at the temple of Śiva, known as Visvanāth, the Lord of the Universe, and visited other sacred shrines. One day, witnessing the evening service at the Śiva temple, she was overwhelmed with spiritual emotion and returned home hardly conscious of the world. Later she said: "It was the Master who brought me

[6] The chronicler of Sri Ramakrishna's talks, published later as *The Gospel of Sri Ramakrishna.*

[7] A young disciple of the Master who later renounced the world and assumed the name of Abhedananda.

home, holding me by my hand." In Benares the Mother and her women companions paid their respects to the well-known holy man Swami Bhaskarananda, who was completely naked. Looking at them, the Swami said: "Don't feel nervous, Mothers. You are all manifestations of the Divine Mother of the Universe. Why should you be embarrassed? Is it because of my genital organ? Why, it is like one of the fingers." The Mother said later: "What an unruffled, great soul! He always remains naked, in winter and summer alike." In Benares she met a woman saint from Nepal who advised her to practise the austerity of "Five Fires" for relief from her anguish of mind.

From Benares the party went to Ayodhya, the birthplace of Rāma and capital of his kingdom. Next they went to Vrindavan. On the way Holy Mother had a vision of Sri Ramakrishna. She was in the habit of wearing on one of her arms Sri Ramakrishna's gold amulet, which had been given him to allay the burning sensation of his body when he practised intense spiritual discipline at Dakshineswar. In the train she lay down with her arm on the window sill, leaving the amulet exposed. The Master suddenly appeared and, looking at her through the window, said: "Why are you keeping the amulet that way? You may lose it." After that vision she took it off and kept it in a tin box with the Master's photograph.

Alighting from the train in Vrindavan, she went to Kalababu's grove, which belonged to Balaram's family, where Balaram's father used to spend his time in prayer and meditation. There she met Yogin-Mā, who had left Calcutta shortly before Sri Ramakrishna's death. She embraced her, crying: "Oh, Yogin!" and both wept. At that time Holy Mother used to weep often for her husband. One night at Vrindavan Sri Ramakrishna appeared again and said: "Why are you crying so much? Here I am. Where have I gone? It is just a change from one room to another—isn't that so?" Repeated visions of the Master during this period somewhat assuaged Holy Mother's grief.

Vrindavan is one of the most sacred places of India, associated with the memory of the youthful Krishna and his consort Rādhikā, also called Rādhā. Here on the bank of the Jumna River, Sri Krishna, Rādhā, and the gopis[8] used to sing and dance, while Sri Krishna played His flute. The bhakti cult of Hinduism was highly developed in Vrindavan, where sensitive spiritual souls feel an upsurge of divine love. Sri Ramakrishna had there experienced many visions recalling various episodes of Krishna's life. Holy Mother spent her days there in spiritual ecstasy. Swami Yogananda, one of Sri Ramakrishna's foremost devotees, has left vivid reminiscences of those days. "One day," in his words, "her women companions found her absorbed in deep samādhi. They repeated the Lord's name in order to bring her mind down to the world. I then repeated Sri Ramakrishna's name very loudly and then the Mother seemed to come down to the ordinary sense plane. During such periods of ecstasy, her manner of speech, her voice, her way of taking food, her mode of walking, and her general behaviour resembled exactly those of the Master. We have heard that in deep meditation the worshipper and the worshipped become one. The scriptures, too, mention a spiritual state in which the devotee feels his identity with God. We have read in the *Bhāgavata* how the gopis, unable to bear their separation from Krishna, became so deeply absorbed in the thought of Him that they forgot for the time being their own individualities and acted as if each one of them were a Krishna. In the same manner Holy Mother forgot her own separate existence and behaved just like the Master, feeling her oneness with him. When I put to her some intricate questions about spiritual matters, shortly after her state of samādhi, she replied in a God-intoxicated mood, very much like Sri Ramakrishna, even using the same easy style of expression with metaphors and parables. We were all surprised to see the spirit of Sri Ramakrishna unified with her. We realized that the Master and the

---

[8] The milkmaids who were playmates of Sri Krishna.

Mother were in essence one, though appearing in separate bodies. The Master told me many times that there was no difference between his body and that of the Mother.

"On one occasion she passed nearly two days in the superconscious state. A great transformation came over the Mother after that experience. Thenceforward she was seen to remain always immersed in bliss. All her sorrow and grief and feeling of separation from the Master disappeared. A serene happy mood took their place. She was then in such a blissful state that at times her yearning for Krishna's presence and her utterance of Krishna's name with intense love reminded us of Rādhā. I have heard from Yogin-Mā and Golap-Mā that the Mother at times openly spoke of herself as Rādhā. At Hardwar, which we visited later, her mood was quite different. Like an ordinary pilgrim she offered worship at different temples on the banks of the Ganges. But at the sight of the Himalayas she stood speechless. At Vrindavan, through the Mother's grace, I could understand and appreciate the divine lilā[9] of Krishna."

At Vrindavan the Mother took long walks alone on the sandy banks of the Jumna River. She often went from one temple to another like a happy girl. One day she saw a corpse decorated with flowers and garlands being carried to the cremation ground. Like an innocent child she said to her companions: "See, how blessed this person is to die in this holy place! I came here to die but haven't had even a trace of fever. And yet how old I am! I have seen my father and my brother-in-law, both of whom died long ago." Yogin-Mā laughed and said: "Indeed, you have seen your father! Tell us, who has not seen his father?"

In a temple of Krishna at Vrindavan, Holy Mother prayed fervently that she might not see other people's blemishes. This prayer, which was literally fulfilled, was only an outer expression of an inborn characteristic of hers which made her an embodiment of compassion and patience. Later in life, when

---

[9] Sport.

she found people around her criticizing others, she would mention her prayer at Vrindavan and say: "Formerly I too used to notice others' faults. Then I prayed to the Master and through his grace got rid of this habit. It is in the very nature of man to see defects. You should learn to appreciate virtues. Man is no doubt liable to err, but you must not take notice. If you constantly find fault with others, you will see faults alone." To Yogin-Mā she said once: "Do not look at the faults of others lest your eyes should become vitiated."

It was at Vrindavan that Holy Mother had her first direct intimation of her future mission. One day Sri Ramakrishna appeared before her and asked her to give Swami Yogananda formal initiation. He even told her the mantra with which she should initiate him. Holy Mother thought it was a freak of her mind. She even felt embarrassed to think that people might criticize her action and say: "See, she has already started to make disciples." But the vision was repeated on each of the two days following. On the third day, she said to the Master: "I do not even speak to Yogen. How can I initiate him?" Sri Ramakrishna asked her to have Yogin-Mā with her at the time of initiation. Swami Yogananda also, in a vision, received similar instruction from the Master. At last the Mother gave him the initiation and Swami Yogananda thus became her first disciple. This was the beginning of a new chapter in her life. She stayed at Vrindavan for a year, practised meditation with clocklike regularity, and experienced many visions and ecstasies about which, however, she remained silent. How happy she was! She once remarked that she and Yogin-Mā would be so absorbed in meditation that they did not notice flies sitting on their eyes and causing sores in them.

After spending about a year at Vrindavan, Holy Mother and some of her companions visited Hardwar, where the Ganges, coming down from a high glacier in the Himalayas, enters the plains of India. There she consigned some of the Master's hair and nails to the sacred river. Next the party went to Jeypore and Allahabad. At the confluence of the Jumna and the Ganges in Allahabad, she deposited the remaining hair of Sri Ramakrishna. To describe the incident in her own words: "Is the Master's hair a mere trifle? After his passing away I carried his hair to Allahabad to offer it at the confluence of the sacred rivers. The water was still. As I held the hair in my hand suddenly a wave rose and carried it away. The spot, already sacred, took the hair from my hand in order to increase its sanctity."

The party returned to Calcutta in August 1887.

Anguish and Reassurances

AFTER HER RETURN from Vrindavan, Holy Mother lived in her mortal body for thirty-three years, which may be roughly divided into three periods. During the first period (1887–1898) she lived mostly out of the public gaze, travelling frequently between Calcutta and Kamarpukur and Jayrambati. Not much information is available about this period. During the second period (1898–1909) she began her spiritual ministry in earnest. It reached its culmination during the third period (1909–1920).

On returning to Calcutta, in August 1887, Holy Mother spent a few days at Balaram's house and then set out for Kamarpukur accompanied by Yogin-Mā, Golap-Mā, and a few other devotees. Before her departure she went to Dakshineswar and paid her respects to the different deities in the temples. Needless to say, she also visited the Master's room and the Nahabat, associated with so many indelible precious memories.

While coming from Calcutta, the party, for want of money, had to walk about sixteen miles from the railway station. Holy Mother became extremely tired and hungry, and Golap-Mā hastily prepared a simple meal by the roadside. As the Mother tasted this plain food she said to the cook: "Golap, what nectar you have prepared!" Soon after their arrival at Kamarpukur her companions returned to Calcutta. Lakshmi decided to live at Dakshineswar with her brother Ramlal, who was working there as the priest of the Kāli temple. Holy Mother was left alone at her husband's parental home. There she spent about a year

(1887–1888), under most trying circumstances, suffering from poverty, loneliness, and people's uncharitable criticism.

At Cossipore Sri Ramakrishna had told his nephew about Sarada Devi's living permanently at Kamarpukur. Ramlal said rather indifferently: "She may live anywhere she likes." At this casual remark the Master scolded him and said: "What do you mean? You are a man and still can say such a thing!" Ramlal not only did nothing to be of any help to Holy Mother; he actually made her pecuniary difficulties much worse. After the Master's death, the temple authorities gave her a monthly allowance of seven rupees. While she was living at Vrindavan, Ramlal told them that Sri Ramakrishna's wealthy devotees were looking after her and that she did not need any other help, and the paltry allowance was stopped. Narendranath pleaded with them in vain. When the Mother heard of it she said, in a spirit of utter dispassion: "Let them stop the allowance. I have lost the Master; what shall I do with their money?" Some of the householder devotees talked of helping her, but it remained a mere pious wish.

Sri Ramakrishna had asked Sarada Devi at Cossipore to live at Kamarpukur, and said: "Grow some greens, eat boiled rice and greens, and repeat Hari's[1] name." What hard days she had to face there! There were times when she had only rice, without even a pinch of salt to flavour it. But she put up with all this, remembering Sri Ramakrishna's admonition that she must not stretch her hand to anyone for money. Most of the young disciples of the Master were then living as wandering monks. They had no idea of her difficulties. Swami Saradananda[2] once remarked: "We did not dream that Mother did not have the means to buy even salt."

We have already said that Ramlal and Lakshmi lived at Dakshineswar. Sivaram, their youngest brother, also lived with

---

[1] A name of God.

[2] A disciple of the Master who later became the Secretary of the Ramakrishna Mission and assumed responsibility for Holy Mother. His premonastic name was Sarat.

them. Sivaram was attached to Holy Mother, who was a sort of godmother to him, and later he visited her now and then at Jayrambati. She had nothing in common with her niece and nephews. Ramlal did not pay her any attention. One day during this period he came to Kamarpukur and made a drastic change in the affairs of the family. He left the house used by Sri Ramakrishna to Holy Mother, and made arrangements about the property and the worship of the family deity. Holy Mother felt terribly alone and helpless, but she steeled herself to face the situation. Her garment was a mere rag. Her mother, Shyamasundari, who was herself in financial distress, during one of the Mother's visits to Jayrambati wept to see her in such straitened circumstances and begged her repeatedly to live with her. But Holy Mother did not agree and only said: "I am now going back to Kamarpukur. We shall see what the Lord ordains for me."

Soon another problem presented itself, as if to add to Holy Mother's misery, which was already great enough. The villagers, who were narrow-minded and fanatical about social traditions, thought it outrageous that she wore a red-bordered sāri and gold bracelets and did not live like an orthodox Hindu widow. Wherever she went she found people's tongues wagging about her. In distress she took off her bracelets. In addition to all this, she never felt happy living away from the Ganges, for which she cherished a life-long reverence. She even thought of taking a trip to the sacred river. But presently she saw, with her physical eyes, Sri Ramakrishna coming along the road by the side of the house, followed by Narendra, Baburam, Rakhal,[3] and other devotees. She also saw that a stream of water, springing from his feet, flowed in front of him in waves. She said to herself: "Why, the Master is everything. The Ganges has sprung from his feet." She quickly plucked some flowers and offered a handful of them to the river. Sri Ramakrishna said to

___
[3] A monastic disciple of the Master who later assumed the name of Brahmananda.

her: "Do not discard your bracelets. Do you know the Vaishnava scriptures?" She said that she knew nothing about them. The Master told her that Gauri-Mā would come there in the afternoon and explain the scriptures of the Vaishnavas to her. Gauri-Mā arrived as he had promised and told her that she could not be a widow, since her husband was none other than the Lord Himself. This vision reassured her. She put on her bracelets again and turned a deaf ear to people's criticism.

One day the village women went to Prasannamayi, a neighbour of Holy Mother's, who was respected by all for her piety and mature judgement, and asked her views about Holy Mother's unorthodox conduct. This lady, who had an insight into the personality of Sri Ramakrishna and Holy Mother, said: "Do not criticize either of them. They possess a divine nature." This silenced the villagers at least for a time.

Holy Mother continued to live at Kamarpukur, fighting poverty, loneliness, and the criticism of the villagers. Now and then visions of Sri Ramakrishna sustained her and gave glimpses of her future mission. Narrating one of these visions, she said later :"I was alone at Kamarpukur. One day I said to myself: 'I have no children. There is no one in this world to call my own. What will happen to me?' Then the Master appeared to me and said: 'Well, you are thinking of children. I have left you so many of them, all jewels. In the course of time you will hear many, many people addressing you as Mother.'"

Embodiment of patience that she was, Holy Mother did not speak of her suffering to anyone, but word of it got out through other sources. A maidservant who used to keep her company at night spoke to the villagers about the Mother's plight, and soon the news reached Jayrambati. Shyamasundari was grieved beyond words. One of her sons, who lived in Calcutta, reported the matter to Golap-Mā, who in turn spoke about it to some of Sri Ramakrishna's disciples, both lay and monastic, who were greatly distressed. They raised a little money and sent it to her with the urgent request that she come at once to Calcutta,

SRI RAMAKRISHNA IN SAMĀDHI

HOLY MOTHER

where she would be taken care of. But this request created a new problem. After all, she was a young widow in her middle thirties, and the disciples of the Master, with few exceptions, were personally unknown to her. The villagers, when apprised of the situation, said among themselves: "How can she live with those young men?" Though her inner voice told her that in the future she would live with the Master's devotees, yet she wanted to sound out the villagers. Some of them approved of her going to Calcutta, while the majority raised objections. Prasannamayi again came to her rescue. When Holy Mother asked her opinion, she wisely said: "Why are you hesitating? Of course you will go to Calcutta. Gadai's[4] disciples are like your own children. Do not listen to the village gossip. Surely you will go." She also sought the advice of her own mother, who, after ascertaining the views of her neighbours, approved of Holy Mother's departure.

After having spent nine months at Kamarpukur, Holy Mother went to Calcutta in April 1888. She stayed for a few days with Balaram Bose's family and then went to Nilambar Mukherji's house at Belur, rented for her by the devotees. Needless to say, the disciples of Sri Ramakrishna, especially the women among them, were overjoyed at her presence. They realized that the responsibility of looking after her now rested with them. It is reported, however, that some of the house-holders at first did not recognize her greatness and rather criticized the excessive devotion of such women disciples as Golap-Mā and Yogin-Mā. But when they were told about her exalted spiritual moods at Vrindavan they soon changed their views. The duty of looking after her devolved mainly upon Swami Yogananda and Golap-Mā.

In February 1889 she returned to Kamarpukur and spent about a year there. She visited Kamarpukur several times before finally settling down at Jayrambati. During one of these visits

---

[4] The nickname by which Sri Ramakrishna was known among the villagers.

to Kamarpukur a painful incident occurred. Harish, a devotee of Sri Ramakrishna, had formerly stayed with the Master from time to time. His wife had been greatly disturbed by his indifference to the family and had given him some medicine to divert his mind to the worldly life. This had affected his brain. He arrived at Kamarpukur one day in a deranged state of mind and began to act queerly. Holy Mother was worried and wrote about him to the young disciples then living at Baranagore. Before they could take any step he became really insane. What happened is best described in the Mother's own words: "One day as I entered the compound of our home from a visit with a neighbour, Harish began to chase me. He was then insane. His wife had brought about this condition. There was no one in our house. In a helpless state I began to walk fast around our granary. He pursued me. After going around it seven times I stopped. I assumed my real form,[5] laid him on the ground, placed my knees on his chest, and slapped him hard. He began to gasp for breath. My fingers became red." Harish was pacified and soon after left for Vrindavan, where he again became normal.

Holy Mother led a quiet life at Kamarpukur. Her financial condition was now slightly improved. A little help came from some of the Master's devotees in Calcutta, and she also received her share of paddy from the family. Thus the fear of starvation was removed. As the occasion arose, she entertained holy men, guests, and beggars, and the devotees of the Master who now and then visited her. Further, she made the necessary repairs on her house and bore her share of expense for the worship of the family deity. But she had to work hard. Her mother at last persuaded her to make Jayrambati her permanent home and live with her and her brothers. But still she

---

[5] According to some, she assumed the form of Bagalā, one of the forms of the Divine Mother. Bagalā is described as the destroyer of demons.

visited Kamarpukur from time to time. Asked about her reason for leaving Sri Ramakrishna's house, where the Master had asked her to live permanently, she once said: "At Kamarpukur I missed the Master very much. It is a very painful experience. That is why I did not live there." Another reason for her living at Jayrambati was, as we shall see later, to look after the brothers' families.

Holy Mother's arrival in Calcutta in April 1888 has already been mentioned. About this time she had some remarkable spiritual experiences. One day, sitting on the roof of Balaram Bose's house, she was meditating when she fell into deep samādhi. Describing this ecstasy she said later to Yogin-Mā: "I found that I had travelled to a far-away country. People there showed me great tenderness. I looked exceedingly beautiful. The Master was there. Gently they made me sit by his side. I cannot express in words the joy I felt at that time. Regaining partial consciousness, I saw my body lying near by like an ugly corpse. I began to worry about entering into it. I did not feel in the least inclined to do so. After a long while I persuaded myself to get into the body and again became conscious of the physical world."

Yogin-Mā and Golap-Mā lived with Holy Mother at Nilambar Babu's house, and some of the monastic disciples of Sri Ramakrishna served as her attendants. One evening, on the roof, Holy Mother was absorbed in meditation with her two companions. After a long time she regained semiconsciousness and said: "Oh, Yogin! Where are my hands? Where are my feet?" Yogin-Mā pressed her limbs and said: "Here are your hands and feet." It took Holy Mother a long time to regain consciousness of her body. This remarkable experience has been described by many as nirvikalpa samādhi, in which one completely transcends consciousness of the body and the world and feels one's identity with Brahman. Of her spiritual mood during that period she once said to a disciple: "At that time my mind used to be absorbed into red, blue, and other lights. My body would not have survived if these experiences had continued long."

At Nilambar Babu's house, Swami Adbhutananda assisted Swami Yogananda in looking after Holy Mother's comfort. Swami Abhedananda also visited her there and one day recited to her a hymn he had composed in her honour. Shortly after, she went on a pilgrimage to Puri, accompanied by Swami Brahmananda, Swami Yogananda, Swami Saradananda, Yogin-Mā and her mother, Golap-Mā, and Lakshmi. They reached Puri in the early part of November 1888. Immediately after their arrival they visited Jagannāth[6] in the famous temple of Puri. One day Holy Mother carried under her sāri a photograph of Sri Ramakrishna and uncovered it before the images on the altar, since the Master had never come to Puri. She believed that a picture is the same as the person it depicts. Later she remarked: "I saw, as it were, a Lion among men seated on the sacred altar, and I was attending Him as His handmaiden."

In Puri Holy Mother showed the utmost humility. When the priest suggested a palanquin to carry her to the temple from her home, she said: "No, you go ahead and show me the way. I shall follow you, walking behind like a helpless beggar." One day in the temple she saw hundreds of devotees worshipping the Lord Krishna and remarked with tears in her eyes: "Ah, isn't it wonderful that all these people will attain liberation!" A moment later it was revealed to her that only one or two, those who were without desire, would be liberated.

The party returned to Calcutta on January 12, 1889. On February 5, Holy Mother went to the birthplace of Swami Premananda together with Swami Vivekananda, Swami Saradananda, and some other disciples of the Master. From there she returned to Kamarpukur, where she stayed about a year. On

---

[6] Literally, "Lord of the Universe," an epithet of Krishna. The images of Krishna, His brother Balarāma, and His sister Subhadrā are worshipped in the shrine.

March 25, 1890, she made a pilgrimage to Gaya to offer the traditional rice-balls and water for the satisfaction of the soul of her mother-in-law. From Gaya she went to Bodh-Gaya, the place of the Buddha's enlightenment, where she saw monks living in affluence in a monastery. Remembering the hardship and poverty of Sri Ramakrishna's wandering disciples, she prayed fervently to God for their physical welfare.

Soon after her return to Calcutta Swami Vivekananda visited her. The great disciple of the Master, feeling a deep longing to realize God, had decided to live alone for a long time, away from his brother disciples at the Baranagore monastery. He came to Holy Mother to take leave of her and said: "I shall see you again if I become a real man. Otherwise, I now say good-bye for ever." "What are you saying!" the Mother interrupted. "No, no," Swami Vivekananda assured her, "I shall soon return through your grace." She said to Swami Akhandananda,[7] who was accompanying Swami Vivekananda: "I am handing my treasure over to you. You know the conditions in the Hima-layas. Please see that Naren does not suffer for want of food."

Between 1890 and 1897 Holy Mother spent a great deal of time at Jayrambati, visiting Kamarpukur and Calcutta now and then. In Calcutta she lived in rented houses. She also visited Benares and Vrindavan a second time and, to improve her health, spent two months at Kailwar, in Bihar, where she was deeply distressed by the poverty of the people.

In 1891 she performed the worship of Jagaddhātri, the Divine Mother, at Jayrambati. It appears from her behaviour at that time that she was then fully conscious of her divine nature. Swami Saradananda and a few devotees of the Master came to Jayrambati with the articles of worship. At the sight of her devotees Holy Mother was beside herself with joy. She prepared the vegetables with her own hands and supervised their meals. Shyamasundari also rose to the occasion, regarding the devotees

---

[7] A monastic disciple of Sri Ramakrishna.

as her grandchildren. She regaled the guests with many stories
of Sri Ramakrishna's life.

Sometime in 1893, at Nilambar Babu's house, Holy Mother
performed the Panchatapā, or "Austerity of Five Fires." It may
be remembered that when she had visited Benares, distressed in
mind, she was asked by a woman ascetic from Nepal to perform the Panchatapā. Later, in a vision, a monk who was a
complete stranger made the same request. But she knew nothing about this austerity and asked Yogin-Mā what it was.
Yogin-Mā explained it to her and said that she, too, would
practise the discipline. Accordingly, on the roof of Nilambar
Babu's house, four blazing fires of dried cow-dung were lighted
about six feet apart. The sun which shone brightly overhead
was the fifth fire. Holy Mother and Yogin-Mā bathed in the
Ganges and approached the fires. They were required to sit
there surrounded by the five fires and meditate from sunrise to
sunset. At first Holy Mother felt extremely nervous, but she
received encouragement from her companion. Keeping Sri
Ramakrishna in her mind, she entered the area surrounded by
the fires and immediately felt that the fires had, as it were, lost
their heat. The two women came out when the sun sank below
the horizon. They went through this ordeal for seven consecu-
tive days from dawn to dusk. Holy Mother felt an inner peace;
her fair complexion, however, became dull. She generally spoke
casually of this austerity. Years later, when a devotee asked her
about the need of it, she said: "Yes, it is necessary. Pārvati, the
Divine Mother, practised the austerity to obtain Śiva as Her
husband." Then, to make light of the whole thing, she added:
"I performed this austerity more or less for show; otherwise
people would say: 'What is extraordinary about her? She eats,
sleeps, and moves about like ordinary people.' This is, you
know, a kind of vow which women love to observe. Yes, they
often observe such religious vows." When an intimate disciple
wanted to know the real reason for her going through this ordeal, she said: "My child, I went through it for the sake of all

of you. Can you practise austerities? This is why I had to do it."
The Panchatapā allayed her mental anguish but it did not
clearly reveal to her the central purpose of her life. This purpose only became known to her through a significant vision
that she had at this time, which also demonstrated to her the
meaning of Sri Ramakrishna's embodiment.

It was a moonlit night. Holy Mother was seated on the steps
leading to the Ganges, looking at the full moon mirrored in
the millions of waves of the sacred river. Suddenly she saw Sri
Ramakrishna come from behind and proceed swiftly to the
river. The moment he touched the water his body dissolved in
it. "The hairs of my body stood on end," Holy Mother said
later, describing the incident. "I looked at the phenomenon
with my mouth wide open, in utter amazement. All of a sudden
Naren also appeared, I don't know from where. Crying: 'Victory
unto Ramakrishna!', he took the water in his two hands and
began to sprinkle it upon innumerable men and women gathered around. Immediately they attained liberation." The vision
was so vivid that for some days after she could not step into the
river where the Master's body had dissolved. It reminded her
also of his words: "You cannot die now. You must live to
awaken people's spirituality. How few I have helped! Many will
come to you. You shall have to assume responsibility for them."
Holy Mother resolved to take care of her body for the sake of
the Master's work. This experience finally convinced her that
Sri Ramakrishna's physical death did not mean he had ceased
to exist. He had been incarnated to fulfil a cosmic purpose,
and she must do her share to bring it about. Thus she came to
realize the central purpose of her own life.

Prior to Swami Vivekananda's sailing for America on May 31,
1893, he was assailed by doubt as to whether he was undertaking the journey to fulfil God's will or to satisfy his own
personal ambition. He had had some supernatural indication of
Sri Ramakrishna's approval of the project, but he wanted a
more concrete sign; so he wrote to Holy Mother for her opin-

ion. Instead of feeling worried about the bold adventure on the part of a penniless young man of thirty, unacquainted with the ways of the world, she saw in it the finger of God and gave him her blessings for the accomplishment of his mission. All trace of Swami Vivekananda's misgivings disappeared. After his triumph in America, he wrote inspiring letters to his brother disciples in India, urging them to broadcast Sri Ramakrishna's message and dedicate their lives to the service of humanity. One day in 1895 one of these letters was read before Holy Mother, who remarked: "Narendra is an instrument in the Master's hand. It is the Master who is working through Naren. What Naren has said is true; in the future his words will be fulfilled."

Swami Vivekananda returned to Calcutta from America in February 1897, and soon after went to Darjeeling for his health. Holy Mother went to Calcutta in April, and about that time Swami Vivekananda also went there. They had not seen each other since 1890. It was indeed a happy meeting after such a long separation. Her mother's heart was full of pride and joy at the triumph of her spiritual child. She waited for him silently near the door of her room, covered from head to foot with a cloth on account of her natural modesty. She did not uncover her face before him nor did she speak to him directly. Golap-Mā acted as intermediary. Swami Vivekananda fell prostrate before Holy Mother but did not touch her feet. He asked his companions not to touch her, with the remark: "If anybody touches her feet, in her infinite compassion she will take upon herself all the iniquities of the devotee and suffer on that account. Open your hearts to her without words, tell her your desires, and ask her blessings. She knows what goes on within you." Holy Mother asked Swami Vivekananda through Golap-Mā: "How was your health in Darjeeling? Are you feeling better now?" Swami Vivekananda said that his health had improved there.

Golap-Mā: "Mother says that the Master is always with you. You have many more things to accomplish for the welfare of the world."

Swamiji:[8] "I clearly see that I am a mere instrument in the Master's hand. I have seen great happenings in the West: the dedication of men and women there to Sri Ramakrishna's teachings and also their generous help to me in my work. All this makes me speechless with wonder. I went to America with Mother's blessings. The success I attained there, and the respect they showed me, convinced me that such impossible things could happen only through the power of her blessings. While I was alone in America I felt that the Divine Power which the Master called 'Mother' was guiding me."

Golap-Mā: "Mother says that the Master is not different from the one whom he called 'Mother.' It was the Master who accomplished all this work through you. You are his chosen child and disciple. How dearly he loved you! He foretold that you would teach men."

Swamiji: "My aim is to preach the message of the Master, and nothing else. And for that purpose I want to start a permanent organization. I feel frustrated because I cannot form it as quickly as I wish."

This time Holy Mother herself said in a whisper: "Do not worry. What you are doing now and what you will do in the future will be permanent. You are born just to accomplish this work. Thousands of people will hail you as a world teacher, a bestower of divine knowledge. I can assure you that the Master will fulfil your desire in no time. You will soon see that the work you want to undertake will be accomplished."

Swami Vivekananda was reassured and deeply moved by Holy Mother's blessings. In the course of this meeting he also

---

[8] The respectful and affectionate term by which Swami Vivekananda is referred to by the devotees and members of the Ramakrishna Order.

said to her: "Mother, I did not clear the ocean this time in one jump.⁹ I went to America in a boat built by Westerners. I discovered there the great glories of our Master. How many good people heard from me, spellbound, about Sri Ramakrishna and accepted his ideas!"

On May 1, 1897, Swami Vivekananda inaugurated the Ramakrishna Mission with Holy Mother's blessings. The Mission held weekly meetings at Balaram Bose's house on Sundays. The Mother attended some of these with several of the women devotees. Often Swami Vivekananda sang when she was present.

On February 3, 1898, the present site of the Belur Math, the permanent headquarters of the Ramakrishna Mission, on the bank of the Ganges, was purchased. One day Holy Mother was taken there to bless the place. She was received with great respect by the monks and the brahmachāris. Three Western disciples of Swami Vivekananda—Sister Nivedita, Mrs. Ole Bull, and Miss Josephine MacLeod—who lived in the neighbourhood, greeted the Mother and accompanied her as she inspected the new grounds. Holy Mother was exceedingly happy. "Now my children have a place to lay their heads," she said. "At last the Master has bestowed his grace upon them." It was about this time (1898) that Mrs. Bull persuaded Holy Mother to have two photographs taken. One of these pictures is now worshipped by her devotees everywhere. She said of it: "Yes, this is a good picture. But before it was taken I was a little stouter. Then Yogen fell ill. Worrying about him day and night, I lost some weight. I was happy when he felt better, but very unhappy when he was worse. Often I wept for him. At first I refused to be photographed. But Sara [referring to Mrs. Ole Bull] pressed me and said: 'I shall take the picture to America and worship it.' In the end I had to agree."

⁹ A reference to Hanumān, the monkey devotee and servant of Rāma. As narrated in the *Rāmāyana*, in order to find Sitā and fulfil the mission entrusted to him by Rāma, he jumped over the water separating Ceylon from India. Swami Vivekananda regarded himself as Sri Ramakrishna's servant.

In October 1898, Swami Vivekananda returned from a trip to Kashmir and visited Holy Mother. He said to her in a rather piqued voice: "Mother, how slight your Master's power is! A holy man in Kashmir became angry with me because one of his disciples was attached to me. He cursed me, saying that on account of stomach trouble I would have to leave the place in three days. And so it happened. Your Master could not help me." Holy Mother replied through an intermediary: "This is the result of psychic powers the holy man had acquired. You must accept the manifestation of such powers. The Master believed in them. He did not come to destroy. He accepted all traditions." Swami Vivekananda, still piqued, said that he would no longer accept Sri Ramakrishna. "My son," she said teasingly, "how can you help it? Even the tuft of your hair is held in his hand."

On November 12, 1898, Holy Mother visited the Belur Math and performed the worship of Sri Ramakrishna in the shrine. Shortly thereafter the Belur Math was formally dedicated and the monks took up residence there.

In a Domestic Setting

HOLY MOTHER MADE JAYRAMBATI her permanent country residence from 1897 till 1920, the year of her death. When she lived there, especially in later years, many devotees from far and near visited the place. This gave the villagers an opportunity to sell their fruits, vegetables, fish, milk, and other articles to add to their meagre income. Holy Mother adored Jayrambati, whose every particle of dust was sacred to her. The place was, at that time, ravaged by malaria, and the comforts of city life were practically unknown. Yet she often grew weary of the restricted life in Calcutta and returned to Jayrambati for relaxation. At Jayrambati she enjoyed freedom of movement among the simple villagers whom she had known from her birth. Also she felt the need of looking after her brothers' families at Jayrambati. And perhaps there was a deeper reason for her choosing her parental home as a place of residence. She thus taught the world how one could be burdened day and night with worldly responsibilities and at the same time lead a saintly life. Here she demonstrated that even the most humdrum duties of the world can be performed as spiritual acts. Since her domestic life was conterminous with her life of spiritual ministry, we shall first consider her relationship to her family.

Holy Mother was the eldest child of the family. She cherished the greatest respect for her parents. Of two of her three uncles, very little is known. The youngest, Nilmadhav, remained a bachelor and served as cook in a wealthy family.

After his retirement he settled at Jayrambati. Since no other relative came forward to assume responsibility for him in his old age, Holy Mother asked him to live with her. She grew fond of this uncle and personally looked after his comforts and needs. He sometimes accompanied her in her travels. When devotees gave her costly things, such as fruits which were out of season, Holy Mother selected the best and gave them to Nilmadhav. If a disciple protested against this excessive kindness, she would say: "Uncle has only a few days to live. Let him fulfil all his desires. I shall live a long time and have many opportunities to enjoy these things." Nilmadhav suffered from asthma. In spite of treatment and Holy Mother's personal nursing the illness became seriously aggravated. On his last day she wanted to remain by his side and refused to eat her midday meal. The devotees told her that death was not imminent and persuaded her to go to the dining room. After quickly finishing the meal, she went to her uncle's sick-bed and saw sadness on the faces of the attendants. Startled, she asked: "Is he then no more?" Everybody remained silent. In a voice shaken with grief and anger she said: "Why did you send me away to eat that trash? I could not see him in his last moments." She wept bitterly, as if she had lost her own father. Placing some flowers from the shrine on his chest and head, she prayed for the peace of her uncle's soul. That was in Calcutta in 1905.

The following year Holy Mother suffered another bereavement, in the death of her mother, Shyamasundari, whom her devoted disciples affectionately called "Grandmother." Even on the morning of her passing away the old lady helped in husking paddy and purchased vegetables in the village for the family. Suddenly she felt sick and lay down on the porch of the house of one of her sons. Addressing a disciple of Holy Mother, she said: "I am feeling dizzy; perhaps this is the end." Holy Mother and the other members of the family rushed to her side. She expressed the desire to eat pumpkin curry, and Holy Mother assured her she would cook it for her when she got well.

Shyamasundari knew her last moment had arrived. She wanted to drink some water, and Holy Mother poured Ganges water into her mouth. She quietly breathed her last and Holy Mother wept loudly, like any worldly person. The usual funeral rites were performed with pomp, and the guests were fed with many dishes, including the pumpkin curry.

In the death of Shyamasundari Holy Mother lost a beloved and intimate relative to whom she had always presented her problems and from whom she received counsel in the discharge of household responsibilities. The villagers also lost a sincere well-wisher and friend. Shyamasundari, strong in body and mind, devoted to God, and resolute and unwavering in the fulfilment of family duties, belonged in the old tradition of sturdy Hindu womanhood. She had gone through many vicissitudes, calmly facing poverty after the death of her husband, and had brought up her children heroically. In her later years the family income increased and she did not feel the pinch of poverty. Swami Virajananda, one of Holy Mother's disciples, who first met her in 1891, said of her: "Grandmother was by nature utterly simple and sweet. Day and night she was busy looking after the cattle, cleaning the cow shed, feeding the workers in the field, cooking for the household, and husking the paddy. But she always kept a smile on her face. Nobody ever saw her lose her temper or reprimand people. Her joy spilled over when we addressed her as 'grandmother.'" After Sarada Devi's marriage her mother had been sad because, along with the others, she thought Sri Ramakrishna was insane. But she lived to see her daughter worshipped as a goddess by rich and poor from all parts of the country. When a devotee came to Jayrambati she would exclaim in joy: "Ah, one of my grandchildren has come!" Her household, she said, consisted of "God and godly people." Now and then Shyamasundari had a glimpse of Holy Mother's divine personality. She once said: "Child, who are you? Do I really recognize your true nature?" Holy Mother replied with a show of annoyance: "Who else do you think I am?

SHYAMASUNDARI DEVI

HOLY MOTHER'S NEW HOUSE AT JAYRAMBATI

HOLY MOTHER ON THE INNER PORCH OF HER HOUSE

Do you see me with four arms?[1] If I were not a human being, why should I have been born of your womb?" Another day Shyamasundari said to her: "May I have a daughter like you in my next birth. My husband will have plenty of money. It is so painful to bring up children in dire poverty." "Why do you drag me in?" Sarada Devi replied. "Do you mean to say that I should again bring up your children?" But the mother insisted that she wanted to have Sarada Devi once more as her daughter. She must have remembered the visions she and her husband had had before their daughter's birth.

Though Holy Mother was blessed with godly parents, she was really unfortunate in her other relatives. Her brothers were greedy, selfish, and quarrelsome, her sisters-in-law jealous of one another, and her nieces always demanding. She had taken care of her brothers during their childhood, bathing them in the river, playing with them, and looking after their general welfare. In after years, though they acknowledged their gratitude, they also constantly demanded money from her, especially when they noticed her affluent disciples helping her in various ways to lead a more comfortable life.

As we have already seen, Holy Mother had five brothers and one sister. Her sister, Kadambini, died soon after her marriage, leaving no offspring. Her brother Umesh died unmarried at the age of eighteen or nineteen. It was he who had persuaded Holy Mother to intercede with the village deity Simhavāhini for a medicine when she was seriously ill of dysentery. Abhaycharan, the youngest, whom she loved most, received a good education. He entered medical school and became friendly with Sri Rama-krishna's disciples Swami Vivekananda, Swami Brahmananda, and Swami Saradananda. Swami Brahmananda helped him to buy his medical books, and Swami Vivekananda sometimes played cards with him. One day the latter remarked: "I didn't know that Mother had such an intelligent brother. Her other brothers are mere priests, practically illiterate and always asking

---

[1] Many goddesses in Hinduism have four arms.

for their priestly fees." Soon after obtaining a medical degree, Abhay died of cholera. His death moved Holy Mother deeply, and once she said regarding her nephews: "Let them remain illiterate." When her sisters-in-law protested about such a peculiar wish, she said: "What do you know? I brought up Abhay nicely, and he left me for good." Abhay was married. After his death his wife gave birth to a daughter, Radharani, who, as we shall see, played a very important part in Holy Mother's life.

The three other brothers, Prasanna, Kalikumar, and Barada, lived to old age. After their father's death they spent some years with relatives but later returned to their ancestral home and lived with their sister until they built their own houses.

Kalikumar was Shyamasundari's third son. A man of short temper, he never got along with his brothers Prasanna and Barada. He loved power and wanted to control the family affairs. His nieces were afraid of him. In the course of time two sons were born to him who were married at an early age. Kalikumar built his own house at Jayrambati and earned his livelihood through priestly duties. Holy Mother took him to Puri on pilgrimage.

Kalikumar often pestered Holy Mother for money. When she lived in Calcutta or elsewhere, the brothers would write to her about their pecuniary wants. Once a disciple said to her: "Mother, please give them plenty of money and pray to the Master about it. Let them have their enjoyment to the full. Then perhaps they will show dispassion." Holy Mother replied: "Will they ever have dispassion? Nothing will satisfy them. Do worldly people ever feel satiated? My brothers tell me nothing but their woes. Kali always demands money. Prasanna is now imitating him. Barada hardly makes any demands. He says: 'Where will sister get money?'" On another occasion she said: "Their sole thought is money. They always say: 'Give us money, give us money.' Not even absent-mindedly have they ever asked for knowledge and devotion. All right, let them have what they want."

Constant friction raged among the three brothers. Each tried to obtain their sister's favour for purely selfish purposes. There was always rivalry among them as to who could extort the most from her. This caused Holy Mother worry and annoyance, which she endured with infinite patience, at the same time helping them financially to the best of her ability. At last she realized that the partition of the family estate was the only thing that might pacify them. Swami Saradananda was asked to arbitrate. He arrived at Jayrambati in March 1909. But the arbitration, too, proved a difficult task. Kalikumar wanted to keep all the documents in his custody, but Prasanna did not agree. The two brothers became so heated that they were about to start a scuffle, but it was somehow stopped by Swami Saradananda. Holy Mother looked on with utter detachment. When asked where she would live after the partition, she replied: "Rats make holes, providing places for snakes to live in. I shall stay a few days with Prasanna and a few days with Kali." In fact, until she moved to her own newly built cottage in 1916, she used to stay mostly with Prasanna. The special reason for this was that she had to look after his two young daughters.

Here is another instance of the friction between the brothers. One morning Holy Mother was seated on the porch of her house when suddenly Kalikumar and Barada began to quarrel about a fence put up by Kalikumar. Soon they were about to come to blows. Their sister tried her utmost to calm them down, blaming both for the quarrel. After a while some of her disciples intervened and persuaded the brothers to stop arguing. Still abusing each other they went away. In an excited mood Holy Mother entered her own house. All on a sudden she burst into laughter and said: "What an illusion Mahāmāyā[2] has conjured up! Here is this infinite world, and what one claims as his possession will be left behind at death. Still men cannot under-

---

[2] The Great Enchantress, an epithet of the Divine Mother of the Universe. Mahāmāyā is the potency of Brahman. In one aspect She casts a veil over the eyes of creatures to perpetuate the creation, and in another She liberates them from the snares of the world.

stand this simple truth." As she uttered these words, she was convulsed with laughter which continued for some time.

In spite of their being greedy, Kali and Prasanna once in a while had glimpses of Holy Mother's real nature. On one occasion Prasanna remarked: "Our sister is a veritable goddess! What hasn't she done to keep us alive! As a child, she husked paddy for us, made sacred threads, fed the cattle, and cooked the meals. For the most part she alone managed the household." To Sarada Devi he said: "Do I not understand how precious you are? I see it all, but I cannot be nice to you for fear of arousing Kali's jealousy. Please bless me so that we may have you as our sister in future births, as we have now. As for me, I want nothing else." Holy Mother replied: "Catch me coming to your family again! I have had enough of it this time. To come again to you! The idea!"

Another day Prasanna said to her: "Sister, I have heard that you appeared to a devotee in a dream, gave him initiation, and also assured him of his liberation. You have nursed us from birth and have brought us up. Shall we remain like this for ever?" The Mother replied: "Things will happen as the Master ordains. Let me tell you something. Sri Krishna played with the cowherd boys, laughed with them, walked with them, and even ate the leavings from their plates. Did they know who He was?" Once Prasanna asked: "Sister, we all were born in the womb of the same mother; shall we not achieve anything?" "True," she assured her brother. "What should you be afraid of?"

Kalikumar, too, sometimes appreciated Holy Mother's non-attachment. One day he said to one of her monastic disciples: "Sister is so much respected by people because she has not the slightest attachment to money. Had she been different they would not have cared for her. She is not a human being but a veritable goddess. You are blessed indeed. You have renounced the world so young and are devoting yourself day and night to her service."

One day Kalikumar had a bitter discussion with Girish Ghosh, a staunch disciple of Sri Ramakrishna, about whether Holy Mother was an ordinary human being or a goddess. Kalikumar naturally regarded her as his sister and said: "It is you who call her the Divine Mother or the Mother of the Universe. But we were born from the same womb. I do not understand what you say." "What are you talking about?" replied Girish firmly. "You are the son of an ordinary brāhmin, born and reared in a village. You have forgotten the duties of your caste, such as worship and study, and are now living as a farmer. If a man promises you a bullock for your plough, you will run after him for at least six months. Is it not possible for Mahāmāyā, who can make the impossible possible, to appear as your sister and hoodwink you for the rest of your life? Listen to me. If you want liberation in this life or afterwards, go immediately to Mother and take refuge at her feet. I urge you to go at once." Girish's words always carried great power. Kalikumar went to Holy Mother and clutched her feet. He begged her grace. She said: "Kali, what are you doing? I am your sister. What are you saying?" Kali returned to Girish the same person he was before. Girish asked him to go back, but he would not. Girish once remarked that Holy Mother's brothers must have performed bone-breaking austerities in a previous life to have obtained her as their sister.

Holy Mother's sisters-in-law and nieces were jealous of one another, and quarrelled about petty things. Her patience with them, as she tried to make everyone happy, defies description. She often said: "One must be patient as the earth, which always puts up with people's transgressions. Men should behave likewise." When Holy Mother's forbearance reached its limit she would say about her family: "I am like a lotus in the midst of a rubbish heap." People often misunderstood her compassion towards her relatives as attachment to them, and criticized her. On such occasions she would say: "How would they understand me? I must look after the family in which I was born.

That is why I feel so intensely for my parents, my brothers, sisters-in-law, and nephews and nieces. I owe them debts which I must pay back. Why, otherwise, should I bother about them? The Master, too, looked after his mother. He even secured a job for his nephew Ramlal in the Kāli temple at Dakshineswar."

Holy Mother's brother Prasanna had by his first wife Ramapriya two daughters, Nalini and Sushila, the latter of whom was called by the nickname Maku. After his wife's death he took a second wife, Subashini, who bore him three children. Nalini and Maku were later married but had unhappy lives. They lived mostly with Holy Mother. The second brother, Kalikumar, married Subodhbala and had two boys. Barada's wife, Indumati, bore him two sons. Radharani, as we have already noted, was Abhaycharan's posthumous daughter. They were all associated in various ways with Holy Mother's life. Her sisters-in-law were much younger than she and she taught them their household duties. She herself trained them in cooking.

Abhay's wife, Surabala, often posed real problems for Holy Mother. Surabala's mother had died during her childhood and she had lived an unhappy life. After her husband's death she became a charge of Holy Mother. She gradually developed signs of an unbalanced mind, and after the birth of her daughter, Radharani, her condition became worse. Once in the early hours of the morning she encountered a thief in the kitchen and fainted through fear. From then on she was really insane. As it was impossible for her to take care of her young daughter, Holy Mother took complete responsibility for her. Surabala was a thorn in her side. Holy Mother, unable to bear with her, sometimes remarked: "Perhaps I once worshipped Śiva with thorny bel leaves and that is why I have this thorn."

Besides being deranged, Surabala was selfish and vituperative. She was jealous of her sisters-in-law and nieces, especially of Nalini. She suffered from many imaginary grievances. She thought that Holy Mother appropriated for herself all the jewellery belonging to her daughter and often created scenes about the matter. Once, after Radharani's marriage, she imagined that her son-in-law had drowned himself in a tank and that Holy Mother was responsible for it, whereas all the time he was playing cards with his friends. She could not bear the idea of Holy Mother's making any gift to her other nieces or sisters-in-law, and wanted her to make ample provision for Radharani before spending money for any other purpose. One day in Benares her abuse of Holy Mother reached the limit. The Mother said to her: "Do not regard me as an ordinary human being. You do not abuse me alone, but my father and mother also. I do not take any offense. I say to myself that you are only making a noise. If I brood on your faults, then who will protect you? As long as I am alive, things will be well with you. Your daughter will remain yours. I shall look after her as long as she cannot stand on her own feet. Why, otherwise, should I show so much attachment to her? This very moment I can cut off all my connections with your daughter. Some day I shall vanish like camphor in the air, and you will not even know it." Surabala changed her tone and said: "When did I show disrespect to your father? I never did. All I meant was that if you wanted to give something to a person you gave him everything." Holy Mother replied: "I have the nature of a child. I cannot calculate. Whoever asks me for something, I at once give it to him." Tormented by the insane sister-in-law, Holy Mother once remarked: "My mind is eager to soar high into a spiritual plane. I feel compassion for them and keep it down. And what do I get in return? Only abuse and insults." Another day she said to Surabala, after finishing her worship: "Many saints and ascetics do not obtain my favour through austerities. And here I am with you and you do not know it."

Surabala could occasionally be humorous, as when one day Holy Mother was decorating the Master's picture with flowers. With a twinkle in her eye Surabala said: "See what she is doing! She is decorating her husband with her own hands." She would even, on rare occasions, show respect to Holy Mother. One day inadvertently the Mother touched her feet with her hand.[3] Surabala cried out: "What will happen to me? Why did you touch my feet?" Holy Mother laughed aloud at this show of respect and said to a disciple: "Rāvana knew fully well that Rāma was Nārāyana Himself, the embodiment of Brahman, and that Sitā was the Primordial Power, the Divine Mother of the Universe. Still he did not refrain from ill-treating Sitā.[4] She [referring to Surabala], too, knows who I am. She knows it well. Yet she must play her part."

Radharani, too, as we shall see in the following chapter, had an abnormal mind, especially after the birth of her son. Besides, she contracted the habit of eating opium to forget some of her physical pain. One day Holy Mother was preparing vegetables when Surabala suddenly appeared and said: "It is you who feed my daughter with opium. You have made her a cripple in order to exercise control over her. You do not allow my daughter and grandson even to come near me." Holy Mother replied with utter detachment: "There is your daughter. Take her away. Have I hidden her anywhere?" But Surabala was determined to pick a quarrel and became flushed with anger. At last she took a piece of firewood in her hand and was about to strike Holy Mother with it. Holy Mother cried aloud: "Is there nobody here? Come and help me. This insane woman is going to kill me." A disciple came and saw the faggot about to fall on the Mother's head. He snatched it from Surabala's hand, expelled her from the room, and forbade her to enter it again. In the heat of the excitement Holy Mother, too, forgot herself for the moment and said: "You mad woman, what were you about to do? Your hand will wither away." The next moment she felt

---

[3] In Hindu tradition a person commits a sin if his feet touch any part of the body of an elder or of a person worthy of worship. The transgressor at once asks forgiveness.

[4] Rāvana had to play a dishonourable part in the life of Rāma in order to bring about the destruction of the demons, of whom he was the leader.

HOLY MOTHER AT FIFTY-TWO

HOLY MOTHER WITH MAKU AND HER CHILD

distressed and said to the Master with folded hands: "Oh, Master, what have I done? My lips have never uttered any curses. At long last that, too, has happened. Why live any more?"[5] She began to weep. The disciple was astonished to see the extent of her compassion. By an inscrutable decree of fate, Surabala, shortly after Holy Mother's death, was attacked with leprosy and lost the fingers of her hand.

We have already mentioned Holy Mother's nephews and nieces. Maku and Nalini, among the nieces, were practically members of her family. Nalini and Surabala never got along with each other. Holy Mother often had to pacify them. She consulted Nalini about family matters. She used to say: "I show these girls due respect for their views. Remaining detached, I watch their movements so that they may not go to extremes. Remaining humble, one should give some amount of freedom to all." Nalini had a morbid mania for cleanliness and purity, and thereby inflicted suffering upon herself and others. Noticing her indifference to her husband, Holy Mother once said: "She feels like her aunt [referring to herself]; that is why she does not care for him." Her nieces' children received their due share of attention from Holy Mother. She gave them gold ornaments and arranged for medical treatment for them when they were sick. A son of Maku was her favourite, and she wept when he died at an early age. She once said of him: "The child must have been a yogi in his previous life. One of his age does not usually show so many good tendencies. He used to gather flowers and worship my feet with them." One day the child asked the Mother who created the red flowers, and she said: "God." He wanted to know the reason for it. The Mother replied: "God likes to wear them." When Holy Mother lost some of her teeth, the child said: "Why don't you take two of mine?"

Some of her relatives received initiation from Holy Mother.

---

[5] This occurred during Holy Mother's last visit to Jayrambati, and a few months later she died.

But she concealed her true nature from the family. One day Nalini said to her: "People say that you know the inmost thought of all."

Mother: "Stop! They say such things out of devotion for me. I am nothing."

Nalini: "I don't believe that. Please tell me what I am thinking just now."

Mother: "Nalini, let us not talk about it. Please pray with me to the Master so that he may completely wipe away from my mind all trace of ego." Forthwith Holy Mother began to pray.

Her compassion knew no bounds and was totally devoid of selfishness. She often said: "If one is without kindness, how can one be called a human being?" The following two incidents illustrate the nature of her compassion and love.

One day Holy Mother was talking at Jayrambati to a devotee who was a high-caste brāhmin. His sacred thread, the sign of his noble lineage, was conspicuous. Just then a young man, who happened to be an untouchable, arrived and begged her for initiation. At her village she carefully observed the local traditions regarding caste, and so she expressed her hesitation to accept an untouchable as a disciple. Thereupon the young man became angry and said in an excited voice: "Don't you remember that evening[6] when you were travelling alone through a lonely meadow and encountered a highwayman who was an untouchable? Out of sheer fear you addressed him as 'Father.' And now you are objecting to being the mother of another untouchable!" Holy Mother burst into a laugh. She brushed aside the consideration of caste and out of kindness agreed to initiate him.

There was a child in Calcutta who gave a great deal of trouble to her family and always demanded attention. She used to visit Holy Mother with her own mother. Whenever she

---

[6] Referring to her encounter, on her way to Dakshineswar, with the highwayman whom she addressed as "Father."

entered the Mother's room she clung to her. The Mother always gave her plenty of sweets to eat. Once Holy Mother was about to leave for Jayrambati and said to the little girl: "Darling, you have been visiting me a long time. Do you love me?"

"Yes, I love you very much."

"How much?"

The girl stretched her arms as wide as she could and said: "That much." The Mother asked: "Will you still love me when I am away at Jayrambati?"

"Yes, I will love you just the same. I shall not forget you."

"How shall I know it?"

"What should I do to make you know?"

"I shall be sure of your love for me if you can love everyone at home."

"All right, I will love all of them. I will not be naughty any more."

"That's very good. But how shall I know that you will love all equally, and not some more and some less?"

"What should I do to love all equally?"

"Let me tell you how to love all equally. Do not demand anything of those you love. If you make demands, some will give you more and some less. In that case you will love more those who give you more and less those who give you less. Thus your love will not be the same for all. You will not be able to love all impartially." The little girl promised to love all without demanding any return. And, indeed, it was reported that from that time her behaviour in the family was exemplary.

Holy Mother's love sought no return. She showed equal love for the righteous and the unrighteous. On one occasion she said that she was the mother of the beasts, birds, and insects, as well.

Holy Mother lived the life of a householder. People saw her involved in family affairs and identified with the weal and woe of her relatives. She taught them the minutest details of their household duties. But few realized her total non-attachment to

the world and her relatives. Even Yogin-Mā, one of her intimate companions, once felt some doubt about it and said to
herself: "Sri Ramakrishna was the embodiment of renunciation, and Mother is engrossed in the world, preoccupied day
and night with the thought of her brothers, sisters-in-law, and
nephews and nieces." One day, soon after, she was seated on
the bank of the Ganges, meditating, when Sri Ramakrishna
appeared in a vision before her. The Master said: "Do you see
what is being carried by the water of the Ganges?" Yogin-Mā
saw the corpse of a new-born baby, smeared with blood, and
with the placenta still attached to it. She also saw that thousands of people were offering worship to the holy water of the
river. The Master said to Yogin-Mā: "Can anything make the
Ganges impure? Regard her [meaning Holy Mother] in the
same way. Never have any doubt about her. Remember she is
not different from this [meaning himself]."

At the death of Maku's son Holy Mother wept like any other
householder. She realized how much people suffer when their
children or other relatives pass away. A disciple asked her:
"Mother, why did you weep like an ordinary person at the
death of that child?" She replied: "I live as a householder. I
must taste the fruit of the tree of the world. That is why I
weep. Sri Ramakrishna once remarked: 'When God is incarnated in a human body, he acts exactly like a man. He feels the
same hunger, thirst, sickness, grief, and fear as others do. Even
Brahman weeps when caught in the trap of the five elements!' "[7]

Holy Mother's life at Jayrambati was a strenuous one. She
shouldered the responsibility for her relatives and also had to
look after the comforts of the many disciples who visited her
there. In Calcutta she was inaccessible to male disciples except
at fixed times. Therefore, many of them preferred to visit her
at her native village. They often stayed for several days. She

[7] Referring to earth, water, fire, air, and ākāśa (or space), which
constitute all physical objects.

cooked meals for them, procuring the necessary vegetables and fish, and tended those who fell ill. Some of her disciples took tea with their breakfast, and early in the morning Holy Mother would go unobserved to the villagers to get milk. Though others were ready to help, she preferred to do many things with her own hands, even during the later years of her life when she suffered from malaria. When one day a disciple protested about her strenuous life, she said: "My child, it is good to be active." Remaining silent for a few minutes she said gravely: "Please bless me that I may serve others as long as I live."

Beginning her household duties at seven o'clock, she spent two hours preparing vegetables. Besides, she supervised the supplies, arranged for the daily worship and performed it, distributed the prasād, looked after the disciples at their meals, kneaded the flour for bread, cleaned the lamps, and did other odds and ends. She did not retire before eleven. She was self-reliant and even in old age disliked the idea of being a burden to others. Her brothers, instead of looking after her physical welfare, became her responsibility. Her regular income from the donations of her devotees and disciples was very limited. But she did her utmost to cater to the tastes of her devotees, rich and poor alike. Often food or money came to her unexpectedly when she needed it.

Swami Premananda[8] often exhorted the young monks of the Belur Math to emulate Holy Mother's example. Once he said to them: "Many people worship her photograph. But in spite of her rheumatism she herself does not accept service from others. How tirelessly she serves the visitors at Jayrambati, known or unknown! She fetches water from the tank and even walks a mile to procure milk and good vegetables. Often she washes their dishes after their meals." When the present writer one day told Swami Premananda that the Mother sat by his side when he ate his meals, and that she herself prepared the vegetables, the Swami said in a moved voice: "She has set the

---

[8] A monastic disciple of Sri Ramakrishna.

example of how to lead an ideal life in the world. How non-attached she is in the midst of her manifold tasks! And never forget that she is the embodiment of the Divine Mother of the Universe."

Jayrambati, as we have already seen, had a special attraction for Holy Mother. Once as she was leaving for Calcutta her aunt said to her: "Sarada, come back soon." With tears in her eyes, she replied: "Of course I will come." By way of reassurance, she touched the floor with her forehead again and again and said, quoting a Sanskrit proverb: "The Motherland, which is none other than the mother, is superior to heaven itself." Though Kamarpukur was her home after her marriage, she first saw the light of day at Jayrambati and grew up there. She loved the very sky and air, the trees, the tanks, and the meadows of Jayrambati. The attraction of the village drew her from the metropolis of Calcutta. Though neither her house nor the village gave her the comforts of her Calcutta home, she felt an ease, naturalness, joy, and freedom there which she found nowhere else. She sighed with relief whenever she left Calcutta, where she felt like a bird in a cage. In the village she was free to do things her own way, but in Calcutta her meals, movements, and interviews were regulated by the clock. She often protested against the formalities observed in the metropolis, and one day she said to a disciple: "In Calcutta I have to weigh my words before uttering them, lest people should take offence. I am much better off at Jayrambati. I bluntly tell the villagers whatever I feel, and they reply to me without any restraint. We do not harbour any ill feeling for each other. But the people of Calcutta feel hurt if I deviate from the formalities even a little."

After the Master's death the people of Jayrambati regarded Holy Mother as one of themselves. Some, no doubt, regarded her as an unfortunate woman—a poor widow, without children and dependent upon her brothers. But before long they were surprised to see how many people visited her from far and near with all sorts of gifts. Some even became jealous. One woman remarked: "Certainly she is a lucky woman, with disciples and attendants, and money and other gifts pouring at her feet. If her brāhminical lineage brings her all these gifts, then why should we be deprived of them? We, too, are brāhmins." Some of the villagers on various pretexts tried to extract money from her.

But many of the villagers held Holy Mother in great respect. Women visited her with their children and grandchildren and were rewarded with sweets and fruits. She helped her neighbours financially by purchasing fruits and vegetables from them. During the days of religious festivals she gave sumptuous feasts to the villagers. There was a village watchman named Ambika, whom Holy Mother had addressed during her childhood as "Brother." He was an untouchable. One day, in later years, he said to her: "People call you a goddess, the Divine Mother, and by other such names. I do not understand all this." Holy Mother said: "You don't have to understand. Just remember that you are my brother Ambika and I am your sister Sarada."

In a neighbouring village lived many Moslem families who some years before had earned their livelihood by making silk. But when that business was ruined because of the competition of imported silk, these Moslems became thieves and dacoits, and people were frightened of them. Then in 1915 a famine broke out, and some of the Moslems supported themselves by assisting in the construction of Holy Mother's new house. Observing their peaceful life, the people of Jayrambati used to say: "By Mother's grace even desperadoes have become devotees of God." Holy Mother was extremely kind to them. One day a Moslem offered Holy Mother some bananas and said: "Mother, I have brought them for the Master; will you accept them?" "Of course I will," Holy Mother replied. "Give them to me. You have brought them for the Master. I shall certainly take them." The man was rewarded with some sweets. A woman devotee who was present was surprised and said to the Mother: "We know he is a thief. How can you offer his things to the Master?" After he had left Holy Mother scolded the woman and said: "I know who is good and who is bad." On one occasion she said: "Men, by nature, often do evil things. How few know how to make them good!"

Another Moslem, Amjad, who was a bandit, built the wall for Holy Mother's new house. One day she invited him for a meal, which was arranged on the porch of her house. An orthodox Hindu in many respects treats a Moslem as untouchable and regards food or drink touched by him as polluted. Nalini, Holy Mother's niece, began to throw the food at Amjad's plate from a distance. Holy Mother noticed this and said: "How can one enjoy food if it is offered with such scorn? Let me wait on him properly." After he had finished his meal, Holy Mother cleaned the place with her own hands. Nalini shrieked: "Aunt, you have lost your caste!" "Keep quiet," the Mother scolded her. And she added: "As Sarat is my son, exactly so is Amjad." Sarat was a direct disciple of Sri Ramakrishna, the Secretary of the Ramakrishna Mission, and a monk possessed of saintly virtues, and Amjad was a man of disreputable character. Her behaviour on this occasion bears out her remark: "I am the Mother of the good and I am the Mother of the wicked."

To complete the story of Amjad, several years later Holy Mother was bedridden with fever. Devotees from distant places came to Jayrambati to visit her. One morning a brahmachāri attending her noticed that an emaciated man of dark complexion, clad in rags and leaning on a stick, had entered the house. As he approached the Mother's room her eyes fell upon him. "Who is there?" she said in a feeble voice. "Is it my child Amjad? Come in." Amjad entered the room and talked with the Mother for some time. In the afternoon when Amjad was returning home, people found him to be a completely different person. He had taken his bath, filled his stomach with food, and put on a new cloth. He carried in his bundle many gifts from Holy Mother. Amjad, who had been starving all this time, soon recovered his health. He now became devoted to Holy Mother and often got her fruits and other articles not easily obtainable in the neighbourhood. He did not, however, give up his profession of a bandit. Once, released from jail, he came to Holy Mother with a gourd from his vine. She said: "I have been thinking of you a long time. Where have you been all these days?" He said that he was in jail because he had stolen a cow. She did not pay any heed to his criminal act and said with great kindness: "I was worried by your long absence." Amjad had been in and out of jail many times. During her last illness, Holy Mother came to know that he was again arrested for burglary and remarked: "I knew all the time that Amjad had not given up his old habits."

There is a village named Koalpara, about three miles from Jayrambati, which is closely associated with Holy Mother's life. It is situated on the road to Vishnupur, where one takes the railway train for Calcutta. There lived at Koalpara a band of Holy Mother's devotees, several of whom later renounced the world. An āshrama[9] grew up there, which she often designated as her "parlour," and she rested there on her way to or from Calcutta. The inmates of the āshrama gave their help whenever the Mother had any construction work to be done or there was a religious festival in progress. They procured vegetables, ran errands for her, and were always at her service. She had a soft corner in her heart for them. A cottage was built for her at Koalpara where now and then she spent a long period of time. Many devotees visited her there. On the altar in the shrine she installed photographs of the Master and herself for daily worship. The inmates of the āshrama were, at the beginning, very much interested in the political movement for India's freedom. Holy Mother advised them to concentrate on spiritual matters and follow in the footsteps of Sri Ramakrishna. She had many visions there. Gradually a charitable dispensary was established

[9] A retreat for the practice of spiritual disciplines.

at Koalpara to distribute free medicines to the people of the neighbouring villages. One day the leader of the āshrama complained to Holy Mother that many people who could afford to pay took advantage of the dispensary and got their medicine free. He asked Holy Mother whether they should be given medicines which were really meant for the poor. She replied: "Whoever comes here to get free medicines should be considered poor. The door of this dispensary must be open to all."

Holy Mother was a living embodiment of the non-attachment taught in the Bhagavad Gītā. In every action, great or small, she practised yoga, or complete union with the Godhead. Her will was one with God's will. Though a householder, she never deviated from the ideal of renunciation laid down for monks. She did not shun disagreeable duties nor did she welcome agreeable ones. Through all her activities she never forgot God. If she had wanted, she could have lived a life of ease and comfort in Calcutta, receiving worship from her devotees and disciples. Yet much of the time she chose to lead an austere life in a malaria-stricken village, performing her duties cheerfully in order to set an example to the world. The secret of her inner peace, poise, and contentment was her unceasing communion with God. Even when her body or sense-organs were extremely active, her heart was directed to God, like the needle of a compass which points always to the north. Again, like an anvil in a blacksmith shop, she remained unmoved by the repeated blows of the world. The events of the outer world may have made slight ripples on her mind, but they could not disturb the peace of her soul. She was like the ocean, into which rivers from all sides empty themselves, causing waves on the surface, but whose inner depths remain for ever serene.

Radhu

O F ALL THE TRIBULATIONS Holy Mother had to endure in her family, the greatest was her niece Radharani. An inscrutable phenomenon, Radhu played an important, though painful, rôle in Holy Mother's life and the fulfilment of her mission. Such troublesome, incongruous, and rebellious characters are necessary, as Sri Ramakrishna once said, to "thicken the plot."

After the Master's death, Holy Mother, as we have seen, had lost all interest in the world. Life seemed insipid and meaningless, and she wanted to give up the body. But several revelations indicated to her that her body was to be preserved to fulfil a special purpose. One day, at Jayrambati, she intensely felt the emptiness of her life and asked the Master why she should keep her body any more. Suddenly in a vision she saw a girl ten or twelve years old, dressed in a red cloth, moving about in front of her. Sri Ramakrishna appeared, pointed to the girl, and said: "Take her as a support and live. Many spiritual seekers will come to you." Immediately the vision vanished. This girl, whom she later recognized in her niece Radharani, became a strong chain to bind Holy Mother's mind, always directed upward and inward, to the relative world in order to carry on Sri Ramakrishna's unfinished mission.

Abhay, Holy Mother's youngest brother, on his death-bed had begged her to look after his wife, who was expecting a child. On January 26, 1900, Surabala was delivered of a daughter who was named Radharani, and called Radhu or Radhi for short. Surabala was nearly insane. Engaging a nurse to look after the baby, Holy Mother went to Calcutta. One evening as she was telling her rosary, she had a vision of Radhu being treated carelessly by her insane mother and saw that the baby's life was in danger. She became extremely worried and returned to Jayrambati. While she was there, one day she noticed that Surabala, with her arms wound around with threads of red, blue, and other colours, was coming across the courtyard dragging some cotton quilts under her arm. She was stark mad. Radhu was crawling in the dust behind her, eating a few grains of dry puffed rice and weeping. In contrast, the other children of the family were well looked after. At this pathetic sight Holy Mother shuddered. She felt choked, like a drowning person, and said to herself: "Who will look after the poor thing if I do not? Her father is dead and her mother insane." She rushed out and took the baby into her arms. Immediately Sri Ramakrishna appeared and said: "This is the girl you saw before. Take her as a support. She is Yogamāyā." From now on Holy Mother's life became inextricably entwined with Radhu's. They were almost inseparable. Holy Mother herself fed Radhu, entertained her, and slept with her. To outsiders she appeared to be inordinately attached to Radhu. One day a disciple said to her: "Mother, why are you so obsessed with Radhu? Day and night you talk of nothing but Radhu. You seem to be terribly entangled in the world. Many devotees come to you and you pay no heed to them. Is such attachment good for you?" Holy Mother had heard similar complaints before and had said with her usual humility: "We are women, and I follow my womanly nature." But this time she replied in a rather animated voice: "Where will you find another like me? Try and see. Let me tell you something. Those who constantly contemplate the Supreme Reality develop a subtle and pure mind. Whatever object such a mind takes hold of, it clings to with tenacity; people regard this as attachment. When lightning strikes a building, the flash is seen in the glass panes and not in the wooden shutters." On another occasion she said: "People think I worry about Radhu and am strongly attached to her. But they do not know that without this attachment my body would not have been preserved after the Master's death. He himself kept the body alive, through Radhu, for the sake of his work. When my mind withdraws from her I shall give up the body." On still another occasion she remarked: "This constant doting of mine on Radhu is a form of attachment. But I can sever it even this moment by my mere wish. I do not do so only because of compassion. How can māyā bind me?" Holy Mother's visions concerning Radhu gave her a reason to live and allowed her to resume her active life. Her joy in life was restored.

Similar phenomena were noticed in the life of Sri Ramakrishna. He often created forced desires to bring his mind down from the high plane of samādhi. He would ask for a smoke or a particular kind of sweetmeat. He prayed to the Divine Mother that he might not remain unconscious in the contemplation of Brahman. If his mind did not dwell on the physical plane, he asked, how would his earthly mission be fulfilled?

In her childhood Radhu was a rather charming girl and attracted people by her air of innocence. She had nothing to worry about for her future and was indifferent to money. She loved Holy Mother very much and affectionately called her "Mother." She kept away from her own mother, whom she addressed as "Baldy Mother" since the latter often had her head shaved after the fashion of Hindu widows. But Surabala felt terribly jealous when Holy Mother gave presents to others. She wanted everything for Radhu. Now and then she would say: "There, she is giving things away again. What will happen to Radhu?" Addressing her daughter, she sometimes said: "My sister-in-law is generous to others. She is keeping nothing for you. Why should you live with her? Come away to my house."

Radhu would be annoyed by these remarks; she would scold her mother and keep away from her. Holy Mother gave her everything she wanted and Radhu was happy.

But as Radhu grew up, her body and mind gradually changed. Physically she turned out to be a valetudinarian and mentally a moron. She became eccentric, petulant, and intractable. She not only disobeyed Holy Mother at every turn but abused her, cursed her, and, in short, treated her in such a way as would have exhausted the patience of any other human being.

At the age of twelve, on June 10, 1911, Radhu was married to Manmatha Chatterjee, a young man of fifteen. The bridegroom came from a rather well-to-do family of a neighbouring village, but was a good-for-nothing fellow. Swami Saradananda spent money without stint for the marriage. Radhu was bedecked with gold and silver ornaments from head to foot. The party of the bridegroom and the people of Jayrambati were entertained with a sumptuous feast.

Radhu did not want to live at her husband's house; so both she and Manmatha stayed most of the time with Holy Mother. Though she was now quite grown up and was expecting a child, her behaviour towards Holy Mother did not improve in the least. One day the Mother said to a disciple: "She was rather pleasant in her childhood. Now she is married and suffers from various ailments. I am afraid this daughter of an insane mother may herself become insane. Alas, am I bringing up a mad person?" Radhu never let slip an opportunity to torture Holy Mother. One day the Mother said to a woman who wanted to adopt a son: "Never do any such thing. Do your duties to all. But love you must not bestow upon anybody except God. If you love men, there will be no end of your suffering. Look at me. How much I am suffering on account of Radhu!" One day Manmatha had gone out and Radhu was restless for him. "Look at the Master's sport," Holy Mother said to someone.

"My mother's family was so noble. And look at my present companions. How totally silly Radhu is! She is standing on the porch, holding on to the railing and eagerly waiting for her husband to return. There you hear some music in a house. Radhu is afraid that Manmatha may enter the place. Day and night she watches him. What attachment! I never dreamt she would be so attached."

Between 1911 and 1917 Radhu developed strong symptoms of neurasthenia. She also suffered from fits of hysteria and could not stand even the slightest noise. It was an anxious time for Holy Mother. As Radhu could not bear the turmoil of the metropolis when she became pregnant, Holy Mother decided to take her to Jayrambati. She said to her disciple Barada: "I am taking with me a turbulent ocean. From now on I shall depend on you children for help." The party went by train to Vishnupur, where an astrologer predicted that Radhu would not have an easy delivery. The Mother and her companions left Vishnupur in six bullock carts. On the road they stopped for lunch. As the cook was taking out the rice-pot from the oven it dropped and the rice was scattered on the ground. Everyone was distressed at this mishap, but not Holy Mother. She realized that to cook rice again would cause great delay; so with a wisp of straw she gathered up some rice to offer to the Master. Then she washed her hands and took out the picture of Sri Ramakrishna from her box. Arranging rice and some vegetables on a leaf-plate, she offered them to the Master and said with folded hands: "Today you have arranged things this way; we can't help it. Now quickly eat some warm food." Her companions watched the whole thing and laughed aloud. The Mother said to them: "We must act according to the situation. Now come and take your lunch."

The party arrived at Koalpara at eleven o'clock at night. They planned to stay there for a day or two and then proceed to Jayrambati. Radhu slept well for two nights and wanted to live in that quiet village. But soon her illness was aggravated and she began to make many demands. Holy Mother had to bring ice for her from Vishnupur. Various treatments, including supernatural ones, were tried. Holy Mother performed her immediate duties to Radhu but maintained an attitude of non-attachment. When someone suggested that a specialist should be brought to look after Radhu's delivery, Holy Mother said: "Dogs and jackals live in the jungle. Do they not give birth to their young ones there?" In 1919 Radhu safely gave birth to a male child, who was named Vanavihari on account of his being born in the jungle (vana) of Koalpara; his pet name was Vanu.

Soon after this Holy Mother went to Jayrambati with Radhu and her child, and some other relatives. Radhu was very weak. She could not stand and crawled about; often she had to be forced into bed. Now her eccentricity reached its height. The following paragraphs from the diary of a disciple convey some idea of Holy Mother's ordeal with Radhu:

"Radhu's baby was now six months old, but still Radhu could not stand up because of weakness. She could only crawl about. To make things worse, she became addicted to opium. Holy Mother, too, of late had not been well. She was having occasional attacks of fever. She tried to wean Radhu from her opium habit. But Radhu was adamant. One morning Holy Mother was cutting vegetables when Radhu came for opium. Holy Mother understood her intention and said to her: 'Radhi, you have had enough of this. Why don't you stand up? It is impossible for me to take care of you any more. For your sake I have given up my devotion and everything else. Can you tell me how I can possibly meet all your expenses?' At these unpleasant words Radhu lost her temper, picked up a big eggplant from the vegetable basket, and threw it at Holy Mother with great force. It struck her hard and immediately she arched her back in pain. Looking at the photograph of the Master, she prayed with folded hands: 'Lord, please forgive her misdemeanor; she is senseless.' Then she took the dust of her own feet, put it on Radhu's head,[1] and said: 'Radhi, the Master never hurt me even with a rude word, and you torture me so much. How can you understand where I really belong? Simply because I live with you all, you do not think anything of me.' Radhu burst into tears. Holy Mother continued: 'Radhi, if I get angry with you, there will be no one in the three worlds[2] to give you shelter.' Addressing Sri Ramakrishna she said: 'O Master, please do not be offended with her.'

"A few days before, a devotee from Bangalore had spent some time with Holy Mother at Koalpara. He gave her some money for Radhu's expenses, and as he was leaving Koalpara said: 'Mother, whenever you need money, please let me know without the slightest hesitation.' At Jayrambati her expenses increased a great deal. Swami Saradananda had written to her that, since he had to procure money from here and there, he found it difficult to send her monthly expenses regularly. Holy Mother said to a disciple: 'I think Sarat does not have much money to spare, or he would not have written that way. The other day the devotee from Bangalore promised to send me money. But how can I write to him about it? Shall I not fulfil the Master's last injunction about not begging money from others?' To Radhu she said: 'Look here, Radhu, I am going to lose everything for your sake! The Master asked me not to stretch my hand to anybody even for a pice. He assured me that I shall never lack simple food and clothing. He admonished me that, if I begged even a pice from any person, I would sell my head to him in return.'"

Several years before Holy Mother's death, she warned the disciples that when her mind would be withdrawn from Radhu,

---

[1] A person greets his superior by touching the latter's feet with his forehead. Sometimes he touches the superior's feet with his hand and then touches his own forehead. This is called "taking the dust of the feet." According to Hindu custom, when a person has insulted or ill-treated a superior, he touches the latter's feet with his forehead in expiation of the sinful act.

[2] That is to say, earth, heaven, and the mid-region.

nothing could tie her down to earth. It appears as if her self-imposed or God-ordained chain was being snapped. Even seven years before her death Holy Mother once remarked: "My mind is not at all inclined to Radhu. I am tired of her illness. I force my mind down upon her. I say to the Master: 'May I keep my mind a little upon Radhu; otherwise, who will look after her?' Such ill health I have never seen before. Perhaps in her previous birth she did not perform the necessary penance to get rid of her sickness." Reminding Radhu of her strange behaviour, Holy Mother said to her one day: "You have been nursed by a lioness, and you are acting like a vixen. I have brought you up with such care, and you have not imbibed any part of my virtues. You have got everything from your mother." Radhu became angry, pulled down her veil, and turned her head away. Holy Mother laughed and said: "You cannot get along without me, and now you are hiding your face from me."

Radhu's torture of Holy Mother was mounting step by step. Once on their way home from Vishnupur in a bullock cart, Radhu began to push Holy Mother with her feet and said: "Get away from here, get away! Get out of the cart!" Holy Mother moved to the back as far as possible and said: "If I move away, how then shall I practise all these austerities through you?" Radhu kicked her again and the Mother said hastily: "What is it you have done, Radhi? What have you done?" Quickly she took the dust of her feet and touched it to Radhu's head.

One day Holy Mother was in a state of despair. She said to a disciple: "I do not remember having committed a single sin since my very birth. I touched the Master at the age of five. I may not have understood him at that time, but he undoubtedly touched me. Why should I suffer so much? By touching him all others have been freed from māyā; why should I alone have so much entanglement? Day and night my mind wants to soar high. I force it down out of compassion for people. And yet I am so tormented!" The disciple said: "Let people do whatever they like. Please bear with us all. A person cannot be angry so long as he is conscious of himself." "You are right, my child," replied the Mother. "There is no greater virtue than forbearance. This is a body of flesh and blood. Sometimes I say something in a fit of anger." As Radhu's conduct became increasingly outrageous, Holy Mother became more indifferent to her. Dispassion began to take the place of her apparent attachment.

We have already mentioned Radhu's son, Vanavihari, or Vanu. At dawn the Mother would sing as Mother Kauśalyā of the *Rāmāyana* did while rousing her son Prince Rāma from sleep:

"It is morning. Awake, my child, Thou who art merciful to
   the gods, men, and sages.
Bathe now and offer the gods cattle, elephants, gold, and
   betel-nuts."

Vanu had his share of love from Holy Mother. Since Radhu could hardly look after her baby, a woman disciple of the Mother was appointed as his nurse. The doctor gave notice that he would not treat him unless he was kept away from his mother. Holy Mother remarked one day: "She cannot even take care of herself. Why should God have given her a child?"

One more incident before we finish the story of Radhu. It happened three months before the curtain was rung down on Holy Mother's life. The evening worship was finished at the Udbodhan. The nurse was sent for to feed Vanu. It was not yet quite his feeding time, but the baby was crying and Radhu wanted to feed him. Holy Mother forbade her to do so. Radhu's temper was ablaze. Abusing her mercilessly, Radhu said: "I shall put fire to your mouth.[3] Why don't you die?" That day Holy Mother's patience reached its limit. Angrily she said: "Oh, yes, yes! You will learn what will happen to you

---

[3] A curse for death. The allusion is to the Hindu custom of cremation. Fire is first put to the mouth of the corpse as it lies on the funeral pyre.

after my death. What a plight you will be in! I do not know
how many kicks and thrashings with a broomstick are in store
for you. Today is the first day of the year. I sincerely wish that
you may die first,[4] and then I shall follow you with a peaceful
mind." This remarkable statement shows Holy Mother's solicitude for Radhu's welfare.[5] Radhu went on with her abuse.
Holy Mother asked an attendant to fan her, since her whole
body burnt, as it were, from Radhu's torment.

Almost since her birth Radhu had hung over Holy Mother's
life like a dark rain cloud with frequent thunder and showers.
But, in spite of her, Holy Mother's real nature shone through,
like the luminous sun in all its brilliance.

Radhu crossed Holy Mother's path to serve, in the main, two
purposes. First, Holy Mother's apparent attachment to Radhu
was self-imposed or, rather, willed by Providence to fulfil
Sri Ramakrishna's divine mission upon earth. Her own spiritual experiences had effaced from her heart every trace of
worldly desire. But a desireless mind cannot function through
the body. The body, after the experience of nirvikalpa samādhi,
falls off like a sere leaf. Radhu's appearance in her life supplied
the worldly element necessary to preserve her for the fulfilment
of her spiritual mission. Second, Holy Mother, through her behaviour towards Radhu and her various relatives, showed the
world how a householder should discharge his worldly duties.
Unlike Sri Ramakrishna, she did not formally renounce the
world, though in reality she was a perfect world-renouncer.
Holy Mother's apparent attachment to Radhu acted as a ballast
to keep her soaring mind tied to the world. More than once

---

[4] According to popular belief a wish made on New Year's Day
comes true.

[5] Nine months after Holy Mother's death, Radhu's husband took
a second wife. Deprived of conjugal love, Radhu went back to
Jayrambati. Manmatha's pecuniary condition took a turn for the
worse. Swami Saradananda had made arrangements for an allowance for Radhu. Manmatha often went to Jayrambati to claim a
share of it, and Radhu could not refuse this financial help.

she remarked: "My body has been preserved for the Master's work through this attachment to Radhu." Devotees came to her with their struggles and afflictions. Day and night she had to listen to their complaints. Once she said to a disciple: "My son, the whole day I wrestle with the devotees. Now comes one disciple, and next another—and always with problems and troubles. My body cannot bear these any more. I pray to the Master to keep my mind on Radhu for support. But I can cut off my shackles any moment. It is only out of compassion that I do not do so. In truth I am above māyā."

A year or two before her death Holy Mother once was in bed with a high fever. Radhu suddenly left for her husband's home against the Mother's will. The Mother said to a disciple: "When Radhu went away I was frightened. I said to myself that perhaps the Master did not want me to live any longer. But I see I still have many things to do." In spite of her seeming attachment, Holy Mother did not really regard Radhu as her own. To quote her own words: "Radhu and these others are not my true relatives. You alone [referring to her disciples] are my own people. Though I feel a strong attraction for you, there is no māyā in it. It is this attraction that drags me down, again and again, to this world." One day at Jayrambati a beggar woman sang a song describing the eagerness of Gauri, the Consort of Śiva, to go back to Her abode in the Himalayas. As Holy Mother listened to it, sitting on the porch of her house, she became still. Even after the singer had left she did not stir. When a disciple asked her to go inside the room, she did not respond. Then she went in and sat on the floor in an abstracted mood. At last she was heard to say to herself: "How long, O Lord, should I tarry here? It is a long, long time since I came."

Through the channel of Radhu, Holy Mother demonstrated the ideal of a karma-yogi as described in the Bhagavad Gītā. In this scripture, the Gospel of Hinduism, the Lord has said that the embodied soul cannot cease from activity. The body cannot survive without work. The seeker performs action for the purification of the mind. And the enlightened soul works for the preservation of the social order.

Holy Mother remained inwardly unaffected by the pain and suffering inflicted by Radhu and her other relatives, because she was in constant touch with the fount of bliss. This bliss she easily transmitted to her devotees. Once she said to a disciple: "The vision of God is in the palm of my hand; I can see Him whenever I like."

HOLY MOTHER AND RADHU IN A BULLOCK CART

HOLY MOTHER AND RADHU

HOLY MOTHER IN HER HOUSE AT JAYRAMBATI

Spiritual Ministry

SRI RAMAKRISHNA, during his lifetime and afterwards, in assigning Holy Mother her place in the scheme of his mission on earth made her his spiritual successor. On her part, she was born with unique spiritual tendencies. To her devotees and disciples she was the embodiment of the Divine Mother or the Primordial Śakti. Sri Ramakrishna, from the beginning of his association with her, gradually prepared her for her future rôle, and he later instructed her in the various phases of spiritual discipline and experience. Her full divinity, as we have seen, was awakened when he formally worshipped her in his room as the personification of the Divine Mother. Even before his death, Sri Ramakrishna told her that she would have to bring light to deluded people groping in darkness. After his death, when Holy Mother lost all interest in the world and even in her body, the Master reminded her, through many visions, of the tremendous task awaiting her. One day he appeared before her and said: "No, no. You must live. There are many things to be done." He certainly did not mean that Sarada Devi was to serve as an Abbess or Mother Superior in a religious organization, which would not have been in keeping with her temperament or nature. All that he meant was that she should be the central guide and mentor of his devotees. At his bidding, she had already given her first formal initiation, to Swami Yogananda in Vrindavan.

It will be useful here to discuss briefly the significance of spiritual initiation, according to Hindu tradition, and also the part a preceptor plays in unfolding a disciple's spiritual life.

Spirituality is awakened by the transmission of light from the living, through the living, to the living. The transmitter is called the guru or teacher, the method of transmission is known as initiation, and the person to whom it is transmitted is called the śishya or disciple. Spiritual truth is the living truth co-existing with and inherent in God Himself. Initiation is the descent of God through a human channel and is bestowed upon a living disciple. This bestowal may be designated as grace. No doubt God, in His real nature, transcends name and form and is present everywhere. But He must attune Himself to our receptivity so that our minds can receive Him. This is a law of the spiritual world demonstrated even by God-men like Krishna, Christ, Chaitanya, and Ramakrishna, who in spite of their divine nature accepted human teachers, as it were, to set an example for the common man. The idea of apostolic succession or the laying on of hands in Christianity seems to be based upon this fact. God is the real guru, but He uses a human instrument to manifest His power. The purer the channel, the clearer the manifestation of the power.

The human teacher must possess qualifications to discharge his task. The Upanishads emphasize that knowledge and realization of Brahman are the primary qualification. Knowledge, which belongs to the domain of intellect, is necessary to dispel the disciple's doubts. Furthermore, the guru must be sinless and free from worldly motive. He should act as a friend of those who, with humility, seek his help. An ocean of infinite compassion, he wants the welfare of the disciple, and helps, unnoticed and unheralded, in unfolding his spirituality, as the spring unfolds leaves and blossoms after the cold and bleak months of winter. No wonder these qualifications of an ideal teacher are fully found only in God-men, who visit earth from time to time. Holy Mother possessed them fully. But an aspirant can obtain help even from a lesser teacher. It would be folly for a beginner in science or art to refuse to start his study unless he obtained the guidance of an Einstein or a Leonardo. Even if such a teacher were available, would the beginner be able to understand him? How many contemporaries of Christ and Ramakrishna availed themselves of the presence of these exalted teachers? The right teacher always appears in the proper time to help the qualified pupil.

Spirituality can be literally handed down like any physical object, if the teacher possesses it and the student is capable of receiving it. A thought can be as vivid and real as a tangible thing. An aspirant can be initiated by a look or a touch or by mystical words. Only the most exalted teacher can awaken spirituality by a look or a touch, and then only in exceptional cases. The imparting of a mystical word, called the mantra, is the usual method of initiation. Real mantras are not created by the human intellect. They exist in the cosmic mind of God and are revealed to a qualified teacher. "In the beginning was the Word." Different mantras are adapted to the different aspects of the Godhead and the needs of the pupil. Through some mantras the pupil can commune with God's impersonal aspect, through some with His personal. Some mantras stimulate a disciple's love of God, some his knowledge, and so on. Holy Mother said: "The mantra purifies the body. One becomes pure by repeating the name of God given by the guru." The mantra is to be regularly repeated by the disciple with concentration and devotion. It has an intrinsic power of its own. It kindles the spark of spirituality in the disciple. A disciple asked the Mother if the mere repetition of the holy word taught by a qualified guru really helped the aspirant, if he did not possess intense devotion. "Whether you jump into water or are pushed into it," she replied, "your cloth will be soaked, will it not?" The mantra is generally chosen by the guru, who sometimes in its selection takes into consideration the feelings of the śishya.

Besides imparting the mantra, the guru teaches through instruction, personal example, and silent influence. The last method can be used only by highly qualified teachers.

An illumined teacher, endowed with direct knowledge of God, assumes responsibility for the disciple's sins and often himself suffers on his account, physically and mentally. The relationship between such a teacher and student is eternal and cannot be severed by death. He stands by the pupil both here and hereafter and does not cease guiding him until he is liberated from the bondage, delusion, and suffering of the world. He is the pupil's father—more real than an earthly father, who gives birth only to the physical body—for it is he who gives him spiritual birth. When, however, a blind teacher guides a blind student both find themselves in the ditch. As Sri Ramakrishna said, when a bullfrog is seized by an ordinary water-snake, there is no end of suffering for both. The frog can be neither easily swallowed nor ejected and it goes on croaking. But when it is seized by a cobra, its agony stops after three croaks at the most. Holy Mother suffered intensely, as we shall presently see, when people with sinful minds touched her feet. When, on the other hand, an earnest seeker touched her she felt soothed in both body and mind.

The knowledge of God which the teacher transmits is, according to the Upanishads, dearer than a son, dearer than wealth, and dearer than all precious things of the world. It should be imparted only to a qualified son or a disciple. It cannot be bartered for any material consideration. Like the teacher, the student also must be qualified. According to Hinduism, besides acquiring a general knowledge of the scriptures he should perform his daily obligatory activities and other duties prescribed for special occasions, and refrain from sinful actions. An advanced student should be able to distinguish between the permanent and the transitory and renounce the transitory. He should be endowed with control of the body and mind, forbearance, non-attachment to the world, faith, and concentration.

These disciplines create the inner purity through which one experiences spiritual truths. Patience is important in spiritual progress. The time factor is involved in the elimination of past worldly tendencies and the creation of spiritual ones. Anyone who has a sincere longing for the higher life and is ready to work for it can approach a teacher. According to the Bhagavad Gitā, the student should have unbounded faith in his teacher. Full of humility, he should put intelligent questions to him. Religious instruction, according to one of the Upanishads, becomes fruitful only when it is obtained from a teacher.

Spiritual experience involves, as already mentioned, the descent of God and the ascent of the soul—the grace of God and the right effort of the seeker. The meeting of a competent teacher and a qualified pupil is an unusual phenomenon. An Upanishad says: "Many there are who do not even hear of Ātman; though hearing of It, many do not comprehend. Wonderful is the expounder and rare the hearer; rare indeed is the experiencer of Ātman taught by an able preceptor."

That Holy Mother was a teacher *par excellence* goes without saying. In her relationship with her disciples she acted as mother, teacher, and Divinity incarnate. But for the most part she covered herself with a veil of humanity. Who can look straight at the blazing midday sun without the help of a coloured glass?

Holy Mother lived for thirty-three years after her return from Vrindavan in 1887. We have seen that during the first eleven of these years she lived a virtually retired life, visiting Calcutta only now and then. During the second eleven years the public began to learn about her and she initiated a few disciples. During the third period (1909–1920), which she spent mostly at her own houses in Calcutta and Jayrambati, devotees thronged to receive her blessings. From the fullness of her heart she bestowed her grace upon all. Men and women of every station and stage of life came to her. Among them there were high and low, young and old, students and lawyers, physicians and teachers, revolutionaries, spiritually evolved souls and people entangled in the world, and some eccentrics as well. With a very few exceptions none went away empty-handed. A silent yearning constantly welled up from her heart: "Come, all of you, I am here for your sake. I shall soothe my heart by showing you the way to liberation." She did not publicly summon the devotees. She did not write books, issue statements, or mount a public platform. The disciples of Sri Ramakrishna were extremely reticent about her. Perhaps they were afraid that ordinary people would take her lightly or not show her proper respect. But drawn by her irresistible attraction they all came. She seemed to be waiting for them. "Let them all come," her motherly heart said. "None will be rejected. Suppose they have lived sinful lives. Will they be deprived of my blessings on that account?" She initiated them in the shrine room and from her sick-bed, on roads and railway platforms, in meadows and under trees. All felt, when with her, that they were in the presence of an affectionate mother and made all kinds of demands upon her—reasonable and unreasonable. To the best of her power she tried to satisfy them. She had hardly any respite even when she badly needed it. If no devotee came to her on a particular day, she would say: "No one has come. This day seems to be passing in vain." Very shortly a seeker would arrive. This went on till nearly the end of her life. One day Holy Mother said seriously to a disciple: "He is unfortunate indeed who does not feel my compassion. I do not know anyone, not even an insect, for whom I do not feel compassion."

How did she give initiation? For the purpose of meditation, prayer, and worship, one requires an Ishta or Chosen Ideal, which may be a Personal God or the Impersonal Brahman. The average aspirant needs a concrete symbol of God. To Holy Mother, Sri Ramakrishna was the manifestation of the Supreme Spirit, the Incarnation for modern times. Most of her disciples accepted him as their Chosen Ideal. But she was not dogmatic. She often asked the aspirant, as she did the present writer, whom he would accept as his Ishta. She also advised seekers to follow their family tradition. When they could not decide, she herself suggested the particular form and name of the Godhead. It is said that, just before the initiation, she herself would meditate and thus discover the mantra suited to the aspirant. It would be revealed in her pure mind. Sri Ramakrishna said that whatever one hears in the pure mind is the word of God. Pure mind and pure Ātman are one and the same.

To the devotees of Sri Ramakrishna she sometimes said: "For you there is the Ramakrishna-loka, the heaven where Sri Ramakrishna is eternally present with his intimate disciples." There, she told them, they would experience eternal communion with the Lord. But to seekers of the Impersonal, she taught that Sri Ramakrishna would provide a wide doorway. To them she would say that finally the Ishta, the guru, and the śishya all merge in the Supreme Spirit.

Some of Holy Mother's disciples were impressed by her motherly solicitude, some by her ability as a teacher to dispel their doubts, and some by her unshakeable reassurance regarding their ultimate salvation, which can be given only by Divinity. But these features must not be compartmentalized. Whenever she appeared as mother, one saw behind her motherhood the power of a teacher, the transmitter of spiritual wisdom. Again, when she acted as teacher, she was not aloof or severe; she attracted her disciples by her motherly love. Finally, her divine nature supplied the foundation of the other two.

While Sri Ramakrishna was alive, as we have seen, Holy Mother sometimes felt sad because she had no children of her own. And the Master had spoken to her about the many disciples who would regard her as their mother. More importantly, Sri Ramakrishna wanted to present through Holy Mother the Motherhood of God; for this relationship hastens the aspirant's spiritual progress. Holy Mother's motherly longing was fulfilled not only through her giving initiation to hundreds of spiritual seekers, but also through the extreme tenderness, compassion, patience, and sweetness with which she ministered to their various other needs. At the Udbodhan, her Calcutta residence, Golap-Mā, Yogin-Mā, Swami Saradananda, and the other inmates kept an eye on her physical comfort and tried to curtail her activities. But at Jayrambati, where she was her own mistress, things were somewhat different. There Holy Mother dedicated herself fully to the physical welfare of her disciples. One day a monastic disciple wanted to wash his own plate, but the Mother would not allow him to do this, remarking: "How little I am doing for you! You are a treasure highly cherished even by the gods." Sometimes her women companions complained: "You belong to the brāhmin caste, besides being their guru. It will be inauspicious for them if you wait on them." The Mother replied in a natural way: "I am their mother. Who will look after the children, if not their mother?" She showed the same feeling towards low-caste disciples and even untouchables. She regarded the devotees as above all caste distinctions. They belonged to Sri Ramakrishna's family. When a disciple arrived at her home after a long journey, many times she herself fanned him to cool him off. She often nursed disciples when they were sick. She knew how difficult it was to come to Jayrambati, especially for people accustomed to the comforts of the city. She once remarked that it was rather easier to visit Gaya, Benares, and other sacred places than Jayrambati. She always insisted that the disciples spend at least two or three days at her home. As good food was scarce in the village, she procured fish, fruit, or vegetables from distant villages. Girish Ghosh at one time spent several days at the Mother's home. He was surprised to see clean linen on his bed every night and on inquiry found out that the Mother herself daily washed his sheets and pillow slips in the village tank. Even in her Calcutta house she would not allow any devotees who arrived at meal time to go away without taking food. This often exasperated Golap-Mā, who was the housekeeper, because she had to provide meals for the unexpected guests. She would complain to Holy Mother: "You are a fine person, indeed! You entertain anybody and everybody who comes to you and addresses you as 'Mother.'" Holy Mother brushed off the complaint with a smile. When a disciple referred to all she did for the comfort of disciples and the gratification of her relatives, she remarked: "I have done more than is necessary so as to set up a model for others."

Once Swami Arupananda, a monastic disciple, had to go to a neighbouring village on business and did not return till late in the afternoon. When he came back he found that the Mother had not taken her midday meal. The disciple complained about her fasting when her own health was bad. But she replied: "You have not taken your meal; how could I?" One day she remarked to a disciple: "If a thorn hurts the sole of your foot, I feel as if a plough-share had gone into my heart."

Whenever a devotee took leave of her at Jayrambati she would be distressed, like an earthly mother, at the thought of parting with her child. She would walk with the devotee some distance from her house and bid him farewell with tears in her eyes. A personal experience comes to the present writer's mind. He and Gauri-Mā were returning to Calcutta. As he was about to take leave of the Mother in her room, she gave him some rice-pudding of which she had touched a little to her tongue, thus making it prasād.[1] She caressed him affectionately, touching his chin. "Mother, I am going," he said. At once she corrected him and said: "Never say that. Say, 'Let me come again.' You come from East Bengal and do not know the custom."[2] The Mother shed tears of grief and fervently prayed to the

---

[1] Food offered to the Deity or partaken of by the guru or a holy man is called prasād. It is believed to be spiritually potent.

[2] The expression "I am going" denotes a kind of final parting, like "farewell" or "good-bye" in English. But the parting words "Let me come again," like the German *auf Wiedersehen*, denotes the possibility of meeting again. A few days before the Master's death, as Yogin-Mā was leaving for Vrindavan, Sri Ramakrishna said to her absent-mindedly, "Go." After she departed he was sorry for having used such an unlucky word. They never met again in the physical body.

Master for their safe trip. She said: "Master, please look after their welfare; they are undertaking a long journey." Gauri-Mā was a dynamic woman, an organizer and lecturer. In her younger days she had travelled all over India as a wandering nun. Vehemently she assured the Mother that it was only a night journey by train and they would return safely to Calcutta. The more she roared, the more humble the Mother became. As the writer watched the scene, he said to himself: "Here is a woman who does not possess a millionth part of the Mother's power and she is bubbling all over. And the Mother has suppressed all her power and is acting like an ordinary mother." Even after a lapse of forty-five years the scene remains vivid with him. On another occasion, in 1920, the writer took leave of Holy Mother at the Udbodhan, probably for the last time. He went out of the house and walked to the end of the street, and as he looked back he saw the Mother standing on the north porch of the house wistfully looking at him.

Often devotees made unreasonable demands upon Holy Mother. Some would ask for a forthright reply to such questions as whether she was the Divine Mother of the Universe, and if so why he did not realize her as such. Some would want an immediate vision of God or of Sri Ramakrishna. She always succeeded in pacifying their restless minds. This happened at Jayrambati, Calcutta, and elsewhere. One day Holy Mother had just finished her daily worship when an unknown devotee appeared with some flowers, evidently to worship her feet. At the sight of the stranger, she sat on the bed wrapping herself with a shawl, as was her habit. The man made an elaborate genuflection, offered flowers, and began to perform breathing exercises and other rituals, as one does before an image. This went on for a long time, and the Mother began to perspire heavily under the shawl. Golap-Mā came to her rescue. She pulled the man up by the hand and said in her usual loud voice: "Do you think she is a wooden image, that you would awaken her spirit by breathing exercises and other rituals?

Don't you see the Mother is getting hot and very uncomfortable?"

A monastic disciple, out of pique because he felt he was not making any spiritual progress, did not visit Holy Mother for two or three years, although he lived within a few blocks of the Udbodhan. Finally he wrote a long letter to her and requested her to take back the mantra with which she had initiated him. The Mother sent for him. When he came she said: "Look here, my child, the sun dwells high in the sky and water remains on the earth. Does the water have to shout at the sun and ask: 'O sun, please take me up'? It is the very nature of the sun to take up the water in the form of vapour. Let me assure you that you will not have to practise any discipline."

Another disciple made a similar complaint and the Mother said to him: "Suppose you are asleep in Calcutta and someone is removing you with your couch to Benares. Will you at that time know that you are on your way to Benares? When you wake up you will be surprised to see where you have come."

One disciple found it impossible to control his mind and said to the Mother with great anguish: "Mother, either remove my inner restlessness or take back your mantra." Her eyes became filled with tears at the disciple's suffering and she said fervently: "All right, you will not have to repeat the mantra any more." These words frightened him and he thought that his relationship with her was severed once and for all. He said: "You have taken away everything from me! What shall I do now? Does it mean that I am going to hell?" Holy Mother said in an animated voice: "What do you mean? You are my child; how can you go to hell? Those who are my children are already free. Even Providence cannot send them to hell."

One morning a disciple, an eccentric young man, came to Holy Mother at Jayrambati and demanded monastic initiation. He also urged her to make him "mad" and give him a vision of the Master immediately. Somehow she pacified him for the time being and sent him home. But his eccentricity increased and he returned to Jayrambati. He felt that the Mother had the power to give him a vision of Sri Ramakrishna but was refusing to do so. He said: "Mother, won't you let me see the Master?"

Mother: "Yes, you will see him. Don't be so restless."

Disciple (angrily): "You are only deceiving me. Here is your rosary. Take it back. I don't care for it any more."

He flung the rosary at her. "All right," said the Mother. "Remain for ever the child of Sri Ramakrishna." He left the place at once. Now he really became insane and began to write abusive letters to the Swamis of the Ramakrishna Mission, without sparing even Holy Mother. One day Swami Arupananda asked the Mother: "Did he return the mantra with the rosary? Can anyone ever return the mantra?" The Mother replied: "Can that ever be possible? The mantra is a living thing. Can anyone who has received it give it back? Can he, once having felt attraction for the guru, give him up? Some day in the future this man will come around and fall at the feet of those whom he now abuses. He once said to me: 'Mother, make me mad.' 'Why?' said I. 'Why should you be mad? Can anyone, without committing much sin, ever be mad?' " This devotee again began to visit the Udbodhan, but was rebuffed by the Swamis. He used to live on the bank of the Ganges and sometimes take his meal on the outer porch of the Udbodhan. One day he was taken to Holy Mother with her permission. Trying to pacify him in various ways, she said: "The Master used to say: 'At the time of death I shall have to stand by those who pray to me.' These are his very words. You are my child. What should you be afraid of? Why should you behave like a madman? That will disgrace the Master. People will say that one of his devotees has become mad. Should you conduct yourself in a way that would discredit the Master? Go home and live as others do. Eat and lead a normal life. At the time of your death, the Master will reveal himself to you and take you to him." The devotee was consoled by the Mother's words and gradually regained his normal state of mind.

Holy Mother often had to put up with such eccentricity. And what patience she showed with these deranged people! One day a woman devotee while taking leave of the Mother bit her big toe. The Mother cried aloud: "Goodness gracious! What kind of devotion is this? If you want to touch my feet, why not do so? Why this biting of the toe?" The woman said: "I want you to remember me." "Indeed!" the Mother replied. "I never before saw such a novel way of making me remember a devotee." Another time a male devotee while saluting her struck her little toe with his forehead with such force that the Mother cried out in pain. Those present asked the devotee the reason for this queer conduct. He replied: "I purposely gave her pain while saluting her so that she will remember me as long as the pain lasts."

The Mother had to deal with many queer demands. One of her intimate disciples was Kanjilal, a physician. His wife one day prayed to her: "Mother, please give your blessings so that my husband's income may increase." The Mother looked at her and said firmly: "Do you want me to wish that people may be sick and that they may suffer? Certainly I can never do that. I pray that all may be well, all may be happy."

We shall conclude this rather bizarre section about the deranged devotees with one more incident. A young man, who later came to be known as Padmabinode, was a student in the school of "M," the compiler of *The Gospel of Sri Ramakrishna*. He had visited Sri Ramakrishna and received his blessings. Afterwards he joined a theatre and furthermore became addicted to alcohol. Padmabinode knew Swami Saradananda intimately and addressed him as "friend." While returning home late at night from the theatre he used to talk incoherently, under the influence of drink. Often he called for his "friend" while passing by the Udbodhan. But the residents of the house

were instructed not to respond for fear of disturbing Holy
Mother's sleep. One night, finding no one paying attention to
his call, he started to sing in a plaintive voice:

> "Waken, Mother! Throw open your door.
> I cannot find my way through the dark;
> My heart is afraid.
> How often I have called out your name,
> Yet, kindly Mother,
> How strangely you are acting today!
>
> Soundly you are sleeping in your room,
> Leaving your poor child alone outside.
> I am all skin and bones from crying,
> 'Mother, O Mother!'
> With proper tone, pitch, and mode, using
> All the three gamuts,
> I call so loud, and still you sleep on.
>
> Is it because I was lost in play
> That you shun me now?
> Look on me kindly, and I shall not
> Go playing again.
> To whom can I run, leaving your side?
> Who but my Mother will bear the load
> Of this wretched child?"

As Padmabinode sang in the street with all his soul, the
shutters of a window of the Mother's room opened. He saw
this and said with great satisfaction: "Mother, so you have
awakened. Have you heard your son's prayer? Since you are up,
please accept my salutation." He began to roll on the ground
and take its dust on his head. Again he sang:

> "Cherish my precious Mother Śyāmā[3]
> Tenderly within, O mind;

---

[3] A name of Kāli.

May you and I alone behold Her,
Letting no one else intrude."

With emphasis, he improvised a new line: "And surely not my 'friend,'" referring to Swami Saradananda. Next day Holy Mother asked about him and was told his story. "Did you notice his firm conviction?" she remarked. At least once more he saw Holy Mother thus. When the devotees complained about the disturbance of her sleep, she replied: "I cannot contain myself when he calls on me in that way."

A few days later Padmabinode became seriously ill and was taken to the hospital. At the hour of death he wanted to hear something from *The Gospel of Sri Ramakrishna*. As he listened tears rolled from his eyes. Repeating the name of the Master, he breathed his last. When the Mother heard about this she said: "Why should it not be like that? Surely he was a child of the Master. No doubt he covered himself with mud. But now he has gone back to the Master's arms, where he belongs."

Holy Mother's love for her disciples was not just like the love an earthly mother feels for her children. It was much deeper. Once a monastic disciple asked her: "How do you regard us?"

Mother: "As God Himself."

Disciple: "But we are your children. If you think of us as God, you cannot regard us as children."

Mother: "I regard you as God and also as children."

Another disciple asked her: "I address you as 'Mother.' I want to know whether you are my own mother."

Mother: "What else am I? I am your own mother."

Disciple: "That's what you say. But I cannot understand it well. Why can't I feel for you the same way as I do for the mother who gave birth to my body?"

Holy Mother said: "Ah, how true it is." Then she added: "It is God, my child, who is our father and mother. He Himself has become our parents. The love they show is God's love."

God has implanted philoprogenitiveness in the hearts of ordinary mothers for the preservation of family and society. In Holy Mother's case the same love showed her spiritual children the way to liberation from the bondage of the world.

Holy Mother's love was not confined to her disciples alone. It was showered upon all who went to her for succour, irrespective of caste and creed, merit or demerit. She helped them with food, clothes, or medicines, according to their need. One day while she was living at Koalpara, an untouchable woman came to her and sought her help with tearful eyes. She had suddenly been discarded by her paramour, for whose sake she had left her own home, and now she was completely helpless. Holy Mother sent for the man and said to him with gentle reproval: "Look here, she has renounced all for your sake. And you have accepted her service for a long time. It will be very sinful for you to reject her now; there will be no room for you even in hell." The couple was reconciled.

The story of Radhu's pet cat gives even more striking insight into Holy Mother's love. She had arranged for it to have a daily ration of milk. The cat used to lie peacefully near her. Sometimes she would pretend that she was going to punish it with a stick, but this only made the animal creep nearer her feet. Laughing, she would throw away the stick, and the inmates of the house would also laugh. The cat, following its own nature, often stole food, and the Mother would remark: "To steal is its dharma. Who is there always to feed it lovingly?" One day a monastic attendant treated the cat roughly and dashed it against the earth. The Mother looked very sad. She said to the monk: "Scold the cat, but do not beat it. Please feed it regularly and see that it does not go to any other house to steal food." She again reminded him solemnly: "Do not beat the cat. I dwell inside the cat too."

In the Rôle of Teacher

GOD HIMSELF is the real teacher. Spiritual light comes from Him alone, generally through a human channel, called the guru or teacher. Like a magnet's attraction is the irresistible and silent attraction of the guru. Yearning souls, afflicted with the world and seeking release from the apparently interminable round of birth and death, feel the power of this attraction. The teacher takes upon himself the burden of sin and iniquity of the disciples, and suffers on their account. He kindles in their hearts the light of spirit and finally takes them to the realm of bliss and immortality.

Holy Mother did not seek disciples. She once said: "Those who care to come to me will do so of themselves after severing the shackles of the world. I shall not send for them." She herself lived a secluded life unknown to the public. Very few knew of her existence. The present writer, in 1916, expressed the desire for initiation to Swami Premananda at the Belur Math and suggested the name of one of Sri Ramakrishna's foremost disciples. The Swami asked him to go to the Mother. In his utter ignorance the writer asked who the Mother was and received a thorough scolding from the Swami. Nothing was written about her, except for a brief mention in *The Gospel of Sri Ramakrishna*. A life of the Master in Bengali which spoke of Holy Mother was read by only a very few. Her pictures were not shown in public. How, then, did people come to know about her?

Some were recommended, as was the present author, by the

disciples of Sri Ramakrishna or other Swamis of the Ramakrishna Mission. Some heard about her from friends or relatives
who had already been initiated. Some came to know of her
through a dream or vision. And there were some who came to
pay their respects to her as a holy person and received her grace
unsolicited. She also initiated people at the request of her own
disciples. Once when Holy Mother was going to Calcutta she
had to wait for the train at the Vishnupur railroad station. A
poor porter came running to her and said: "You are my Jānaki.[1]
How long I have been searching for you! Where have you been
all this time?" With these words he began to weep profusely.
Holy Mother consoled him, asked him to bring a flower to offer
at her feet, and initiated him then and there. Some received
initiation from her in a dream. When they told her about it,
she explained the meaning of the mantra to them and asked
them to continue to repeat it, and sometimes she gave an additional mantra. In the choice of her disciples Holy Mother
looked into their hearts and did not consider their race or social
position. Thus among them one finds not only Bengalis, who
naturally form the majority, but also men and women of South
India, Europeans, and a Parsi. It may be mentioned that she
neither understood nor spoke any language except her mother
tongue, Bengali.

One of the remarkable features of Holy Mother's spiritual
ministry was her catholicity. She did not ask all her disciples to
accept Sri Ramakrishna as their Ishta or Chosen Ideal, though
she often emphasized the fact that one's spiritual life would be
more easily unfolded through the Master, who was the greatest
manifestation of Divinity in the present age. She knew that the
austerities practised by Sri Ramakrishna were not for his own
sake but for the welfare of the world. As the Master taught,
while excavating an old city an archaeologist may find a rare
coin of great value, a precious museum piece, but it cannot be

---

[1] A name of Sitā, the consort of Rāma.

used for everyday purposes, for one can transact business only with modern currency. Holy Mother often asked her future disciples about the deities worshipped in the family and initiated them in accordance with that tradition. Sometimes a seeker would not be sure about the choice of a spiritual ideal and would ask the Mother to select one for him. Before giving initiation she would become introspective and thus discover what would be best for the disciple. In these moments of introspection she would often come to know about the disciple's spiritual future. When the present writer went to Holy Mother for initiation he was a college student and lived with his family. After the ceremony, he placed a silver coin near her feet as the customary fee. The Mother said that she did not accept any money from her monastic disciples. The writer protested that he was not a monk. Still the Mother refused to accept the fee, giving the same reason. Thrice the disciple offered the money, and each time he received the same reply.

During the second decade of the present century there was a great political ferment in the country. Many young men joined revolutionary societies organized to achieve India's freedom. They were under the constant surveillance of the police, who also kept watch on anyone who gave them shelter. One such revolutionary young man went for initiation to Koalpara, where Holy Mother was then living. For fear of incurring the displeasure of the Government, the local devotees arranged for him to spend the night in a private house, being nervous about keeping him in the āshrama. Early next morning Holy Mother was going to visit Radhu when the young man met her on the road and received initiation.

Here we shall make a slight digression to narrate a few incidents about Holy Mother's attitude towards some religious-minded political suspects and also towards the oppressive measures of the British rule in India. Many revolutionaries were inspired by the patriotic fervour of Swami Vivekananda and read his books and *The Gospel of Sri Ramakrishna* for inspiration.[2] Some of them later joined the Ramakrishna Order. For a long time the police kept a close watch on the Ramakrishna Mission.

There were two young ladies, sisters-in-law, who bore the same name of Sindhubala, one of whom was a political suspect. They hailed from the district where Holy Mother was born. By mistake the police first arrested the innocent one and then the other. One of them was pregnant. They were made to walk on foot in public. The mistake of the police was pointed out and suitable conveyance was suggested for their transportation. But the police refused and insisted on their walking. In addition, the request for bail was refused. The ladies were subjected to various humiliations. When the matter was reported to Holy Mother she shuddered and then said in an extremely angry voice: "What does all this mean? Has it been done by the order of the Government or is it an act of smartness of the police officers concerned? We never heard of such cruelty to innocent women during the reign of Queen Victoria. If the

---

[2] The head of the Criminal Investigation Department of the Government of Bengal, who was in charge of the political prisoners and *détenus,* once visited the present writer in his internment camp. The officer saw a set of *The Gospel of Sri Ramakrishna* in the original Bengali on his desk and said: "I find that almost every *détenu* keeps these books. I learnt the Bengali language to read them in the original but I did not find a single statement against the British rule." The writer told the police officer that the patriotism of the revolutionaries was inspired by religion.

A commission appointed by the Government of India to investigate the activities of the Indian revolutionaries remarked in course of its report that the revolutionaries carried in one pocket the Bhagavad Gītā and in the other a bomb. To the fighters for Indian freedom India was a spiritual entity, the birthplace of the eternal truths of the Hindu religion and philosophy. During the thousand years of foreign domination the spiritual ideals declined. In order to revive those ideals, the country had to be politically free. Therefore one found a strong spiritual element in the struggle for India's political freedom.

Government is responsible for the matter, then it will not last long. Was there no young man near who could slap the police and snatch away the girls?" A little while after, her brother told her that the ladies had been released. Then she became some-what pacified and said: "If I had not heard of their release, I could not have slept tonight."

A disciple of Holy Mother, a quiet and spiritual-minded young man, was harassed for nothing by the police. One day as he came out of the shrine room after meditation, the police arrested him and took him away without giving him time to take refreshment. Holy Mother was very sad to hear about it and said: "This was certainly an unjust action on the part of the English. He is one of my good children, and for nothing he is being harassed. He could not take even a little prasād. Will the British rule last long?"

Another disciple of the Mother was interned with the present writer. Unable to bear the rigours of internment he committed suicide. After the writer's release he told the Mother about the young man's death. With a sigh she said: "O God, how long will You put up with the iniquity of this Government?"

Holy Mother was patriotic in her own way, and cherished the welfare of the country. During the First World War people suffered intensely, especially the women, from scarcity of clothes. Many of them could hardly go out in public. News-papers often reported the news of their suicide. One day, after hearing several reports of these heart-rending episodes, Holy Mother could not control herself. Weeping bitterly she said: "When will the English go? When will they leave our country? Formerly we had spinning wheels in every house. People used to make yarn and weave their clothes. There was no scarcity of wearing apparel. The British have ruined the whole thing. They tricked us and said: 'You will get four pieces of English cloth for a rupee, and one piece extra.'[3] All our people took to an easy life, and the spinning wheel disappeared. Now, what

---

[3] This is how Indians were lured to buy British cloth.

has happened to these fops? There is no end to their misery."
She asked a disciple to give her a spinning wheel.

But all this protest against injustice did not interfere in the
slightest with her innate generosity. It was the time of the
Durgā Pujā,[4] when new clothes are presented to both men and
women. Holy Mother asked one of her brahmachāri attendants
to buy clothes for her nieces. The brahmachāri was a patriot
and he purchased coarse native clothes. But the girls wanted
fine English stuff and refused to wear what was bought. There
was a heated argument. The Mother listened to the discussion
and said with a smile: "The English people, too, are my children. I must live with all. I cannot be exclusive." She asked the
attendant to buy the British goods.

To resume the narrative of Holy Mother's method of initiation. Generally the Mother needed only a few minutes to
initiate a disciple. Someone later asked Swami Saradananda
why he took half an hour to perform this task. The Swami said
that Holy Mother could tell by a glance or a touch whether the
Master had accepted the aspirant, whereas he required long
meditation to be assured of this acceptance.

It is recounted that in a very few cases she declined to give
initiation. Perhaps the candidates were not ready, or perhaps
such initiation would have drained too much of her spiritual
strength. She herself once said: "Embodiment limits the power
of the Spirit." Sometimes she would say: "This body will one
day surely perish. Let it go now, if it must, but let me give
initiation." With what poignancy she felt for people's affliction
can be realized from one of her remarks: "Now and then I
think if this body, instead of being such a small frame of bone
and flesh, were a big one, how many people I could help."

We have already mentioned Holy Mother's physical suffering. It is said that the price of sin is suffering. But the Mother
was sinless. She herself said that she did not remember ever
having committed a sinful act, and explained the cause of her

---

[4] Worship of Durgā, an aspect of the Divine Mother.

suffering as her taking on herself the iniquities of her disciples. It was vicarious atonement. Regarding initiation Holy Mother said: "The power of the teacher enters into the disciple, and the power of the disciple enters into the teacher. That is why, when I initiate and accept the sins of the disciples, I fall sick. It is extremely difficult to be a teacher. On the other hand, by leading a virtuous life the disciple does good to the teacher." Initiation, the Mother said more than once, had made her rheumatism chronic.

In 1916 Holy Mother went to the Belur Math to attend the worship of Durgā. On the second day of the worship many devotees saluted her by touching her feet. Afterwards it was noticed that she was washing her feet time and again with Ganges water. "What are you doing?" warned Yogin-Mā. "You will catch cold." The Mother replied: "How shall I explain it to you? When some persons touch my feet I feel as if my body has been set on fire. Ganges water alone refreshes me." One day she suffered excruciating pain from the touch of the devotees and said to Swami Arupananda: "This is why I fall ill. Tell the devotees to salute me from a distance. But do not mention this to Sarat, otherwise he will not allow them to salute me at all."

A disciple has recorded a striking example of this phenomenon at Jayrambati. Holy Mother's attendant had gone out on some business. After his return he found her lying on a straw mat on the verandah. At the sight of the attendant she said: "A rather elderly man came here. Seeing him from a distance, I entered my room and sat on my bed. He was very eager to touch my feet. Though I protested, he saluted me by touching my feet by force, as it were. Since then I have been almost at the point of death because of a pain in my feet and my stomach. I washed my feet three or four times; still I cannot get rid of the burning. Had you been here, you could have forbidden him to touch my feet." Many instances like this could be recounted.

Holy Mother did not really mind this excruciating physical pain. Her motherly love and the consciousness of her mission made her regard suffering as a privilege. At Koalpara a disciple hesitated to touch her feet, thinking this would cause her pain. The Mother said: "No, my child, we are born for this purpose. If we do not accept others' sins and sorrows and do not digest them, who else will? Who will bear the responsibilities of the wicked and the afflicted?"

When she felt the urge to give initiation, the Mother was heedless of all considerations of health and comfort. Once when she was suffering from malaria at Jayrambati, Swami Saradananda asked her attendants not to allow anyone to approach her for initiation. Then a devotee from a far-off part of the country arrived just for that purpose. The attendants refused to take him to the Mother. A heated argument ensued. The Mother came to the door and asked her attendants why they were not allowing the devotee to see her. When they told her of Swami Saradananda's order, she said: "Who is Sarat to prohibit my giving initiation? I am born for this purpose."

Holy Mother often said: "I initiate people purely out of compassion. They do not leave me alone. They weep. That moves my heart. Out of kindness I give initiation."

One morning three devotees arrived at Jayrambati with a letter from Swami Brahmananda in which he requested Holy Mother to initiate them. When informed of the content of the letter she said: "Alas, Rakhal has sent me this stuff. A son generally sends his mother good things." At first she did not agree to initiate them and told them to go back to the Belur Math. Afterwards she relented and said, addressing Sri Ramakrishna: "O Lord, yesterday I prayed to You that I might not spend a day in vain. And at last You have brought this to me. All right. As long as the body lasts I shall continue to do Your work." The devotees received their initiation. When the matter was afterwards reported to Swami Brahmananda and several other senior Swamis, the former became very grave. Swami

Premananda said with a deep sigh: "Grace! Grace! By this unique grace the Mother has been protecting us. I cannot describe in words the poison which she swallows. If we had done so, the very suffering would have burnt us to ashes." People came to Holy Mother after having committed all kinds of sin. "But," she said, "when they address me as 'Mother,' I forget everything and they get more than they deserve."

At one time some of her attending disciples thought that the Mother was too generous in the matter of initiation, and one of them said to her: "Mother, you give initiation to so many people; certainly you can't remember them all. You cannot always think what happens to them. A guru should constantly look after the welfare of the disciples. Wouldn't it be more prudent of you to initiate only as many as you can remember?" To which she replied: "But the Master never forbade me to do so. He instructed me about so many things; could he not have told me something about what you have said? I give the responsibility for my disciples to the Master. Every day I pray to him: 'Please look after the disciples, wherever they may be.' Further, I received these mantras from the Master himself. They are very potent. One is sure to attain liberation through them." But she did concern herself with her disciples in a more active sense. Daily she practised japa[5] for their spiritual welfare. This continued till the end of her life. She slept very little. One night she was up at two o'clock in the morning. Asked for the reason, she said: "What can I do, my child? All these children come to me with great longing for initiation, but most of them do not repeat the mantra regularly. Why regularly? Many do not repeat it at all. But since I have taken responsibility for them, should I not see to their welfare? Therefore I do japa for their sake. I constantly pray to the Master, saying: 'O Lord, awaken their spiritual consciousness. Give them liberation. There is a great deal of suffering in this world. May they not be born here again!' "

---

[5] Repetition of a name of God.

At the Udbodhan, during her last illness, she said to a disciple: "Even after my death, do you think I shall have respite until every one of those for whom I have assumed responsibility has been liberated? Since I have taken charge of their good and evil, I must always remain with them. Is it a joke to give initiation? What a heavy responsibility the teacher assumes! How much worry he suffers! Can you understand everything? If you did, my burden would have been considerably lightened. Sri Ramakrishna is playing his game with different people in different ways. I have to bear the brunt of it. I simply cannot let down those whom I have accepted as my own."

Another time Holy Mother said: "I am the mother of the virtuous; I am the mother of the sinful." No repentant sinner was ever deprived of her grace. She was incapable of seeing others' faults. To one disciple she said: "Why are you afraid, my child? Always remember that the Master is behind you and also that I am there. What should frighten you as long as I, your Mother, exist? The Master said to me: 'At the end, I will appear to those who come to you, and lift them up, holding them by the hand!' The Master must reveal himself to you at the hour of death, no matter what you do or how you live. God has given you hands, feet, and organs, and they will play their part."

One woman of a respectable family became morally delinquent. Coming to realize her mistake, she went to the Udbodhan, stood in front of the Mother's room, and said to her: "Mother, what will happen to me? I am not entitled even to enter this shrine room." Holy Mother came forward, encircled the lady's neck with her own arms, and said tenderly: "Come in, my child, come inside the room. You have realized that you have sinned and are repentant. Come in, I shall initiate you. Offer everything at the feet of the Master. What is there to fear?"

A young man, a householder, said to the Mother one day: "Mother, I have suffered a great deal from the world. You are my guru, you are my Ishta. I do not know anything else. Truly,

I have done such vile things that I am ashamed to tell you about them. I am still here only on account of your grace." The Mother affectionately stroked his head and said: "To the Mother, a child is always a child." Deeply moved by her compassion, he said: "It is true, Mother. I have received so much of your kindness. But may I never feel that such kindness is easy to win."

All these incidents bear out what the Lord said in the Bhagavad Gītā: "Even if the most sinful man worships Me with unswerving devotion, he must be regarded as virtuous; for he has made the right effort."

To her disciples Holy Mother showed love, forgiveness, and compassion in a transcendent degree, and gave them her assurance of final liberation. She said: "Those who have been initiated by me need not practise spiritual austerities for their salvation. At the hour of death all will realize God; surely they will see Him. But those who want immediate results will have to practise discipline. The more they practise, the quicker they will get them. Those, however, who idle away their time will have to wait. Even those who give up all spiritual effort will realize God at the hour of death; there is no doubt about it." She often spoke of her disciples' present birth as being their last one.

Holy Mother did not, however, promise all her disciples liberation in the present life.[6] "If I freed everyone immediately," she said, "my spiritual strength would be sapped and my body

---

[6] Swami Saradananda once explained the meaning of the term "last birth" to the present writer. He said that Holy Mother did not say to all her disciples that after this present birth they would not be born again. If she gave this assurance to a particular disciple, the latter would of course be liberated at the hour of death. But in this very life he would practise God-consciousness intensely to get a foretaste of the bliss of which he was assured hereafter. The Swami said further that the term "last birth" need not be taken literally. What she perhaps meant was that in the case of her disciples a limit had been put to the apparently endless chain of births and deaths. They might have to be born a few times more. As for worldly-minded people, there was no knowing when they would attain liberation.

would not be able to help many seekers. It would fall off after those few had attained freedom." To some disciples the Mother remarked: "Why do you worry so much? Fulfil all your worldly desires; afterwards you will enjoy abiding peace in communion with Sri Ramakrishna. For you he has created a new heaven." She assured the disciples that they were the heirs to the spiritual treasures earned by her and the Master. We shall refer to this again in the following chapter.

Holy Mother knew the spiritual capacity of her disciples. One day Yogin-Mā said to the devotees, in front of the Mother: "Mother may show us very much love, but still it is not as intense as the Master's. What compassion and love he showed for his disciples! We saw that with our own eyes. Words cannot describe it." "What is there to wonder at?" the Mother replied. "He accepted only a few chosen disciples, and those too after much testing. And to me he pushed a whole row of ants." How true are the words of a great householder disciple of Sri Ramakrishna: "Mother is more kind than Father!"[7]

As to whether all people really want liberation, the Bhagavad Gitā says: "Only a rare one, among thousands, seeks perfection." How can God liberate one who still wants to enjoy the fun of the world, or, as Sri Ramakrishna said, one who, "being infatuated with the red toys of physical pleasures, has forgotten the Divine Mother?" There was a worker at the Udbodhan, a householder, Chandra by name, who often ran errands for Holy Mother; he was one of her disciples. He was very fond of eating and the Mother loved to feed him. Whenever he came to her he got something to eat. One day a senior Swami said to Chandra: "You always go to the Mother for prasād; can you ask her for something I am going to suggest?"

Chandra: "Surely."

Swami: "Can you say to her: 'Mother, I want liberation'?"

Chandra: "Surely I can. I shall do it right away."

[7] Referring to Sri Ramakrishna.

Chandra went upstairs and found Holy Mother engaged in worship. Slowly he entered the shrine room. But his body began to tremble. A little later Holy Mother looked at him and asked: "What do you want?" Chandra felt as if someone was choking his voice. "Prasād," he blurted out. The Mother pointed out to him some food under the couch.

Here is another example of the Mother's compassion and thoughtfulness. It was the occasion of the Śivarātri, the Night of Śiva, when devotees spend the night in meditation, religious singing, and the reading of various episodes from the life of Śiva. The inmates of the Udbodhan, as was the custom, were fasting the whole day and night. In the morning someone had teased Chandra, asking him to observe the fast too. At first he raised objections, but at last he was prevailed upon to go without food along with the rest. In the evening he went to the Mother's room to offer his salutation to her. The Mother looked at his pale and hungry face and asked him what was the matter. In a sad voice Chandra said that he was compelled to go without food on account of the persuasion of the inmates of the Udbodhan. At once Holy Mother asked him to take food. When he objected that in that case he would not derive the merit of fasting, she said: "I will fast for you and you will have the merit." Chandra beamed with pleasure and at once ate to his heart's content. And the Mother went without food.

We shall now briefly describe Holy Mother's attitude towards the life of monks and of householders, and towards marriage. In her one finds all these three elements present. She herself was married. Surrounded by relatives, she lived a householder's life. But at the same time she was a living demonstration of the monastic ideals of compassion, service, purity, non-attachment to the world, and constant communion with the Supreme Spirit.

There were both monks and householders among the Mother's disciples. She imparted the spirit of brahmacharya and sannyāsa to the members of the Ramakrishna Order, sometimes giving them the appropriate robe, and asked them to perform the formal ceremonies under the guidance of Swami Brahmananda, who was then the President of the Ramakrishna Order.

Her advice to her disciples about whether they should remain householders or embrace the monastic life differed according to their temperaments and competency. Holy Mother cherished a soft corner in her heart for her lay disciples who, despite all their worries and difficulties in the world, sincerely practised spiritual disciplines. When some of them spoke of envying the monastic life, she would say to them: "Is the ochre robe everything? You will realize God without it. What is the need of taking the ochre robe?" She also pointed out the dangers of the monastic life, especially the pique which a monk might feel if he was not shown proper respect by householders. She said: "It is much better," pointing to her own white cloth, "to dress like this. It is rather nice." When one day a young man, out of temporary dispassion, expressed unwillingness to marry, she said laughingly: "How is that? God has created things in pairs: two eyes, two ears, two legs—and likewise, man and woman." To another young man hesitant about marriage she said: "Why can't one lead a good life if one is married? The mind alone is everything. Did not the Master marry me?" One disciple said to her that he had tried to lead an unmarried life, but now found it impossible to remain a celibate. The Mother gave him assurance and said: "Don't be afraid to marry. Sri Ramakrishna had many householder disciples. Go and marry. Don't worry." In some cases she strongly discouraged the attempt to lead a monastic life. One married disciple, with children, wanted to become a monk and urged his wife to live with her father's family. When the helpless woman wrote to the Mother about the matter, she said with annoyance: "See how unjust he is! Where will this poor girl find shelter for her tots? He wants to be a monk; why then did he marry at all? If he must renounce the world, let him first provide for his family." Sometimes she refused to give her opinion about marriage and would say: "I won't say anything about it. If after marriage a man is troubled by the worries of this world he will blame me for them."

But Holy Mother never had any doubt about the supreme value of the monastic life. How often she said to the monks: "Look at the suffering of the householders! You have renounced the world and can at least enjoy peaceful sleep!" She also said: "Will a man who has strong desires for worldly pleasures listen to me if I ask him to renounce them? But if a fortunate soul has realized the world to be the sport of māyā and God alone to be real, shall I not help him a little? Is there any end to the suffering in the world?"

She held her monastic disciples in high respect. Once a householder devotee quarrelled with a monk and used harsh words towards him. Holy Mother reprimanded him and asked him to show respect to the monks. "For," she said, "an unkind word or thought on the part of a monk may injure a householder." She scolded her niece Nalini severely for speaking slightingly of the monks. One of her disciples, a college student, wanted to renounce the world, and the Mother encouraged him. Nalini said: "Look at our aunt's strange conduct. Here is a bright young man studying for his B.A. degree. His parents have worked hard to defray his expenses. Now he wants to join the monastery instead of earning money and supporting his parents in their old age." "How little you know of him!" said the Mother sharply to Nalini. "He is not a young crow, but a cuckoo.[8] When the cuckoo fledgeling grows up, it recognizes its mother and flies to her, leaving the adopted mother behind." This young man afterwards became a monk.

On another occasion a young disciple received the ochre robe of a monk from Holy Mother's hand and was exceedingly happy. One of her sisters-in-law remarked: "There! She has

---

[8] It is said that the female cuckoo lays her eggs in a crow's nest, where they are hatched. The mother crow regards the young cuckoos as her own offspring and brings them up. But when the cuckoos grow up they return to their own mother.

made him a monk." A niece added: "With what high hopes his parents have brought him up! Now all this is shattered. Marriage is also a duty. If our aunt goes on making monks, Mahāmāyā will certainly be angry with her. If anyone wants to renounce the world, let him do so of his own accord. Why should Aunt be the instrument?" The Mother said in reply: "Look here, child, these are my godly children. They will live in the world, pure as flowers. Can anything be grander than this? When I see the suffering of the householders my very bones are scorched."

Holy Mother encouraged worthy disciples to become monks. A young man with an M.A. degree came to her at Jayrambati and presented his problem to her. He wanted to embrace the monastic life and had received encouragement from Swami Shivananda. But "M," a lay disciple of the Master, asked him to wait a while in order to avoid giving a shock to his family. Holy Mother heard the story but did not at once say anything to the young man. Afterwards she said to an attending disciple regarding him: "He lives near 'M's' house and has his mother and brothers at home. That is why 'M' is hesitant about his becoming a monk. But Tarak[9] is urging him to be one. After all, 'M' is a householder and Tarak is a monk. One needs good fortune, indeed, to accept the ideal of renunciation taught by the Master. Tarak is right. How few can be rescued from the world once they are entangled in it! The boy has real strength of mind." Next day when the disciple again spoke to the Mother about his sincere longing to join the monastery, she said: "My child, may your desire be fulfilled. Tarak has said the right thing."

A mother whose married son had renounced the world became bitter towards Holy Mother and complained to her about it. The Mother said: "He has not done anything wrong. Rather he has followed the right path. I have heard he has made provision for his family."

---

[9] The premonastic name of Swami Shivananda.

Holy Mother respected the high ideals of monastic life and rebuked the monks if they deviated from them. Once she said about one of them: "I understand he was ill. But why did he live with a householder? There are monasteries. A monk must not lower the ideal of renunciation. Even if a wooden image of a woman lies upside down in the road, he must not turn it the other way, even with his foot, to look at its face. It is dangerous for a monk to save money. Money can create all kinds of trouble, even endanger one's life." About another monastic disciple who had not seen the Mother for several months and felt sad about it, she said: "Why should he feel so? A monk must sever all the chains of māyā. A chain of gold is also a chain. He must not be attached. This idea of the 'Mother's love'—this moaning that one has not obtained it—is pure nonsense. I do not like my male disciples to hang around me constantly. After all, I have a human body. To regard it as divine is not easy."

A monastic disciple had arranged to go to Benares with Girish Ghosh, who had agreed to pay his fare. Holy Mother said to him: "You are a monk. Won't you be able to procure your passage money? After all, Girish is a householder; why should you travel with him? As you both will occupy the same compartment in the train, he may ask you to do something or other for him. You are a monk; why should you take orders from him?"

Holy Mother could not bear any slight to a disciple who had renounced the world, no matter from what quarter it came. Once Golap-Mā was displeased with a brahmachāri at the Udbodhan and said harshly that she would not live there if he stayed in the house. She was about to leave in anger when the matter was reported to Holy Mother. The Mother said in an animated voice: "Who is she? A householder, after all. Let her go away if she wants to. The brahmachāri is living here after renouncing everything for me."

Holy Mother was often heard to say: "Ah, with whom shall I live except those who have renounced the world for God?"

Renunciation to her was the basis of spiritual life, and a true monk was its living example.

The Mother fully approved of women's renouncing the world if they were ready. A young girl refused to marry, and her mother wrote to Holy Mother to persuade her to remain in the world. The Mother replied: "How much a woman suffers during her whole life as a slave of her husband, always catering to his whims."

Men and women of various temperaments and natures became the Mother's disciples. Some visited her many times, though they did not render her any personal service and made no demands on her kindness. Many of them practised spiritual austerities. Holy Mother said of them: "I regard all the disciples as my children. But with these I have a special relationship. They visit me always and look on me as their own." Some householders, and their number was considerable, were satisfied to receive initiation from the Mother. They did not visit her frequently, nor did they particularly devote themselves to meditation and prayer. But they had the firm belief that they need not worry about liberation, which surely would be attained after death, if not earlier. They surrendered themselves to her and performed their ordinary duties in the world. Two statements of Holy Mother's may apply to them. First: "Even if my disciples do not practise any disciplines, they will surely realize God at the hour of death." Second: "To surrender oneself to God and cherish sincere faith in Him is in itself a spiritual discipline." There was a third group of disciples, few in number, who suffered terribly if they did not see the Mother or had to live away from her. For many years they frequented her place and rendered her personal services. Some of them attended her with unbelievable devotion. This service was their spiritual austerity. Certainly they were needed to help the Mother in her work and for the very preservation of her body. Referring to them, she said: "Those who are my own are born with me in every cycle." And lastly, there were those monks who were quiet and serious, and who led an austere life. Though they believed that Holy Mother was the Divine Mother of the Universe, they seldom bothered her, once having been initiated by her. They felt that the contact of the soul was the real contact, the outer contact being only a means to it. They further felt that the Mother's blessings and grace became fruitful when this inner contact was made. That is why they seldom visited her after initiation, and when they visited her they were satisfied with mere prostration. They did not want to bother her with many questions. One such disciple, Swami Madhavananda, who was a former General Secretary of the Ramakrishna Mission, remarked that though he had lived at the Udbodhan for over three years, he seldom talked to her. He was satisfied to take the dust of her feet daily along with the others. It was enough for him to feel that she was there in the house. Holy Mother was exceedingly pleased to see such disciples and said: "May I obtain children like them in every birth."

It had been much the same with Sri Ramakrishna's devotees. Broadly speaking, those who visited him may be divided into three groups. All regarded him as a great yogi, an illumined saint who could fulfil their desires. One group sought the Master's blessings for success in their worldly life and for relief from suffering. A second group prayed to him to guide them in their spiritual practices. No devotee ever went away empty-handed. There was a small number of devotees whom the Master designated as his inner circle: these did not care for spiritual visions or even liberation. They felt an eternal relationship with the Master and were attracted by his irresistible love. They surrendered themselves to him completely: body, mind, and soul. Sri Ramakrishna often treated them as his playmates and companions from birth to birth. One of them, Swami Brahmananda, asked Sri Ramakrishna one day, at the request of another devotee, to teach him meditation and other spiritual disciplines. The Master at once burst into tears and reprimanded him for acting as if he were a beggar, adding that he would naturally inherit, like a prince, all that the Master had earned. He exhorted these intimate disciples never to forget who he was, who they were, and what was the nature of their unique relationship with him. These devotees afterwards became potent interpreters and bearers of his message.

Divinity

REApers OF THE FOREGOING PAGES must have observed how
the Divine Power of the Universe functioned through
Holy Mother. God played, as it were, a game of hide-and-seek
through her body and mind. Her divine nature was confirmed
by Sri Ramakrishna himself and by his disciples. The Master
referred to her as the Goddess Sarasvati, the bestower of wisdom. As we have seen, he worshipped her formally as the
Divine Mother. We have also observed the manifestation of
her divine power when confronted by demented Harish and by
the highwayman. Here is another instance.

One day, not long after Sri Ramakrishna's death, Holy
Mother was going to Jayrambati from Kamarpukur. Her
nephew Sivaram, who was a mere boy at that time, accompanied her with her bundle. As they neared Jayrambati, he
thought of something and stopped. The Mother was surprised
and asked him to follow.

Sibu:[1] "I shall only move if you tell me something."

Mother: "What?"

Sibu: "Will you tell me who you are?"

Mother: "Who else am I? I am your aunt."

Sibu: "Then you can go yourself. You have come near your
home. I won't go."

Mother: "Don't be silly. Who do you think I am? I am a
human being, your aunt."

Sibu: "Very good. Then why don't you go?"

---

[1] Sivaram's pet name.

185

Seeing Sibu still standing there, the Mother said: "People say I am Kāli."

Sibu: "Are you really Kāli? Is it true?"

Mother: "Yes."

Sibu was pleased and said: "Let us go, then."

Now and then Holy Mother herself spoke about her real nature, though these occasions were infrequent. At such times her voice and her actions would be quite different from what they were normally. One night at Jayrambati, her cook said she had touched a dog and needed a bath.[2]

Mother: "It is rather late in the evening. Don't bathe now. Wash your hands and feet and change your cloth."

Cook: "How would that help?"

Mother: "Then touch some Ganges water."

But even that did not satisfy the cook's fastidious nature.

Finally the Mother said: "Then touch me."

One day a devotee was taking leave of the Mother at Kamarpukur. Her nephew Ramlal and her niece Lakshmi were present. As the devotee was about to depart, suddenly the Mother said: "Call on me." The next moment she controlled her feelings and said: "I mean, call on Sri Ramakrishna. That will serve your purpose." Lakshmi heard Holy Mother's remarks and said: "Mother, what do you mean? This is not fair. What will the devotees do if you hoodwink them in this way?"

Mother: "Why? What have I done?"

Lakshmi: "A minute ago you said to the devotee: 'Call on me,' and now you say: 'Call on Sri Ramakrishna.' "

Mother: "If a person calls on the Master, is there anything more for him to do?"

But Lakshmi explained to the devotee that the Mother had just made a most significant statement and that he should pray to her.

----

[2] Orthodox Hindus regard a dog as an unclean animal. After touching it they bathe or change their clothes to get rid of the pollution.

One day, before a disciple, Holy Mother referred to Sri
Ramakrishna as Bhagavān, God Himself. The disciple asked:
"If the Master is God, then what are you?" "Who else am I?"
the Mother replied without any hesitation. "I am Bhagavati,
the Divine Mother of the Universe."

A woman devotee asked her: "Why can't we realize that you
are the Divine Mother?" The Mother replied: "Can everybody
recognize divinity? There lay a big diamond at a bathing place.
People thought it was an ordinary stone and rubbed the soles
of their feet against it after finishing their baths in order to
remove the dry skin. One day a jeweller went there, saw the
precious stone, and realized that it was a valuable diamond."
Many disciples prior to meeting her had dreamt of Holy
Mother as a goddess, and some felt so at the time of initiation.
Very often devotees worshipped her feet, regarding her as the
Divine Mother, and she accepted their worship. One day at
Jayrambati, vexed with her relatives, she said angrily: "Do not
torture me too much. If He who dwells inside this body [point-
ing to her own body] hisses but once, not even Brahmā,
Vishnu, or Śiva will be able to save you." On another occasion
she said to a woman disciple, referring to Radhu's tormenting
her: "Look here, child, this body is a divine body. How much
more torture can it bear? Can a human being, unless he be
God, put up with all this? Let me tell you something. No one
will understand me as long as I am alive. They will know only
afterwards."

But Holy Mother was generally reticent about her divinity.
There was no limit to her humility. One day a woman disciple
said: "Many of us address the Mother as the Divine Mother of
the Universe. But the Lord alone knows the extent of our conviction. The reiteration of sceptics like us of her divinity is a
sort of parrotry." "How true," said the Mother with a smile.
The disciple continued: "Utter absence of egotism is the convincing proof of the Mother's divinity. A human being is full
of ego. Every day we see hundreds of people prostrating them-

selves before the Mother and calling her the Mother of the Universe. Had she been a mere human being, she would have been puffed up with pride. Has a human being the power to digest so much honour?"

An amusing incident may be mentioned here to emphasize her humility. One day a woman disciple was extolling her spiritual power by addressing her repeatedly as the guru. Holy Mother said with a smile: "Please do not drown me that way. Let me tell you a story. A disciple was crossing a river when he found he was being swept away by the strong current. Thinking about the omnipotence and divinity of his guru, he repeated the guru's name several times and was saved. The next day he told the guru about his wonderful power and how he had saved his life. The guru was pleased and went to the river to test his own power for himself. But he did not know how to swim. Finding himself about to be drowned by the strong current, he began to repeat 'I,' 'I,' but was drowned."

A very remarkable incident clearly revealing Holy Mother's divine nature happened when she was staying with Balaram's family at Kothar in Orissa. A disciple went into the inner quarters, where the women lived, and found the Mother seated alone in a secluded corner with her legs stretched out, absorbed in deep thought. Her eyes were wide open, but indrawn. The disciple stood still and looked at her face. After about fifteen minutes Holy Mother noticed him and said: "When did you come?" and then she added: "I do not like to be shut in; that is why I am here. It is now midday and all are asleep." In an abstracted mood she continued: "This repeated journey to the earth! Is there no escape from it? Wherever is Śiva there is Śakti. They are always together. It is the same Śiva again and again, and the same Śakti too. No escape.

"People do not understand how much the Master suffered for their sake. All those austerities! Did he need them for himself? Still he performed them for people's welfare. Can they themselves practise spiritual disciplines? Where is that power,

HOLY MOTHER AT FIFTY-SIX

HOLY MOTHER AT FIFTY-EIGHT IN HER HOUSE AT JAYRAMBATI

Swami Virajananda

Swami Arupananda

Sarajubala

that vigour? That is why the Master did all that. Do you know that song?"

Devotee: "Which one?"

Mother: " 'Behold, the Lord of the lowly has come for the lowly!' Really my children are mere beggars. Can He remain still if they call on the Mother? At once the Lord comes down."

Devotee: "Is Chaitanya,[3] too, God?"

Mother: "Yes, yes. It is the same God. He comes down again and again. It is the same moon that shines in the sky night after night. No escape. He is in the clutches of His creatures. They are His own. Who will look after them if not He? He said: 'Whenever you call on Me, I shall appear before you.' Remember this and never forget it. If you call on Him, you will realize Him. He is the Wish-fulfilling Tree."

Devotee: "I know only my Mother."

Mother: "It is the Master who taught the name of Mother. Did people know before that God is Mother? It is Her creation. She gives birth to all beings and again swallows them. To swallow means to give liberation. It is all Her sport, Her play."

Just then Radhu came in and then left again. The Mother continued: "It is said: 'I come again and again. There is endless suffering. How long shall I bear it?' But who really suffers? Is it the Master or the creature? It is the Master's suffering. That's what I have been thinking about. I realize that there is no end to it. Who can understand how much the Master suffers?"

Devotee: "Why should the Master alone suffer? You too. You and the Master are one."

Mother: "Shame upon you! You must not say that, my stupid child. I am his handmaid. Have you not read in *The Gospel of Sri Ramakrishna*: 'You are the operator, I am the machine; You are the dweller, I am the house; I do as You make me do?' Everything is the Master. There is nothing be-

---

[3] Followers of Sri Chaitanya (born A.D. 1485) regard him as God's Incarnation. Sri Ramakrishna, too, regarded him in that light.

sides him. Once in a while I ask myself if the creature will ever pay back his debt. Then I think: No, this debt can never be paid, not even by biting straw.[4] The creature is his alone."

Devotee: "Is that why you give initiation to anyone and everyone, no matter who seeks it?"

Mother: "How much grief and suffering a creature goes through! Moved by this pain and sorrow, the Master is restless and comes to the earth. Who but the Master will relieve the creature of this anguish? He is a sympathetic kindred soul. He suffers more than the creature. That is why he understands his suffering. Do you know what I see now and then? It is the Master who has become all this. Whichever way I look I see him alone. He is the blind, he is the crippled. There is none else but he. Then I realize that he is the whole creation; he alone has become everything. It is not the creature who suffers; it is he who does. Therefore whoever comes weeping, I must liberate him. I offer him what is really his.

"They ask me to enjoy my sleep. Where is sleep? How can I sleep? It seems to me that the time I might sleep away should be devoted to japa; that will do good to the creatures. Now and then I say to myself: 'If, instead of this small body, I had a much bigger one, how much more good I could do to others!'

"An ant crawled along and Radhu wanted to kill it. Do you know what I saw? I saw it was not an ant but the Master; I saw in it his hands, his feet, his face, his eyes. I stopped Radhi. I thought: The Master alone has become all. It would be right if I could look after all."

The bells and conch shells sounded in the temple. Like one waking from a dream, Holy Mother said: "It is dusk; let me go and offer worship to the Master. How much I have chattered!"

The devotee saluted the Mother and she blessed him. As she walked away she said with a smile: "Mother and child, mother and child."

---

[4] A Bengali expression denoting the humility and the gratitude of the debtor to the creditor.

Holy Mother was conscious that she was not different from Sri Ramakrishna. One day she said: "The Master told me that he would dwell in my body in a subtle form." And yet what humility she showed in her words and action! One day a disciple addressed her as Jagadambā, the Divine Mother of the Universe. Immediately she asked her to leave the place. She often said to her disciples: "As you have all come to Sri Ramakrishna, so did I. As he has been showering his grace upon all of you, so he gave me shelter at his feet. I am his handmaid; I feel blessed to be his handmaid."

Swami Premananda, in the course of a moving letter to a devotee, once wrote: "Who has understood Holy Mother? She does not reveal the slightest trace of the power in her. The Master showed the power of knowledge. But what do you see in her? Even that power is effaced. But with all that, what great power she possesses! Hail, Mother! Hail, Mother! Victory unto you, the fountain of all power! The poison we dare not swallow, we push to her. And Mother welcomes it. What infinite power! What immeasurable compassion! Hail, Mother! How insignificant we are! We did not see even the Master behaving that way. How much he tested people before he accepted them! And what do we find here? Strange. Surprisingly strange. She gives shelter to one and all. She eats food offered by everyone, and digests it all. Mother! Mother! Hail, Mother! Remember her infinite compassion in pleasure and pain, in prosperity and adversity, in scarcity and epidemic, in war and turmoil. Hail, Mother! Hail, Mother!"

Three Reminiscences

THE FOLLOWING ACCOUNTS of three of Holy Mother's disciples of their meeting with her illustrate her methods of initiation and teaching.

In 1891, Kalikrishna[1] met Holy Mother for the first time. As mentioned earlier, together with Swami Saradananda, Yogin-Mā, Golap-Mā, and two other devotees of the Master he went to Jayrambati to attend the worship of Jagaddhātri. He was then only nineteen years old. At the sight of the devotees, Holy Mother's joy knew no bounds. She at once accepted young Kalikrishna as her own child and caressed him by touching his chin. Daily she cooked meals for them, and she sat near them while they ate. Kalikrishna was given the privilege of running errands for her and had unrestricted admission to the inner apartment of the house. Holy Mother's mother, Shyamasundari, was then alive.

One day a wandering minstrel entertained the family with the following song, which touchingly reflected Holy Mother's own life. The words of the song are uttered by the Mother of Umā:[2]

---

[1] Later Kalikrishna renounced the world and received the name of Swami Virajananda. He served as the President of the Ramakrishna Order from 1938 to 1951.

[2] An Incarnation of the Divine Mother, also known by such epithets as Gauri (She of the Fair Complexion) and Annapurnā (She Who Fills All with Food). Annapurnā is worshipped in Benares as the Consort of Śiva, who is regarded there as the eternal King of Benares. Śiva is also depicted as a world-renouncing

O Umā, my darling, what good tidings I hear!
People say you are adored in Benares as Annapurnā. Is it
   true?
O Gauri, when I married you to Śiva,
He went as a beggar from door to door for a morsel of
   food.
But today how glad I am to hear
You are now Queen of the World, seated by His side.
And they called my naked Śiva a madman:
How much abuse I had to bear with from everyone!
Now I hear that doorkeepers guard His palace
And gods like Indra, Chandra, and Yama[3] hardly can see
   Him.
Śiva used to live in the Himalayas;
Many a day He got his food by begging;
Now He rules over Benares and is as rich as Kuvera.[4]
Is it you who have brought him all this good fortune?
No doubt He is very rich now,
Else why should Gauri be so proud?
She does not cast her eyes even upon her own children,
And turns her face away from Radhika.[5]

The song recalled Holy Mother's early life to the listeners'
minds. The singer received his reward and left. Shyamasundari,
who also listened to the song, said to the devotees: "In those
days everyone regarded my son-in-law as insane and felt pity for
my poor Sarada. People flung hard words at me and I almost
died of grief. And now, you see, many an aristocrat worships
Sarada's feet as if she were a goddess."

Three days after the worship the devotees from Calcutta became bedridden with malaria. There was no limit to Holy

---

mendicant, eccentric and uncouth, who goes about naked, with
ghosts and demons as his companions. Umā was a princess and her
mother had to suffer from people's ridicule for marrying her
daughter to an eccentric. Śiva occupies a most exalted place among
the Hindu deities.
   [3] Indra is the king of the gods, Chandra the moon-god, and
Yama the ruler over death.
   [4] The god of wealth.
   [5] The writer of the song.

Mother's worries. Every now and then she stood outside the door and looked at the patients. Milk was scarce in the village. Kalikrishna found out that she went from door to door, pot in hand, to procure a little milk to nourish them. The devotees were aware of the Mother's difficulties and wanted to return to Calcutta as soon as the fever left them. But she pressed them to spend a few days more for convalescence. Finally she agreed to let them go. When they were ready to take their leave, Kalikrishna saw tears flowing unceasingly from Holy Mother's eyes. Her face became red and swollen with weeping. Kalikrishna, too, cried. As the bullock cart moved on, she followed it, stopping awhile every few paces. At last they persuaded her not to go any farther. But they saw that she kept looking at the cart until it was out of sight. Kalikrishna remarked: "We returned to the monastery with empty hearts. From the very little I had heard of Mother, I could realize some measure of her love. But I never thought she would completely steal our hearts and souls and make us dearer to her than her own self. To be sure, I loved my own mother, and she, too, loved me very much. But Holy Mother is my mother from birth to birth, the Eternal Mother."

Two years later, Holy Mother was living in a rented house at the village of Belur. One day Kalikrishna called on her, and she asked him to spend the night at the house. The next day when he was about to take leave of her, she said to him: "I feel very sad, looking at you. You used to be healthy and plump. Now how sickly you look on account of repeated attacks of malaria! Those who live at the monastery are mendicants. How will they feed you properly? You had better spend a few days at home." At this command, the young man became sad at heart at the thought of living away from the holy atmosphere of the monastery. But the Mother persuaded him to go home and gave him initiation. As he left by a ferryboat, he cast his eyes at Holy Mother's dwelling and saw her standing on the roof in the rain, watching the boat with unwavering eyes.

A brief account of some of the visits of Sarajubala, a woman disciple, is given below, as far as possible in her own words.

The whole day before her first meeting with Holy Mother in January 1911, Sarajubala had been filled with such an exuberance of joy that she could hardly sleep that night. She had been living in Calcutta for the previous fourteen or fifteen years, and at last she would be blessed by touching the Mother's feet. She went to the Udbodhan in a hired carriage with her sister Sumati, who was a student and had seen the Mother before. When they reached the house, they saw the Mother at the door of the shrine room, one foot on the door-sill and the other on the door-mat. Her left arm was raised high and placed on the door, while the right arm was hanging at her side. The upper part of her body was bare. She had been looking wistfully as if expecting somebody. As soon as Saraju prostrated herself at her feet the Mother asked Sumati about her. Sumati introduced her as her elder sister. Casting her glance at the newcomer, Holy Mother said: "Look here, my child, how much I am troubled by my relatives! My sister-in-law and her daughter Radhu are both down with fever. I do not know who will look after them. Will you wait a minute? Let me wash my hands. I shall return presently." After she came back she offered the two sisters handfuls of sweets and asked them to eat. The visit lasted for five minutes and the Mother asked them to come again.

February 12, 1911. About a month later Saraju went to the Udbodhan when Holy Mother was visiting with Balaram Bose's family in the neighborhood. After her return the Mother said to Sarajubala, in the course of their talk: "You haven't come for a long time. I was worried about you and thought you might not have been well." The devotee was deeply moved to think that the Mother had not forgotten her though they had met only once for five minutes. Tears came to her eyes. Suddenly Holy Mother said: "You were here; so I was feeling restless at Balaram's house." Saraju was astounded to think of Holy

Mother's kindness. Soon the Mother sat on her bed and said to her: "Sit by me. It seems, my child, that we have known each other a long time." "I do not know," Saraju said. "I was here one day only for five minutes." When the time for departure came, Holy Mother said: "Can you go alone, or shall I come down with you?"[6] She accompanied her to the head of the stairs and bade her come another day in the morning. "What wonderful love!" Saraju said to herself.

Sarajubala visited Holy Mother again at the Udbodhan. It was a hot summer day. The Mother was surrounded by devotees. As soon as Saraju prostrated herself before her the Mother took a small fan from the top of the mosquito net and began to fan her. She said to Saraju anxiously: "Take off your blouse quickly so that your body may be cool." She began to caress her before the other devotees, and Saraju felt embarrassed. All eyes were fixed on her. The more Saraju begged her to give her the fan, the more the Mother insisted on doing the fanning herself. She said: "That is all right. Be a little refreshed." She brought a glass of water and some sweets. As Saraju partook of them the Mother looked happy.

August 3, 1911. This day Saraju was to receive initiation. She took a few articles with her for the purpose. When she arrived at the Udbodhan, she found Holy Mother absorbed in worship in the shrine room. She sat by her side. The Mother asked the others to leave and then said: "Now tell me the mantra which was revealed to you in a dream." At the time of initiation she explained to Saraju the meaning of the mantra. She first asked her to repeat the dream mantra and then communicated to her a new one. She advised her to repeat the second one and then to meditate. Saraju saw the Mother in deep meditation before the initiation. The disciple's whole body began to tremble and she began to weep. As Saraju saluted her, the Mother said: "May you attain devotion to God." When they were taking their meal, Holy Mother first ate three morsels of food and

---

[6] The interview took place on the second floor of the house.

then distributed the prasād to the devotees. Now she became her old self again—very jolly.

June 15, 1912. It was time for the afternoon worship. Holy Mother changed her clothes and sat on the carpet before the image of Sri Ramakrishna. She made, with her own hands, some garlands to decorate the Master's picture. Rashbehari,[7] a young brahmachāri, had placed the garlands near some sweets for the offering, and ants had gathered around the sweets. Some of them were found in the garlands. The Mother said with a laugh: "See what Rashbehari has done! The Master will be bitten by these ants." She removed the ants and tenderly decorated the picture of the Master with the garlands. Seeing her thus decorate the picture of her husband with flowers before others, Surabala, her crazy sister-in-law, laughed.

Another day Saraju went to the Udbodhan and found the Mother resting after lunch. She was gracious enough to request the disciple to fan her and thus render personal service. Suddenly she heard the Mother say to herself: "Well, you have all come, but where is the Master?" The disciple said in reply: "We could not meet him in this life. Who knows in which birth to come we shall see him? But this is our rare fortune—that we have been able to touch your feet." "That is true, indeed," was Holy Mother's brief reply. Very seldom did she speak of herself in such a way.

One evening two pretty young ladies had been talking to Holy Mother privately on the north porch of her room when Saraju went there, not having found the Mother anywhere else. She heard the Mother saying to them: "Lay the burden of your minds before the Master. Tell him your sorrows with tears. He will place in your laps the object of your desire." Saraju realized that the ladies were praying to her to be blessed with children. A few months later she again met them in the

_____

[7] Later he became a monk and received the name of Swami Arupananda. After the Mother's death he compiled her conversations in two volumes. The reminiscences of Sarajubala have been adapted from the account given in one of the volumes.

Mother's house and was glad to notice that their desire was going to be fulfilled.

September 8, 1912. After finishing her bath in the Ganges, Holy Mother entered her room, sat on her bed, and said to Sarajubala: "Look here, my child, I have finished my bath." The disciple understood that the Mother had come to know of her secret desire to worship her. She said to herself: "Thou art ever pure. It is not necessary for Thee to bathe in the Ganges to purify Thyself." She then worshipped her feet with flowers and sandal-paste and bowed down before her. Afterwards the Mother had breakfast. She made the disciple sit near her and gave her, with infinite love, half of every article of food she ate. The disciple felt greatly blessed.

It was the day of the sacred Car Festival.[8] At four o'clock, Sarajubala, accompanied by Gauri-Mā, came to the Udbodhan, and they bowed before the Mother as she finished the afternoon worship. The disciple had brought a silk sāri for the Mother. Placing it near her feet, she asked timidly: "Mother, will you kindly put it on?" "Oh yes, my dear," Holy Mother replied with a laugh. Just then some men devotees came in and prostrated themselves before her. One of them brought with him some hibiscus flowers, roses, a garland of jasmine, and some fruits and sweets. He placed these offerings near her feet and began to worship her. It was a soul-enthralling sight. The Mother sat quietly, a sweet smile playing on her lips. The garland was hanging round her neck. The flowers adorned her feet. After the worship, the devotee took a little from every fruit and sweetmeat and begged of her to partake of it. Gauri-Mā said with a laugh: "You are in the grip of a staunch devotee; you must eat a little of everything." The Mother also laughed and said: "Just a little, please. I can't eat so much." She ate a little from every offering. The devotee took the prasād

---

[8] On this occasion the images of Sri Krishna, His brother Bala-rāma, and His sister Subhadrā are taken in procession in a car which is drawn by devotees.

in his hand and touched it with his forehead, beaming with indescribable joy. After prostrating himself before the Mother he took his leave. She removed the garland from her neck and gave it to Gauri-Mā.

October 1912. Nalini, Holy Mother's niece, was angry. The Mother reprimanded her and said: "Women should not get angry so easily. They must practise forbearance. In infancy and childhood their parents are their only protectors, and in youth their husbands. Women are generally very sensitive; a mere word upsets them. And words are so cheap now-a-days. They should have patience and try to put up with their parents and husbands in spite of difficulties."

Radhu was sitting near with her sāri pulled up above her knees. The Mother reproved her and said: "Dear me! Why should a woman pull her sāri above her knees?" She recited a verse and said: "When the cloth is pulled above the knees, a woman is as good as naked." There were a few women devotees in the adjacent room. Two of them had put on the ochre robes of a nun. One of them asked the Mother: "Is there any truth in image worship? Our teacher does not approve of it. He instructs people to worship fire and the sun."

Mother: "You should not doubt the words of your own teacher. Why do you ask me about it when you have heard the opinion of your guru?"

The nun: "We want to know your opinion."

At first the Mother refused to give any opinion. But the nun pressed her. Finally the Mother said: "If your teacher were really an illumined soul—excuse me for the remark—he would not have made such a statement. From time out of mind, innumerable people have worshipped images and thus attained spiritual knowledge. Can you deny this fact? The Master never cherished dogmatic views. Brahman exists everywhere. Prophets and Incarnations are born to show benighted humanity their way. They give different instructions to suit different temperaments. There are many ways to realize truth. So all these instructions have their relative value. For instance, many birds are perched on the branches of a tree. They are of different colours: white, black, red, yellow, and so on. Their sounds, too, are different. But when they sing we say that the sounds are made by the birds. We do not designate one particular sound only as the sound of the birds, and refuse to acknowledge the other sounds as such." After the visitors left, Holy Mother said: "It does not become a woman to argue like that. Even the wise can hardly realize the nature of Brahman through reasoning. Is Brahman an object of argument?"

Golap-Mā objected to Radhu's going to school, as she was then a grown-up girl. The Mother said: "No, she is not that grown-up. Let her go to school. She can do immense good to others if she becomes educated and learns something useful at school. She was married in a backward village. Through education she not only will improve herself but will be able to help others."

In answer to a few personal questions, Holy Mother said to Sarajubala: "Do not make any distinction between the Master and me. Meditate on your Ishta and pray to Him. The meditation begins from the heart and ends in the head. Neither mantra nor scripture is of any avail; bhakti, love, accomplishes everything. The Master is everything—both guru and Ishta. He is all in all."

One evening when the disciple went to the Udbodhan, Holy Mother kindly asked her to spread her small carpet on the floor and fetch her rosary. The Mother soon became absorbed in meditation. Across the lane was an open space. A few labourers lived there in huts with their families. One of the men began to beat a woman severely. Then—though a child was in her arms—he kicked her with such force that she was thrown to a distance. Again he started kicking her. The Mother could not proceed with her meditation. Though she was extremely shy and would not usually talk loud enough to be heard by people on the ground floor, she now went to the porch of the second floor, stood by the iron railing, and cried aloud in a tone of sharp reprimand: "You rogue! Are you going to kill the woman outright? I am afraid she is already dead!" Hardly had the man looked at her when he became still, like a snake before a charmer, and left the woman alone. The Mother's sympathy made the woman burst into loud sobs. Her only fault was that she had not cooked the meal in time. Afterwards the man wanted to make peace with her. Holy Mother saw this and returned to her room. As Saraju was leaving for home, the Mother called her aside and said: "Progress becomes easier if both husband and wife agree in their views regarding spiritual practice."

November 1913. The disciple arrived at the Udbodhan with a large number of flowers from her garden, and Holy Mother was pleased. The Mother was about to perform the worship. Saraju arranged the flowers and the Mother sat on the prayer rug before the image. But she forgot to put aside some flowers for worshipping Holy Mother's feet. The Mother anticipated the disciple's desire and herself kept some flowers separate in the tray. After the worship she said to the disciple: "Now, my child, I have kept those flowers for you. Bring them here." Just then a devotee came to see the Mother with a large quantity of fruit. She was very much pleased to see him. After putting a mark of sandal-paste on his forehead, she caressed him by touching his chin. Sarajubala had never seen her express her affection for any man devotee in such a manner. Next the Mother asked her to hand him a few flowers. As he accepted them, his whole body trembled with devotional fervour. With great joy he offered those flowers at her feet, and then left the room after accepting the prasād. She sat on the bed and asked Saraju to come near her. The disciple worshipped her feet. Very tenderly the Mother placed her hand on Saraju's head and kissed her. The disciple was deeply touched by her blessings.

After a while Saraju found the Mother on the roof drying her hair in the sun. She invited the disciple to come near and said: "Take your sārī off your head and dry your hair; otherwise your health may be affected." Golap-Mā came to the roof and requested the Mother to make the food offering. Holy Mother came down from the roof and was followed by the disciple to the shrine room. Like a bashful young bride she said to Sri Ramakrishna in a soft voice: "Come now, your meal is ready." Then she went to the image of Gopāla and said: "O my Gopāla! You come, too, for your meal." The disciple was behind her. Suddenly the Mother looked at her and said: "I am inviting them all for their noon meal." Her earnestness and devotion made it apparent that the deities listened to her words and followed her to the adjacent offering room.

One day a disciple asked Holy Mother: "Does the Master really partake of the food you offer him?"

Mother: "Yes, he does."

Disciple: "But we see no sign of it!"

Mother: "A light comes from his eyes and touches all the articles of food.[9] Why is it so? Does the Master really require any food? Certainly not! He eats the food offered to him for the satisfaction of the devotees. The sacred prasād purifies the heart. The mind becomes impure if one eats food without first offering it to God."

June 8, 1918. Sarajubala, on her arrival, found Holy Mother absorbed in meditation. Presently five or six women devotees came in. One of them suffered from an abdominal tumour and had come to Calcutta for treatment. She was very nervous about the operation. Holy Mother did not allow them to touch her feet and asked them, for some unknown reason, to salute her from a distance. One of the women asked the Mother to bless the sick woman so that she might be cured. The Mother said: "Bow before the Master and pray to him with sincerity. He is everything." She seemed to be nervous and asked the

---

[9] The idea that the deity touches the food with a ray of light from his eyes is also expressed in an Upanishad. *See Chhāndogya Upanishad* III. vi. 1.

devotees to go home as it was getting late. After their departure she ordered someone to sweep the place and sprinkle it with Ganges water. Then she lay down and said to Saraju: "My child, please fan me a little. My whole body is burning. My salutations to Calcutta! People come here and lay before me the whole catalogue of their troubles. Again there are others who have committed many sins. There are still others who have procreated twenty-five children! They weep because ten of them are dead! Are they human beings? They are veritable beasts. No control of the body or of the mind!"

August 22, 1918. It was evening. Holy Mother was lying on the floor near her couch. A brahmachāri entered the room and said to the Mother that a woman devotee wanted to see her. She was very tired and said with annoyance: "Dear me! Am I to see another person? I shall die." She sat up. A little later, a well-dressed lady came in and bowed down to her. Holy Mother asked her about her welfare and was told that her husband was suffering from diabetes. The lady said to the Mother: "The doctors say that the illness is serious. But I do not care for their opinion. You must cure him, Mother. Please say he will be cured."

Mother: "I do not know anything, my child. The Master is everything. If he wills, your husband will be all right. I shall pray to the Master for him."

Devotee: "Now I am very happy, Mother. Sri Ramakrishna can never disregard your request."

The lady began to weep, putting her head on the feet of the Holy Mother. The Mother consoled her and said: "Pray to the Master. He will cure your husband."

She soon took her leave. After her departure the Mother said: "Her husband is so dangerously ill and she has come here to pray to God for his recovery. Instead of being prayerful and penitent, she has covered herself with perfumes. Is it becoming to come to a shrine in this manner? Ah, such is the nature of your modern people!"

August 23, 1918. Sarajubala went to see Holy Mother in the evening. Referring to a woman devotee, the Mother said: "She imposes very strict discipline upon her daughter-in-law, but she should not go to excess. Though she has to keep an eye upon her, she should also give her a little freedom. The daughter-in-law is young. Naturally she wants to enjoy nice things. If the mother-in-law becomes over strict, she may go away from home or even commit suicide. What will she do then? The girl painted her feet a little. Is it a crime to do that? Alas, she cannot even see her husband, who has become a monk. I saw my husband with my own eyes, attended him, cooked for him, and went near him whenever he permitted."

September 3, 1918. In the course of conversation Holy Mother began to speak about Sri Ramakrishna. She said: "How fine his teachings are! How little we knew at that time that things would take this turn! What a great soul was born! How many people are being illumined by his words! He was the embodiment of bliss. All twenty-four hours of the day were devoted to religious music, merriment, laughter, teaching, and story-telling. So far as I remember, I never saw him worried about anything. Often he would give me nice words of advice. If I had known how to write, I would have noted them down." Holy Mother continued in a low voice: "Do you notice this human body? Today it is and tomorrow it is not. And the world is full of misery and pain. Why should one be eager to have another birth? The body is never free from its attendant troubles. . . . A monk is like a bleached cloth. One does not notice spots on a black cloth so much, but even a drop of ink looks so vivid on a white cloth. The whole world is engrossed in lust and gold. The monk should always practise renunciation and dispassion. Therefore the Master used to say: 'A monk must always be alert and careful.' I have heard that the Englishman begets children according to his income. After the birth of the children he wants, the husband and wife live separately, each one busy with his or her work. And look at our race!

"Yesterday a young woman came to see me. She had a lot of children, some hanging from her back, some clinging to her arms. She could hardly manage them. Can you imagine what she said to me? She said: 'Mother, I do not enjoy worldly life at all.' I said: 'How is that, my child? You have got so many young ones!' She replied: 'That is the end of it. I will not have any more!' I said: 'It would be nice if you could carry out your intention!' " The Mother began to laugh.

September 30, 1918. It was the time of the midday worship, when a party of three men and some women, from a distant part of Bengal, came to pay their respects to Holy Mother. They were very poor, all their possessions consisting of one piece of cloth each. They had had to beg their travel money to Calcutta. One of the party—a male devotee—was having a private talk with Holy Mother. There seemed to be no end to the conversation. It was getting late for the worship and the Mother was to perform it. The inmates of the Udbodhan became annoyed. One of them asked the devotee, rather sharply, to leave the Mother alone and continue his talk downstairs with a senior Swami. But the Mother said firmly: "It does not matter if it gets late. I must hear what he has to say." She continued to listen to him very patiently. In a whisper she gave him some instruction. Then she sent for his wife as well. It became known that they must have experienced something in a dream. After about an hour they took leave of the Mother. She said: "Alas, they are very poor. They had to put up with a great hardship to come here."

It was four o'clock in the afternoon. A European lady had come to pay her respects to Holy Mother and had been waiting for a long time downstairs. The Mother sent for her. As the latter bowed down before her, Holy Mother clasped her hand as one does in shaking hands. Then she kissed the lady by touching her chin. The lady knew Bengali and said: "I hope I have not inconvenienced you by this visit. I am in great difficulty. My only daughter, a very good girl, is seriously ill. I have come here to crave your favour and blessings. Please be gracious to her so that she may be cured. She is a nice girl. I am praising her because one seldom finds a good woman among us now-a-days. I am sure many are wicked and evil-minded. But my daughter is of quite a different nature. Please be kind to her." Holy Mother said: "I will pray for your daughter. She will be cured." The lady was much encouraged by this assurance from Holy Mother and said: "When you say she will be cured, she will certainly be cured. There is no doubt about it." She spoke these words three times with great faith and emphasis. Holy Mother with a kindly look said to Golap-Mā: "Please give her a flower from the altar. Bring a lotus." Golap-Mā brought the lotus. The Mother took the flower in her hand and closed her eyes for a few moments. Then she looked wistfully at the picture of Sri Ramakrishna and gave the flower to the lady, saying: "Please touch it to your daughter's head." The lady accepted the flower with folded hands and bowed down before the Mother. "What shall I do with the flower afterwards?" she asked. Golap-Mā said: "When it dries up, throw it into the Ganges." "No, no," the lady protested, "this flower belongs to God. I cannot throw it away. I shall make a bag from a new piece of cloth and preserve the flower in it. I shall touch it daily to my daughter's head and body." Holy Mother approved. Now the lady was about to leave and said: "I have taken much of your valuable time. Please forgive me." "No," said the Mother, "I am very pleased to talk to you. Come here again on a Tuesday." The lady bowed down and departed. She kept her promise and visited the Mother, who not only received her kindly but gave her initiation. The daughter was cured of her illness.

We give below a brief account from the diary of one of her monastic disciples, Swami Arupananda, who first met Holy Mother in 1909 and served as one of her personal attendants for a number of years until her death in 1920.

When Arupananda first arrived at Holy Mother's home at

Jayrambati, he was told by her brother that the Mother wanted to see him. He went into the inner apartment and found her standing at the door of her room awaiting him. He saluted her and she asked him where he came from. She also inquired if he was reading the teachings of Sri Ramakrishna. She talked to him as if she had known him for a long time. He remembered her first tender and affectionate look for the rest of his life. Next she gave him some refreshments which had been offered in the shrine.

She sent for him again when the midday worship was over. Afterwards he sat for his meal, which was served by Holy Mother herself. As he was eating, the Mother said: "Eat well. Don't feel shy. Remember what I say." After the meal she gave him a betel leaf.

In the afternoon Arupananda went to Holy Mother again and found her kneading the flour for bread. She was seated on the floor near the stove, facing the east, her legs stretched out in front of her. Casting a benign glance upon him she said: "What do you want?"

Disciple: "I want to talk to you."

Mother: "What do you want to talk about? Sit down."

Disciple: "Mother, people say that our Master is God Eternal and Absolute. What do you say about it?"

Mother: "Yes, he is God Eternal and Absolute to me." As she said "to me," the disciple remarked: "It is true that to every woman her husband is God Eternal and Absolute. I have not asked the question in that sense."

Mother: "Yes, he is God Eternal and Absolute to me as my husband, and in a general way as well."

The disciple thought that if Sri Ramakrishna was God Absolute, then she, Holy Mother, must be the Divine Power, the Mother of the Universe. She must be non-different from her divine consort. They must be like Sitā and Rāma, Rādhā and Krishna. The disciple had come to her cherishing this sort of belief. So he asked her: "If that is so, then why do I see you preparing bread like an ordinary woman? It is māyā, I suppose. Isn't that so?"

Mother: "It is māyā indeed. Why, otherwise, should I be in this state? But God loves to sport as a human being. Sri Krishna was born as a cowherd boy, and Rāma as the son of Daśaratha."

Disciple: "Do you remember your real nature?"

Mother: "Yes, now and then I do. At those times I say to myself: 'What is it that I am doing?' Then I look at the house [pointing to it with her hand], buildings, and children, and forget my real self."

The disciple visited the Mother almost daily in her room. She would talk to him, lying on her bed, Radhu asleep by her side. Sometimes a maidservant rubbed her feet with medicinal oil. The Mother suffered from rheumatism.

One day Holy Mother said to Arupananda in the course of conversation: "Whenever I think of a disciple and long to see him, then he either comes to me or writes to me. You must have come here prompted by certain feelings. Perhaps you have been thinking of the Divine Mother of the Universe."

Disciple: "Are you the Mother of all?"

Mother: "Yes, I am."

Disciple: "Even of those subhuman beings, birds and animals?"

Mother: "Yes, of those also."

Disciple: "Then why should they suffer so much?"

Mother: "In this birth they must have these experiences."

One evening the Mother and the disciple had the following conversation:

Mother: "You have all come to see me because you are my own."

Disciple: "Am I your own?"

Mother: "Yes, my very own. Is there any doubt about it? If one person is another's very own they remain inseparable through successive cycles of time."

Disciple: "All address you as *āpani*,[10] but I cannot do so. I cannot utter that word while addressing you. May I address you as *tumi*?"

Mother: "That will be good. It denotes an intimate relationship."

In the course of the conversation the disciple said to Holy Mother: "You must have assumed responsibility for those whom you have initiated. Then why do you say, when we request you to fulfil a desire: 'I will speak to the Master about it'? Can't you take on responsibility for us yourself?"

Mother: "Indeed, I have taken on responsibility for you."

Disciple: "Please bless me, Mother, that I may have purity of mind and attachment to God. I would be grateful if I could give the Master a fourth of the love I once felt for one of my schoolmates."

Mother: "Ah me! That is true indeed! Well, I will speak to the Master about it."[11]

Disciple: "Why do you always say that you will speak to the Master? Are you different from him? My desires will certainly be fulfilled by your blessings alone."

Mother: "My child, if you can obtain perfect knowledge

---

[10] In Bengali there are three personal pronouns by which one can refer to another. The word *āpani* is used in addressing a superior person entitled to respect. It is a rather formal term. *Tumi* is used to address an equal. It is a term of intimacy and endearment. *Tui* is used to address inferiors: children or servants.

[11] Parallel instances can be given from the lives of Sri Ramakrishna and Jesus Christ. When a devotee asked a favour of Sri Ramakrishna he often said that he would speak to Mother Kālī about it. When Jesus healed the sick or the crippled, he asked them to offer worship in the temple as a mark of gratitude. But this does not detract from their divinity. They themselves often assured the disciples of their salvation. Sri Ramakrishna said that he would reveal himself to his disciples at the hour of death, if not earlier. Christ also said that he was the Resurrection and the Life. While making those statements they felt their oneness with the Godhead.

through my blessings, then I bless you with all my heart and soul. Is it possible for a man to free himself from the clutches of māyā without the Master's grace? He performed spiritual austerities to the utmost and gave their results to mankind for its liberation."

Disciple: "When shall I have a vision of the Master?"

Mother: "You will certainly see him. You will see the Master at the right time."

About herself, she said: "Balaram Babu used to refer to me as 'the great ascetic, the embodiment of forgiveness.' Can you call one who is devoid of compassion a man? He is a veritable beast. Sometimes I forget myself because of compassion." At that time the disciple lived at his own home with his relatives, though he had been cherishing an intense desire to embrace the monastic life. Often he said to himself: "Perhaps in the future it will be possible for me, through Mother's grace, to be a monk and live near her." Holy Mother said to him: "I feel very free with you. See me in Calcutta and stay with me." A short while after, through her blessings and through arrangements made by Swami Saradananda, the disciple joined the Belur Math. On being informed of this, the Mother said to him: "That is very good. You have come under the spell of monastic life. Live at the Belur Math. May you obtain love for the Master. You have my blessings."

By way of testing the disciple, the Mother one day said to him: "Why don't you return home? Live in the world, earn money, and bring up a family." "But, Mother, please do not say that," the disciple said. He wept as he spoke. Holy Mother replied with great tenderness: "My child, please do not weep. You are a living God. Who is able to renounce all for His sake? Even the injunctions of destiny are cancelled if one takes refuge in God. Destiny strikes off with its own hand what it has foreordained for such a person. What does a man become by realizing God? Does he grow two horns? No, what happens is that he develops discrimination between the real and unreal, obtains spiritual consciousness, and goes beyond life and death.

God is realized in spirit. How else can one see God? Has God talked to anyone who is devoid of spiritual fervour? One envisions God in spirit, talks to Him, and establishes a relationship with Him in spirit."

Disciple: "No, Mother. There is something else besides. One obtains a tangible vision of God."

Mother: "Only Narendra had that. What else is spiritual life besides praying to the Master, repeating his name, and contemplating him? [With a smile] And the Master? What is there after all about him? He is our own eternally."

Disciple: "Mother, please see that I obtain right knowledge. May I realize that Sri Ramakrishna is my own."

Mother: "Must I repeat it? You will certainly realize him as your own. Certainly you will."

At first the disciple had felt a sort of hesitation in addressing Holy Mother as "Mother"; his own mother had died during his childhood. One morning Holy Mother sent him to a certain person on an errand. As he was about to leave, she asked him: "What will you say to him?" The disciple said: "Why, I shall say to him: 'She asked me to tell you such and such.'" "No, my child," corrected Holy Mother. "Tell him: 'The Mother asked me to tell you such and such.'" She emphasized the word *Mother*.

One evening while Holy Mother was seated on her porch preparing betel leaves, the disciple said to her: "In the future, how many people will practise spiritual disciplines just to propitiate you!"

Mother (with a smile): "What do you mean? Everyone will say: 'Mother had the gout; she used to limp like this.'"

Disciple: "You may say that."

Mother: "That's all right. The Master used to say, when he was lying ill at the Cossipore garden: 'Those who came to me expecting some earthly gain have disappeared. They said: "Ah, if he is an Incarnation of God how can he be ill? This is all delusion." But those who are my own suffer a great deal when they see the pain.'"

What Holy Mother Taught (I)

As we have seen, Holy Mother in her spiritual ministry acted as mother, teacher, and Divinity. Her motherly solicitude for the physical welfare of her disciples was expressed in her prayers to God when she visited the holy places during her pilgrimage. She once remarked that, as was natural to a mother, she always asked the Lord to see that they never suffered from any physical privation, being inwardly assured that Sri Ramakrishna himself would look after their liberation. To the disciples she often said: "Whenever you are in danger or trouble, remember that you have a mother," or, "Do not be afraid; the Master is behind you, and I am, too, as your mother." As Divinity she bestowed her grace, without which liberation is impossible. Holy Mother once said that whatever was needed for the disciples' liberation she had given them at the time of initiation, when she transmitted the spiritual power to them. She also said again and again that they would have spiritual illumination at the hour of death or after a few more births.

As teacher, Holy Mother stressed the need of sādhanā, or spiritual discipline, without which there could be no spiritual attainment. Disciples came to her with doubts and problems, and she had to solve them in order to discharge her responsibility as their guru. In this chapter we shall consider what she taught.

All prophets and saints have emphasized the practice of spiritual disciplines. Religion is not a mere acceptance of dogmas or beliefs, nor does it consist in mere study of the scriptures or observance of moral laws or performance of rituals. The main purpose of religion is to help a man bring out his potential divinity and apply the knowledge of this divinity to his every-day life. Rituals, dogmas, moral disciplines, prayer, meditation, and scriptural study are only helps. From time out of mind spiritual seekers have practised disciplines to curb their senses, control the mind, and realize the ultimate unsubstantiality of the phenomenal world. Man considers the world to be real and is trapped in it because he directly perceives it with his senses. But his knowledge of God, through study, is indirect and mediate. Only through practice of spiritual discipline does he obtain, by the grace of God, direct and immediate knowledge of Him, and so is no more deceived by appearances. Hence for the average man there is no way to a higher life except through earnest, sincere, and wholehearted practice of spiritual discipline.

But meditation and prayer contain a certain element of ego. The ubiquitous ego is present even in the practice of spiritual austerities. When an aspirant has passed through the entire gamut of austerities, he realizes that God is still far away. Then he totally surrenders himself to God, seeking His mercy. Genuine self-surrender is not possible without prior self-effort. Only through self-effort does one come to know that God cannot be realized through self-effort. Then God reveals Himself to a man in His own good time. Neither meditation nor spiritual effort can compel this revelation. God's grace is showered when a seeker is completely free from desire or ego. Yet when the revelation comes, the seeker will not recognize God unless he has made himself ready through prior self-effort.

Spiritual unfoldment may be compared to the transformation of a larva into a butterfly or a seed into a plant. The larva goes on eating leaves, and, with the help of air and sunlight, changes into a chrysalis and then silently into a beautiful butterfly. So, too, a seed draws nourishment from earth, water, and air, till finally a sprout emerges and from it a large tree. Likewise the spirituality transmitted even by a competent guru becomes fully unfolded only with such extraneous help as meditation, japa, prayer, and other practices. That grace and self-effort are complementary in spiritual realization will become clear from Holy Mother's teachings, some of which are given in this chapter.[1]

Time and again Holy Mother said: "The aim of life is to realize God and remain immersed in contemplation of Him. God alone is real and everything else is false. God is one's very own, and this is the eternal relationship between God and creatures. One realizes God in proportion to the intensity of one's feeling for Him. He who is really eager to cross the ocean of the world will somehow break his bonds. No one can entangle him."

To her God was both Pure Spirit, or Brahman, and also the Universal Energy, or Śakti, and Sri Ramakrishna was the Divine Incarnation of modern times. "The Master is the embodiment of all deities and of all mantras," she said. "Really and truly, one can worship through him all gods and goddesses." And she continued: "Sri Ramakrishna assumed this human body to remove the sorrows and sufferings of others. He moved about in disguise, as a king walks through his capital. The moment he became known he disappeared." On another occasion Holy Mother said: "He who has prayed to the Master even once has nothing to fear. By praying to him constantly one obtains ecstatic love, through his grace. This love is the essence of spiritual life. The Master used to say to his devotees: 'I have made the mould; now you may cast the image.' To 'cast the image' means to meditate on the Master, to think of the various incidents of his life. Contemplate the great suffering the Master had to undergo because of taking upon himself the

---

[1] These teachings have been culled from the "Conversations of Holy Mother," in Book II of *Sri Sarada Devi*, Madras, India: Sri Ramakrishna Math, 1958. They were given to different disciples on different occasions.

results of the bad karma done by others, and then you will find
that your body and mind have been purified. Your grief and
misery will disappear if you only remember how the Master,
though Divinity Itself, suffered for the sake of others and yet
did not miss even for one moment the ecstatic joy he experienced from the contemplation of the Divine Mother." Thus
she advised her disciples to meditate on Sri Ramakrishna and
repeat his name; through his grace every desire of the seeker
would be fulfilled. Those who pray to him, the Mother taught,
"will never suffer from want of food or other physical priva-
tions, and will also easily gain love and knowledge of Brahman."

But she was not dogmatic. Once Swami Arupananda said to
her: "Those who are obtaining your blessings are fortunate indeed. What will happen to people in the future?" "What do
you mean?" the Mother asked with great surprise. "Why will
not they too succeed? God exists everywhere and at all times.
Are people not realizing God in other countries?" On another
occasion she said: "Holy men are born on earth to show people
the way to God. They teach differently. There are many paths
leading to the same goal. Therefore the teachings of all the
saints are true." Realization of God, according to Holy Mother,
does not mean anything peculiar or abnormal. It enables a man
to discriminate between the real and the unreal, deepens a
man's knowledge and consciousness, and enables him to pass
beyond life and death. Sounding a higher note, she said: "In
the course of time God and other such things disappear. After
the attainment of knowledge one realizes that the Master and
other forms of God are māyā. They come and they go. Once
Naren said to me: 'Mother, nowadays I see everything vanish-
ing away.' I said to him: 'But do not make me vanish.' He
replied: 'Where shall I stand if you vanish? If knowledge
effaces the lotus feet of the guru, then what will be its support?' " Then the Mother added: "God and His forms disappear

after the awakening of knowledge. There remains only the Mother.[2] One finally sees that Mother alone exists, pervading the whole universe. All differentiation is effaced. This is the simple truth."

A disciple once asked: "How does one attain the knowledge of Brahman? Should one practise it step by step or does it come all at once?" The Mother replied: "The path leading to Brahman is very difficult. It is quite natural for a man to forget God. Therefore whenever the need arises, God becomes incarnated on earth and shows the path by practising spiritual discipline Himself. This time, too, God has shown the example of renunciation."

Holy Mother emphasized renunciation as the unique feature of Sri Ramakrishna's life. One day a disciple asked her about the special message of Sri Ramakrishna. Was it not the harmony of religions that he experienced and taught? The Mother replied: "My child, what you say about the harmony of religions is true. But it never occurred to me that he had practised the disciplines of different faiths with the definite idea of preaching this harmony. Day and night the Master remained overwhelmed with divine rapture. He enjoyed God's sport by following the paths of the Vaishnavas, Christians, Mussalmāns, and the rest. But it seems to me, my child, that the chief characteristic of the Master's sādhanā was his renunciation. Has anyone ever seen such natural renunciation? Renunciation is his great ornament."

Holy Mother's life, too, was an example of true renunciation, though outwardly she lived as a householder. She was neither entangled in anything of the world nor attached to anything. Thus she inspired advanced aspirants, especially young seekers, with the ideal of renunciation. She would say to them: "Many think of God only after receiving blows from the world. But blessed indeed is he who can offer his mind, like a fresh flower,

---

[2] She meant the Universal Energy which projects all names and forms, including the divine. This energy, or māyā, is the power of Brahman. The guru is a symbol of it.

at the feet of the Lord from his very childhood. One should practise renunciation in youth. In old age the body deteriorates and loses strength. The mind does not possess vigour. Is it possible to do anything then?"

She emphasized the transitoriness of the human body, to which all are attached, and taught: "Today the human body is, tomorrow it is not; even the shortest span of life is beset with pain and misery. He who is able to renounce all for God's sake is a living God." A devotee pointed out sorrowfully: "Mother, the Master loved renunciation, but how little we practise it!"

Mother: "That is true. But you will acquire it slowly. You can make some progress in this life, a little more in the next, and so on. It is the body that changes. Ātman always remains the same. Lust and gold must be renounced. The Master used to say: 'I can cover the whole village of Kamarpukur with gold; but what good will that do? Those alone who belong to a high plane of existence can take to monastic life, and free themselves from all bondage. Again, there are those who are born to enjoy a little taste of worldly pleasure. I say that such persons should see it through. Otherwise, there is no knowing when they may fall victims to unfulfilled desires.'

"Everything is illusory—husband, wife, even this body. These are the great shackles of māyā. Unless you can free yourself from these shackles you will never be able to cross to the other shore of the world. Attachment to the body, this identification of the self with the body, must go. What is this body, after all, my child? It is nothing but three pounds of ashes when it is cremated. However strong or beautiful this body may be, it ends up in those three pounds of ashes. Yet people are attached to it. What māyā!"

A disciple wanted to know if all men can get rid of desires. The Mother replied: "How can they? If they could, then the creation would come to an end. The world is going on because not all can be free of desires. People with desires are born again and again."

Another disciple, a monk, complained that many insignificant desires cropped up in his mind. How could he get rid of them?

Mother: "In your case these are not real desires. They are only fancies that appear and disappear. The more they do so, the better for you."

The disciple complained that in spite of his practising spiritual disciplines, the impurities of his mind were not growing less. The Mother explained this by referring to the tendencies created by past karma. "Suppose you have rolled a thread of different colours—red, black, and white—on a reel. While you unwind it you will see it come out in exactly the same order. You will find only one or two persons who are free from all desires. Though a man obtains a new body determined by his desires, yet if he has performed righteous action in his previous birth, he does not completely lose spiritual consciousness.

"A person may have no relatives anywhere, but Mahāmāyā may make him keep a cat and thus make him worldly. This is how She plays!

"One should desire of God desirelessness. Desire is the obstacle to liberation."

Disciple: "Do those who give up their bodies in a state of unconsciousness attain to a higher spiritual state afterwards?"

Mother: "The thought that is uppermost in the mind before one loses consciousness determines the course of one's soul after death."

Holy Mother constantly emphasized the need for regular practice. Real progress is made by steady effort and not by sudden spurts. She once remarked: "As you smell the fragrance of a flower while handling it or the smell of sandalwood while rubbing it against a stone, so you obtain spiritual awakening by constantly thinking of God. If you become desireless you can realize Him right now." But this desirelessness is not possible without the practice of disciplines and without God's grace.

A devotee asked if one who had been blessed by Holy Mother as his guru needed to practise any spiritual discipline.

Mother: "You may be right. But the real point is this: there may be different kinds of food-stuffs in the storeroom, but one must cook them. Whoever cooks earlier gets his meal earlier. Some can eat in the morning, some in the evening, and some may have to fast because they have been too lazy to cook. The more intensely a person practises spiritual discipline, the more quickly he attains God. Even if a devotee does not practise spiritual discipline, he will attain God in the end—surely he will. If he spends his time idly, without practising prayer and meditation, he will take a long time to realize God."

As concrete spiritual disciplines Holy Mother prescribed daily prayer and devotions. After listening to letters from some of her disciples, she once said: "Did you notice what these children have said? One writes: 'We have been practising so much of japa, meditation, and prayer but we are not achieving anything.' Again, others write about their sufferings and sorrows, poverty and worries. I cannot listen to their complaints any more. I always pray to God: 'O Lord, please protect them here and hereafter.' What else can I pray for, as their mother? But how many are there who truly want to realize God? No doubt they talk of great devotion and longing, but they feel satisfied when they get a tiny bit of worldly enjoyment. Then they say: 'Oh, how kind God is!' "

On another occasion the Mother said: "How infinite God's creation is! If you do not pray to God, what does it matter to Him? There are many, many people who do not even think of God. If they do not call on Him, it is their misfortune. Such is God's māyā that He has made people forget Him. He says to Himself: 'They think they are quite all right as they are; then let them feel that way.' "

Disciple: "If God is our very own, why doesn't He reveal Himself to His devotees by His mere will?"

Mother: "That's a good question. But who has the faith that God is his own? People practise this or that discipline because they think it their duty to do so. But how many truly seek God?"

Holy Mother gave a high place to japa and meditation in the

practice of daily devotions. Japa purifies the mind, creates inner calmness, and leads to meditation. Meditation is a difficult discipline, especially for beginners. The Mother used to say that it is more arduous to concentrate the mind on the Chosen Ideal than to dig the earth with a spade. Without acquiring mental purity one cannot properly meditate. Japa should be combined with meditation. There is a saying that as the plant is hidden in the tiny seed, so also is the Lord hidden in His name. "When a pure soul performs japa," the Mother said, "he feels as if the holy name bubbles up spontaneously from within himself. He does not have to make an effort to repeat the name."

A few of her statements regarding the efficacy of japa and meditation are given below:

"As wind removes a cloud, so does the name of God disperse the cloud of worldliness."

"The mind will be steadied of itself if aspirants repeat God's name fifteen or twenty thousand times a day. I myself have experienced it. Let them first practise; if they fail, then let them complain. One should practise japa with devotion, but this they do not do. They will not do anything; they only complain, saying: 'Why don't I succeed?' "

"No doubt you must do your duties. This keeps your mind in good condition. But it is also necessary to practise japa, meditation, and prayer. One must practise these at least in the morning and evening. Such practice acts like the rudder of a boat. When a man sits in the evening for prayer, he can reflect on the good and bad things he has done in the course of the day. Then he should compare his present mental state with that of the previous day. Next, while performing japa, he should meditate on his Chosen Ideal. In meditation he should first think of the face of his Ideal, and then meditate on the entire body from the feet upward. Unless you practise meditation morning and evening, along with your work, how can you know whether you are doing the right thing or the wrong?

"The natural tendency of the mind is to run this way or that.

Through japa it is directed to God. While repeating God's name, if one sees His form and becomes absorbed in it, then the japa stops."

Devotee: "Why is it that the mind does not become steady? When I try to think of God I find it drawn to worldly objects."

Mother: "It is wrong if the mind is drawn to worldly objects. By 'worldly objects' I mean money, family, and so on. But it is natural for the mind to think of the work in which one is engaged. If meditation is not possible, repeat God's name. If a meditative mood comes, well and good; but by no means force your mind to meditate. Real meditation is spontaneous."

Regularity should be observed, Holy Mother taught, in the practice of japa and meditation. It is true that there are certain auspicious moments when the mind becomes easily collected. But no one can say when the auspicious moment will come. It comes so suddenly that one has no hint of it beforehand. Therefore one should be regular about spiritual practice, no matter how busy one may be with one's duties. The conjunction of day and night, in Holy Mother's view, is the most auspicious time for calling on God. Night disappears and day arrives, or day disappears and night arrives—this is the conjunction of day and night. At those times the mind is pure.

Sometimes the Mother discouraged excessive meditation, for the mind can become deranged if one goes to extremes. "If the mind is deranged," she warned, "one's life becomes useless. A man's intelligence is a very sensitive thing. It is like the thread of a screw. If the thread is crooked, then the screw jams. If a man's meditation is not directed properly, he goes crazy or becomes trapped in the net of delusion. He feels he is quite all right. If meditation is correctly practised, then one enjoys peace and happiness. How many are there who can practise meditation and japa all the time? Very soon their brains get heated on account of their constantly sitting on their prayer rugs. They become vain. They also suffer from mental worries by brooding on different things. It is much better to work than to allow the mind to roam aimlessly. When the mind is given free scope to wander, it creates much confusion. Repeating the name of God once, when the mind is controlled, is equivalent to a million repetitions when the mind is away from God. You may repeat. the name for the whole day, but if the mind is elsewhere it does not produce much of a result. The repetition must be accompanied by concentration. Only then does one obtain God's grace."

God's name should be repeated with the utmost love, sincerity, and self-surrender. "Before commencing your daily meditation, first think of your utter helplessness and then slowly begin to meditate as directed by your guru."

A disciple asked if the effect of karma performed in previous births could be cancelled by the repetition of God's name. "One must experience the effect of past action," the Mother replied. "None can escape it. But japa minimizes its intensity. For example, a man who, as a result of his past karma, is destined to lose his leg, may instead suffer from the prick of a thorn in his foot."

She asked the disciples to be careful about the practice of breath-control and postures. "The mind," she said, "is restless by nature. Therefore at the outset one may begin meditation by regulating the breath a little. This helps to make the mind steady. But one must not overdo it; otherwise the brain gets heated. Be careful about yogic postures. If you continue these exercises a long time, the mind may be diverted to the body. Again if, once having started them, you give them up, your health may be affected. Therefore you should use discretion."

Love of God is essential for spiritual progress. "If you love a human being, you will have to suffer for it. He is blessed, indeed, who can love God alone. There is no suffering in loving God. Be devoted to God and take shelter at His feet. It is enough to remember that there is someone—call Him Father or Mother—who is always protecting you."

Like a magnet, God is constantly attracting His creatures to

Him. We do not feel the force of His attraction because our minds are filled with impurities. This perennial attraction nevertheless exists. It is experienced in the depth of contemplation when the mind's impurities are removed. For purifying of the mind Holy Mother stressed the value of truthfulness, love of solitude, magnanimity, self-surrender, and the other disciplines found in the teachings of all the great religions. She said: "God is purity itself and cannot be realized without the practice of control of the body and mind." In answer to a question of a disciple, she stated: "Can anyone destroy lust altogether? A little of it remains as long as one has a body; but it can be subdued, as a snake can be subdued by means of dust.[3] If you are constantly in contact with objects of enjoyment, you are likely to succumb to their influence." "Don't be afraid," she assured another disciple. "In this Kaliyuga mental sin is no sin. Free your mind from all worries on that score. You need not be afraid."

Food plays an important part in creating inner purity. One must not, Holy Mother advised, eat food which has not been offered to God. "As your food is," she said, "so will your blood be. From pure blood you will get bodily strength and a pure mind. A pure mind begets ecstatic love for God."

Solitude, Holy Mother taught, deepens one's spiritual mood. "If you practise spiritual discipline for some time in a solitary place, you will find that your mind has become strong, and then you can live in any place or society without being in the least affected by it. When the plant is tender it should be hedged around. But when it has grown big not even cows and goats can injure it. Spiritual practices in a solitary place are essential."

Holy Mother emphasized the practice of truthfulness. "The Master used to say that truthfulness alone is the austerity of the present age. One attains to God by holding to the truth."

_____

[3] Referring to the charmed dust used by the snake-charmers of India.

An embodiment of magnanimity, Holy Mother could not find fault with anybody or hurt others by thought, word, or deed. At one time she fervently prayed to God that she might not notice others' shortcomings. By constantly seeing blemishes in others, she taught, one's eyes become contaminated and one finds nothing but faults. There was a slum in front of the Udbodhan, and the people who lived there did not always follow the conventional moral code. Once the mistress of one of the men there became seriously ill and he nursed her day and night. Referring to him, Holy Mother said: "How wonderfully he waited on her! Such devotion I have not seen before. This is real service, true attraction." A woman who had once lived an immoral life used to visit the Mother. Some of the respectable ladies did not approve of her coming and one of them expressed her annoyance to Holy Mother. She said that if the fallen woman frequented the Udbodhan, it would be impossible for others to go there. The Mother replied firmly: "Those who have taken shelter with me are always welcome. If that stops the visits of some others, I can't help it." One day, praising the respect and devotion of some of the actresses of a theatre, who were slighted by others, the Mother said: "These girls have real devotion. Their love of God, no matter how little it may be, is wholehearted and sincere." A monk living at the Udbodhan objected to visits by a certain class of immoral women. The Mother replied: "If they are prevented from coming here, I will leave the place." On another occasion she remarked: "The mind is everything. It is in the mind alone that one feels pure or impure. A man first makes his own mind guilty and then sees another's fault. Can you injure anybody by enumerating his faults? You only injure yourself. I cannot see anybody's shortcomings. If a man does a trifle for me, I try to remember even that. To see faults in others! Forgiveness is a great religious austerity. There is no virtue higher than forbearance."

One day an inmate of the Udbodhan was severely taken to

task for his wrong conduct. Holy Mother was asked to reprimand the guilty man. "I cannot do it," she firmly remonstrated.
"I cannot see others' faults. I am simply not made that way.
There are enough people eager to criticize others. Surely the
world will not come to an end if I refrain from doing so." Holy
Mother was gentleness itself and asked the devotees not to hurt
others even by a harsh word. "One must not speak unpleasant
truths unnecessarily. By indulging in rude words one's nature
becomes rude. One loses sensitivity without control over one's
words."

Humility, a natural trait of Holy Mother, must not be confused with mere politeness or courtesy. True humility is based
on spiritual perception. Holy Mother said: "In the fullness of
spiritual realization, a person finds that the God who resides in
his heart resides in the hearts of all—the oppressed, the perse-
cuted, the lowly, and the untouchable. This realization makes
one truly humble."

Holy Mother always extolled modesty as a great virtue in a
woman. One day a well-dressed woman devotee came to visit
her. After her departure the Mother said to the other ladies:
"I want to tell you something. A woman's only ornament is her
modesty. A flower is indeed blessed when it is offered at the
feet of the deity; otherwise it were better for it to wither away
on the plant. It pains me very much to see a dandy make a
bouquet of beautiful flowers and gently put it to his nose,
saying: 'Ah, how sweet it smells!' Perhaps the next moment he
drops it on the floor and may step on it, without even looking
at it." It was reported that this particular woman was later
deserted by her husband.

Devotees constantly came to the Mother with their problems
and difficulties, their worries and sorrows. She was not a shallow
optimist who denied the existence of such things. She accepted
the reality of suffering and said: "The creation contains both
misery and happiness. Could anyone appreciate happiness if
misery did not exist? Besides, how is it possible for all persons

to be happy? No one can suffer all the time, either. Every action brings its own result, and one gets one's opportunities accordingly. However spiritual a person may be, he must pay the tax to the last penny for the use of his body. Difficulties always come, but they do not last for ever. You will see that they pass away as water passes under a bridge." But is misery an unmitigated evil? Is not its presence a reminder to men of the ultimate reality of God? The Mother said: "Misery is truly a gift of God. I believe it is a symbol of His compassion." The remedy for misery or worry does not lie in turning away from it, but in cultivating love of God and facing it squarely. Listening day and night to people's worries, one day she remarked: "Many people come to me to tell me their worries. Thereupon the thought flashes in my mind: 'Why do they say all this? Am I, then, a superhuman being? I never know what worry is.'" We have noted how much she had to suffer on account of Radhu and her mother. But all this did not really affect her, since, to use her own words, the vision of God lay in the palm of her hand and she could have it whenever she wanted.

What Holy Mother Taught (II)

As we have already seen, Holy Mother's disciples included both householders and monks. She advised householders who wanted to lead a spiritual life to practise inner renunciation and not run away from the world. The rich householder should serve God and His devotees with money, and the poor, by repeating His name. But she admonished householders to lead a life of self-control. To one of her nieces who criticized her for giving monastic initiation to a certain young man, the Mother said: "You have seen for yourself what kind of happiness life in the world can give. What have you learnt from me all these days? Why so much attraction to the worldly life? Why so much animal propensity? What sort of happiness do you derive from it? You cannot conceive the ideal of a pure life even in a dream, can you? Can't you and your husband live now as brother and sister? Why this desire to lead a piggish life? The misery of the world has been gnawing into my bones. An unmarried person who leads a pure life will advance towards God with rapid strides, whether he prays to Him or not. The others, being tied hand and foot, find it difficult to extricate themselves from the bondage of worldliness, even though they try to think of God."

But even about such matters the Mother could be witty on occasion. A young wife visited Jayrambati accompanied by her husband, and said to Holy Mother: "Mother, please bless me that we may have no children. Please destroy our physical cravings for ever." The Mother showed surprise and said: "What do you mean, my daughter? How will our devotees multiply if you have no children?"

But she was strict about both the outer and the inner renunciation of a monk. To a monastic disciple she once said firmly: "People cannot give up attachment even to a brass pot; is it an easy thing to renounce the world? A monk must always be alert. The path of the monk is slippery. While one is on a slippery road, one should walk tiptoe. If you had so desired, you could have married and lived as a householder. Now that you have given up such an intention, the mind should not be allowed to think of worldly things. What has been spat out is not eaten again. The ochre robe protects a monk as the collar protects a dog. No one molests a dog with a collar, as it belongs to somebody else. The monk with his ochre robe belongs to God. All gates are open to a monk. He has admission everywhere. A monk should be above attachment and jealousy. He must remain unruffled under all circumstances."

To another monastic disciple, pointing out the entanglement of a worldly person, she said: "What is there in the worldly life? How attached people are to it! See how many are born out of one person, and how his attention and energy are dissipated! Is it possible for a person to attain spiritual greatness under such conditions? Have you not seen crabs? The mother crab peeps out from her hole every so often, and then goes back. She struggles hard to be free, but fails. Why is this so? Because of her attraction to her numerous young ones living in the hole. This attraction draws her back in spite of her efforts. So it is with those who are immersed in worldly life."

The Mother gave a third monastic disciple a stern warning about money: "Such is the fascination of money that if you are too much involved in it, you will not be able to resist its attraction. You may think that any moment you may leave your money behind. No, my child, never harbour any such foolish thought. Through a tiny loophole the attachment to money will enter into your mind and then strangle you gradually, without your knowing about it. Always remember Sri Ramakrishna's saying that money is at the root of all the disasters you see in the world. Money can lure one's mind into other temptations. Beware."

The Mother admired a genuine monk who was endowed with scholarship. She compared him to an elephant's tusk adorned with gold.

Holy Mother urged her devotees, whether monks or householders, to lead an active life. She herself never spent an idle moment. When asked by a disciple why she did all kinds of work herself without accepting anyone's help, she replied: "My child, it is good to be active." And then she added solemnly: "Bless me that I may work as long as I live." On another occasion she remarked: "One must always do some work. Only through work can one remove the bondage of work. Total detachment comes later. One should not be without work even for a moment. Work helps one to fend off idle thoughts. If one is without work such thoughts rush into one's mind." As we shall see later, she admired the various activities of the monks of the Ramakrishna Mission. Once there was a heated discussion among the monks living at the Udbodhan as to the usefulness of public activities. Besides being Holy Mother's Calcutta residence, the Udbodhan was a busy publishing centre. The monks working there had to sell books, keep accounts, correct proofs, and look after the publication of books. Someone said that Sri Ramakrishna had discouraged such activities and emphasized meditation, prayer, and other spiritual practices. When the matter was referred to Holy Mother, she said: "Never listen to such ideas. Sri Ramakrishna's case was quite different. Mathur Babu always provided him with his milk and butter. If you do not work who will supply you with your morning cup of tea?" Many monks of the Ramakrishna Order came from middle-class families and were used to a few simple amenities like tea or cigarettes, which they had to get from the public. But why should people provide monks with these harmless comforts if they did not render them some form of service in return?

Holy Mother emphasized self-surrender as the penultimate stage before God's grace bestows final liberation. It has already been stated that genuine self-effort, by which mental impurities are removed, leads to self-surrender. This is followed by His vision. What is self-surrender? It is the surrender of the individual soul to the Universal Soul or God. Dualists conceive of God as an extra-cosmic reality, a person, to whom one should surrender one's words, deeds, and thoughts. According to the Vedāntists, Ultimate Reality is universal spirit, or universal consciousness, or universal intelligence, which alone exists. Man has separated himself from the Universal Self because of ignorance. And this separation is the cause of desire, selfishness, greed, anger, passion, fear, suspicion, and all the other evil propensities which cause his suffering. They all spring from a narrow view of the self. The aim of spiritual disciplines is to realize the oneness of the individual soul and the Universal Soul, which is its true nature. This realization is finally achieved by means of self-surrender. True self-surrender means the complete effacement of illusory individuality; it makes a man a channel for the expression of the power, wisdom, and majesty of the Godhead. It removes all his weakness caused by the idea of separateness. The great powers displayed by saints are derived from self-surrender, or the absence of the sense of individual agency.

Holy Mother, conscious of the helplessness of average seekers, put before them the ideal of self-surrender in the language of dualism. "Be devoted to God," she urged her disciples, "and take shelter at His feet. Blinded by egotism, people think of themselves as independent agents in regard to their work. They do not depend on God. God protects one who relies on Him." But a man is fooled by his puny brain. Holy Mother said: "How little intelligence a man possesses! He may want one thing, but asks for another. He starts to mould an image of Śiva and often ends by making the likeness of a monkey! It is therefore best to surrender all desires at the feet of God. Let Him do whatever is best for us. But one may desire devotion and non-attachment. These are not harmful desires." The age-long doubt persists: if everything is done by God's will, where is man's freedom or responsibility? A devotee asked the Mother: "Is it not true that God inspires man to every action?" "Yes," she replied, "it is true. But is man conscious of it? He thinks in blind infatuation that he is the doer; he does not rely on God. Whoever surrenders himself to God is saved." On another occasion she said: "Everything, no doubt, happens by God's will, yet man must work because God expresses His will through man's action. Do not relax your spiritual practices."

Grace directly follows self-surrender and brings about the fulfilment of man's spiritual aspiration. A profound mystery surrounds the concept of grace; it cannot be solved by reasoning. "Do you know," Holy Mother said, "what God's grace is like? It is like a piece of candy in a child's hand. Someone begs the child to part with it, but he does not care to give it to him. Yet he easily gives it to another whom he likes. A man performs severe austerities throughout his whole life but he does not succeed, and yet another obtains realization with practically no effort. It all depends on God's grace. He bestows His grace upon anyone He likes. The man who receives God's grace perhaps has done many meritorious deeds in a past life. Therefore God's grace descends upon him."[1]

A man must not try to fit grace into the framework of his own understanding. "There is no rule," the Mother counselled again, "that God's grace will fall on one simply because one is practising austerities. In olden times, it is said, the ascetics practised austerities for thousands of years, with their feet up and heads down and a lighted fire burning under them. Even then, only some of them received God's grace. God is not like fish or vegetables, that you can buy Him for a price."

---

[1] Grace, no doubt, is the essential element in the attainment of liberation. But this does not mean that the seeker should neglect the practice of meditation, prayer, and other disciplines. Holy Mother constantly reminded her disciples not to slacken their efforts. While living with the Master at Dakshineswar, she herself repeated the Lord's name daily a hundred thousand times, in spite of her preoccupation with many household duties.

The following excerpts from conversations between the Mother and a devotee will shed further light on the subject of grace.

Devotee: "How does one cultivate love of God? If one's own son is brought up by someone else, the son does not recognize his own mother."

Mother: "Yes, that is true. God's grace is the one thing needful. One should pray for God's grace."

Devotee: "How can we speak of one person's deserving grace, and another's not deserving it? Grace should apply to all."

Mother: "If a man wants to cross a river he must pray sitting on the river bank. He will be taken across in proper time."

Devotee: "If everything happens in proper time, where does God's grace come in?"

Mother: "Must you not sit with a fishing-rod in your hands if you want to catch fish? A deer does not simply walk into the mouth of a lion which is fast asleep."

On another occasion the Mother remarked: "In the relative world all creatures act and suffer according to their past karma. But if God so wills, He can shorten the period of a man's evolution."

Holy Mother warned that an aspirant must not give his reliance on grace as an excuse for idleness or sloth. Self-effort adds something to the enjoyment of divine communion. "A seeker," she said, "can realize God any moment by God's grace. But there is a difference between such realization and what comes in the fullness of time, as between mangoes that ripen out of season and those that ripen at the proper time. The out-of-season ones are not very sweet." A man can sometimes stumble upon a spiritual experience without working for it. But he enjoys it more if he earns it by his own efforts. A man certainly enjoys more the fortune he has built up with his own hands than what he inherits from his father.

We have already said that the idea of the last birth need not be taken literally. To a disciple who asked complainingly why he did not see the Master, in spite of his having received her grace, Holy Mother replied: "Keep on praying without losing heart. Everything happens in time. For how many cycles did the ascetics and hermits of olden times practise austerities to realize God; and do you believe that you will realize Him in a flash? If not in this life, you will attain Him in the next. If not in the next, you will attain Him after that. Is it easy to realize God?"

After the devotee's departure she said: "He is so deeply engrossed in worldliness and still he says: 'Why do I not see the Master?' Many women used to come to the Master and say to him: 'Why can't we concentrate our minds upon God? Why can't we steady our minds?' and things like that. He would say to them: 'You are like a new-born babe and still smell of the lying-in room. First get rid of that smell. Why are you so worried about realizing God now? Everything will happen in course of time.' "

On another occasion she said to a devotee: "People say to me: 'Please show me God.' The sages practised austerities for ages upon ages and still could not realize God. And now people will not practise any disciplines or undergo any austerities, but they want the vision of God immediately! I cannot help them."

Devotee: "There are devotees who surrender themselves to God but do not practise disciplines. Will they be spiritually awakened?"

Mother: "If they truly surrender themselves to God and place complete trust in Him, that is their spiritual discipline."

If one can regard God as one's own and call on Him without seeing Him, that is God's grace, Holy Mother once remarked.

Holy Mother's teachings do not differ from those of Sri Ramakrishna or of true Hinduism. While imparting them she assumed that the devotees had already read the teachings of the Master. It must not be forgotten, however, that although she made Sri Ramakrishna the centre of her instruction, she did not do so in a narrow or dogmatic sense. Whenever necessary, she advised disciples to accept as their Chosen Ideals other aspects of the Godhead. Where appropriate, it will be in keeping with the spirit of her teaching to substitute the word "God" for Sri Ramakrishna. Followers of Christ or Buddha or other religious traditions may thus deepen their spiritual consciousness by pondering her teachings.

While speaking to her disciples Holy Mother used language that was concise, clear, and free from ambiguity. It went straight to the heart of the problem and carried with it conviction and compelling power. Here are a few examples.

Devotee: "How shall I meditate?"

Mother: "Think of God."

Devotee: "How shall I practise spiritual disciplines?"

Mother: "The mind itself finally becomes the teacher. The practice of disciplines means to fix the mind constantly on the lotus feet[2] of God and remain absorbed in the thought of Him."

Devotee: "What is the goal of life?"

Mother: "To realize God and remain immersed in Him."

On another occasion she remarked: "Suppose people are engaged in both holy and sinful talk; those present will partake of both the good and the evil."

Devotee: "How is that possible?"

Mother: "Listen, my child, how it happens. Suppose a person has spoken to you about his virtuous and sinful deeds. When you recall him, you will naturally think of his good and evil deeds. Thus both good and evil will leave some impression on your mind. What do you say, my child? Isn't that so?"

Holy Mother tried to instil a feeling of fearlessness into her disciples' minds.

Devotee: "Mother, I cannot practise any spiritual disciplines. It seems that I shall never be able to do so."

Mother: "Don't worry. Do whatever you can. Always remember that Sri Ramakrishna is behind you, and that I am too."

---

[2] The term is used as a mark of deep veneration.

Devotee: "Mother, I can't meditate at all."

Mother: "Never mind. Just look at the picture of the Master." To another devotee she said: "Do not worry about meditation. Just try to remember the Master; that is enough."

Devotee: "However I may try to remove evil thoughts, I do not succeed."

Mother: "This is the result of what you have done in your past life. Can one get rid of it by force? Cultivate good company, try to be good, and in time you will succeed. Pray to the Master. I, too, am here."

Devotee: "How much longer can I fight with my mind? One desire disappears and another pops up."

Mother: "As long as I-consciousness remains, desires will certainly arise. Those desires will not hurt you. The Master will protect you. He will commit a great sin if he does not protect those who have taken refuge in him and have taken shelter at his feet. Depend upon him and so lead your life. Let him make you better or let him drown you. But you must follow what is good, and that too according to the power God has given you."

Holy Mother's teachings were interspersed with apt illustrations and analogies. About the vision of God she said: "The moon is in the sky, but it is hidden by a cloud. The cloud must be slowly blown away by the wind, and then you will see the moon. Can anything happen abruptly? The vision of God is also like that. Slowly one gets rid of one's past karma." About men's experiencing weakness of the mind the Mother taught: "That is nature's law. Haven't you noticed the new moon and the full moon? The mind, likewise, sometimes feels pure and sometimes impure."

The Mother spoke in colloquial language. In Calcutta she used the city dialect, and at Jayrambati the village *patois*. She often mixed up both, but the village accent was more noticed. Frequently she used illustrations which gave her conversation a living quality. At the death of Swami Yogananda, Holy Mother said very sadly: "Yes, a brick has come out of the building." A disciple fell sick at Jayrambati and was nursed by the Mother. Deeply moved, he said: "Shall I always get this affection?" "Yes, my child," replied the Mother. "In my love there is no ebb tide or flood tide."

Her simple words often revealed her deep intuition, refinement, and inborn culture, though she had no academic education whatever. After the First World War someone read to Holy Mother the Fourteen Points submitted to the Peace Conference by Woodrow Wilson, President of the United States of America. Her comment was: "What they say comes from their lips; it would be wonderful if the words came from their hearts." When the war was going on, with its accompanying cruelty, violence, and death, a disciple asked the Mother how one could reconcile such wanton destruction with the advent of a God-man like Sri Ramakrishna, a messenger of peace. She replied: "A God-man first uses a broomstick to remove the rubbish and dust accumulated through the ages and then soothes the world by pouring nectar from the pitcher of peace."

Sister Nivedita observed in her an "instant power to penetrate a new religious feeling or idea." When one day some Easter music was sung before her by Nivedita and another Western devotee, she evinced swift comprehension and deep sympathy with those resurrection hymns, unimpeded by any foreignness or unfamiliarity in them. Again, when the same disciples described a Christian wedding to her, she was exceedingly delighted. On hearing the marriage vow: "To have and to hold from this day forward, for better for worse, for richer for poorer, in sickness and in health, to love and to cherish, till death us do part," she exclaimed joyously that these were "dharmic" words, righteous words.

Here is one more example of the Mother's broad-mindedness and deep understanding. The Advaita Āshrama at Mayavati, a branch of the Ramakrishna Order in the Himalayas, does not allow formal worship. Its inmates are not permitted to worship even the picture of Sri Ramakrishna. The Āshrama is dedicated to the study and contemplation of the nameless, formless, non-dual Brahman. At one time an inmate of devotional temperament installed a picture of the Master in his room and performed his devotions before it. The monk in charge remonstrated in vain. Finally the matter was referred to Holy Mother, and the worshipper now felt sure that, on account of her unswerving devotion to Sri Ramakrishna, she would permit him to worship the picture. In her reply the Mother said that Sri Ramakrishna represented both dualism and non-dualism and that therefore the Mayavati Āshrama should enforce its own rule.

Sister Nivedita wrote these vivid words about Holy Mother: "In her one sees realized that wisdom and sweetness to which the simplest of women may attain. And yet to myself the stateliness of her courtesy and her great open mind are almost as wonderful as her saintlihood. I have never known her hesitate in giving utterance to large and generous judgement, however new and complex might be the question put before her. Her life is one long stillness of prayer. Her whole experience is of the theocratic civilization. Yet she rises to the height of every situation. Is she tortured by the perversity of any about her? The only sign is a strange and quiet intensity that comes upon her. Does one carry to her some perplexity beyond her ken? With unerring intuition she goes straight to the heart of the matter, and sets the questioner in the true attitude to the difficulty."

As we have seen, the Mother had a sense of humour too. One day a relative said to her at the Udbodhan: "Mother, I have no desire to live any longer. I shall leave you all my property." Holy Mother laughed aloud and said: "Tell me, when will that be?" Of course she reprimanded the woman later for her silly remark.

Sister Nivedita once said to her: "Mother, you are our Kāli." Sister Christine, who was present, nodded her agreement. Mother said with a laugh: "No, children, I can't be Kāli or

any such thing; otherwise, I shall have to stick out my tongue!"[3]
Then the devotee said: "No, you won't have to take that
trouble. We shall regard you as our Mother; Sri Ramakrishna
is our Śiva."

Another day a disciple said: "Mother, formerly I used to
think of you as Kāli; but now I regard you as mother." "What
a relief," replied the Mother. "Then I won't have to show my
tongue."

When Holy Mother finished her meal the devotees eagerly
awaited her prasād, consisting of rice, milk, fruits, and sweets.
At one time she was sick in bed with malaria and the physician
prescribed sago water as her diet. A devotee came to her room
to remove the cup; she said with a smile: "What's the matter?
No one is eager for the prasād today?"

When a person made a stupid remark and was ridiculed by
others, the Mother too enjoyed the fun, but she also showed
the unfortunate victim her sympathy. One day a distant cousin
of hers visited her and the Mother gave her a pomegranate for
her sick old mother. Just then a variety of fruits sent by devotees arrived. Looking at them, the cousin said with a sigh:
"How unlucky I am! When Sri Ramakrishna's relatives were
looking for his bride, my name was proposed. But Father rejected the idea because Sri Ramakrishna was then known to be
insane. If he had married me all these gifts would have come
to my home." Those present laughed at these stupid words.
The Mother too smiled and said to her: "Take all you want."
She offered the cousin a large quantity of fruit.

---

[3] In the usual representations of Kāli, the Divine Mother is
shown standing on the prostrate figure of Śiva, Her Consort. In
India a person generally bites the tip of his tongue as a sign of
embarrassment when doing something improper. It is highly improper for a woman to touch her husband with her feet. This picture of Kāli, sticking out her tongue, is symbolic. It signifies the
Divine Mother, the potency of Brahman, arising out of the Absolute to project the relative universe. One is led to infer that the
Divine Mother felt embarrassed for disturbing the eternal peace of
Brahman in order to precipitate the creation.

Holy Mother did not care much for book-learning if it did not lead to faith in God and love for Him. "Does one get faith," she asked, "by the mere study of books? Too much reading creates confusion." She did not argue or reason, though she stressed the value of discrimination between the real and unreal, between God and the world. Whatever she taught came from her heart and her inner experience. Once, asked for a proof of God's existence, she said: "Why argue about something which you clearly see to exist?" She said to a devotee: "Give up dry discussion, this hotchpotch of philosophy. Who has been able to know God by reasoning?"

The Ramakrishna Order

O N DECEMBER 9, 1898, the Belur Math was formally dedicated and Swami Vivekananda carried on his head the
sacred urn containing the relics of the Master and placed it on
the altar of the new shrine room. Sri Ramakrishna, one day
shortly before his death, had said to the Swami that he would
dwell wherever his beloved disciple Naren carried him. When,
on January 2, 1899, the Math buildings were completed, the
monks went there to live permanently. Holy Mother, who lived
in a rented house near by, visited the Belur Math several times
about this period. On one of these occasions Swami Vivekananda said to her: "Mother, this is your own place. Please feel
at home here and wander about the grounds in perfect ease."
Regarding the site, she had once remarked: "I always noticed,
long before the acquisition of this ground, that Sri Ramakrishna was, as it were, dwelling here." She added in a happy
mood: "Now my children have a place to lay their heads. At
last the Master has bestowed his grace upon them."

In 1890, as we have already mentioned, Holy Mother had
visited Bodh-Gaya, where Buddha attained Nirvāna. There she
noticed how comfortably the members of a local monastery
lived, with all their physical wants supplied. At once the picture
of the monastic disciples of Sri Ramakrishna appeared before
her mind. Some of them were leading a wretched life of penury
at the Baranagore monastery, and some were wandering about
the country, begging bowl in hand, and practising austerities.
The contrast was painful. A fervent prayer went forth from her

Swami Vivekananda

The Belur Math

heart for the physical welfare of her spiritual children. She also felt the need of an organization for carrying on Sri Ramakrishna's mission. "Ah," she said later, "how much I wept, how often I prayed to the Master! That is why you see all these monasteries established by his grace. Immediately after his passing away, the children renounced the world and sought out a temporary shelter. But soon after, they began to wander about independently. I felt very sad and prayed to the Master: 'Oh, Master, you came down to earth, had fun with a few companions, and then departed in a happy mood. Was that the end of everything? If so, what was the need of assuming a human body and going through all this suffering? I have seen many sādhus at Benares and Vrindavan who live on alms and seek shelter under trees. There is no dearth of sādhus like them. I cannot bear the sight of my children, who have renounced everything in your name, going from door to door for a morsel of food. I fervently pray to you that those who give up the world in your name may not lack simple food and clothes. Let them live together, with you and your teachings as their centre. Those who are afflicted with the sorrows of the world will come to them and obtain peace by listening to your teachings. That is the purpose of your advent, isn't it so? I cannot control myself when I see them drifting about helplessly.' Afterwards Naren slowly organized all this."

The inmates of the Belur Math celebrated their first worship of Durgā in 1901, and Holy Mother attended the festival. She stayed next door at Nilambar Babu's house. The worship of Durgā is the great national festival of Bengal. It is performed for three successive days and on the fourth day the image is immersed in water. Everywhere there is great rejoicing. Religious music, dancing, dramatic performances, and fireworks enliven the occasion. People are fed sumptuously. In later years Holy Mother participated in several of these religious festivals. The devotees made offerings of flowers at her feet as they did at the feet of the image. During the worship in 1912, as Holy Mother entered the gate of the Belur Math accompanied by some women devotees, the monks, led by Swami Premananda, unhorsed her carriage and pulled it themselves. Golap-Mā helped her out of the carriage and the Mother remarked with a laugh: "See, everything is spick and span. We, too, have come here dressed like Mother Durgā." Several devotees received initiation from the Mother.

On the last day of the worship Golap-Mā said to Swami Saradananda: "The Mother is highly pleased by your loving care of her and sends you all her blessings." "Is that so?" replied the Swami in a serious voice and said to Swami Premananda: "Brother, did you hear that?" The two Swamis embraced each other joyously. In 1916, on the second day of the worship, the Mother was walking around when she saw some of the young Swamis and brahmachāris preparing vegetables for feeding the people. She said with a smile: "The children know how to cut vegetables very well." One of the Swamis replied: "Our aim is to gratify the Divine Mother of the Universe, whether through spiritual practices or the preparing of vegetables." After the evening worship Swami Saradananda gave a gold coin to a brahmachāri and asked him to offer it at the feet of the Mother. The latter thought that the offering was meant for Mother Durgā and wanted to be sure about it. The Swami said: "You will find the Mother in the house of the garden next door. It is she who has received our worship through the image of Durgā." Describing the occasion, Swami Shivananda wrote to a devotee: "The presence of Holy Mother made the worship vivid. Though it rained constantly during the three days of the worship, everything went off smoothly through her grace. The rain stopped whenever the devotees sat for their meals. We were all surprised. We learnt later from Yogin-Mā that just at the time of meals Holy Mother used to pray: 'O Mother, how will the devotees eat their meals in this rain? The leaf-plates will be washed away. O Mother, please save the situation.' Really, her prayer was answered during all the three days." Whenever the Mother attended the Durgā Pujā at the Belur Math, the joy of the devotees exceeded all bounds. When they saw her happy they thought that the Divine Mother surely accepted their worship. On one occasion Swami Brahmananda worshipped her with one hundred and eight lotuses.

Holy Mother cherished a special feeling for the village of Belur. Even before the establishment of the monastery, she had lived in rented houses in that locality and practised spiritual austerities there. Reminiscing about those days, she once remarked: "How happy I was at that time! It is a peaceful place. I was always in a meditative mood. That is why Narendra wanted to build the monastery there." Holy Mother visited the Belur Math on many occasions other than those of the worship of Durgā. Once she said that to live at the Belur Math was in itself a religious austerity.

In this chapter we shall discuss particularly the Mother's relationship with the Ramakrishna Order. We shall first describe her relationship with Koalpara.[1] As already mentioned, the Mother used to spend a few days there during her trips between Calcutta and Jayrambati. Gradually a permanent residence was built there for her comfort. Radhu's child was delivered at Koalpara. Many sādhus and devotees visited her there and found opportunities to associate intimately with her. The devotees of Koalpara cheerfully did much manual labour in the āshrama during religious festivals and on other occasions, carried vegetables to Jayrambati, and ran various errands for her. She depended upon them a great deal even while living at Jayrambati. At Koalpara, as in Jayrambati, she lived a natural life among the villagers, being free from the routine and restrictions of Calcutta. One day a zealous devotee arranged for a palanquin for her convenience, though the distance to traverse was very short. The Mother scolded him and said: "This is a

---

[1] An āshrama still exists there, supervised by some householder devotees of the Mother.

village and I regard the āshrama as a part of my home. The devotees are my own people. I want to lead a free life at Koalpara. I give a sigh of relief here to be free from my cage in Calcutta. There you keep me confined and I am always cautious about my movements. I simply will not be controlled here at every step. If you like you may write to Sarat about it. I shall certainly not follow the clock here in my activities." She encouraged her local disciples to learn English as, she told them, many white foreigners would later visit the place. She kept her eyes on the health of the inmates and asked the leader to give them nourishing food.

At one time the devotees of the Koalpara āshrama were influenced by the patriotic fervour that swept over the country. Instead of engaging in any really constructive activities, they often wasted time in futile criticism of the English or in merely uttering slogans. The Mother warned them against useless excitement and asked them to spin and weave native cloth. One day the leader of the āshrama remarked: "Swami Vivekananda encouraged us to engage in patriotic work and inspired the young people to dedicate themselves to unselfish service of the country. Had he been alive, what an inspiration he would be to us today!" The mention of Swami Vivekananda's name moved the Mother deeply and she said: "My child, if Naren were living now, do you think the Government would have left him free? They would have kept him behind the bars of the jail. I could not have borne it. He moved about like an unsheathed sword." Holy Mother tried to give the thoughts of the young devotees a spiritual turn and remarked: "What will mere patriotism accomplish? The Master alone is our ideal. Whatever you may do, you will never go wrong if you cling to him."

At Koalpara Holy Mother did not deviate from her regular meditation and prayer. She experienced various visions there. One day she went into samādhi simply on uttering the word "Master." After the devotees had sprinkled her eyes and face with water, she regained normal consciousness. Nalini asked:

"Aunt, what happened to you?" "Oh, nothing," the Mother replied. "I felt a little dizzy when I was threading your needle." Years later, referring to the incident, she said: "I was physically weak at that time and was seated on the porch at noon. Nalini and the other girls were sewing near by. It was a very hot day and the sun was bright. I suddenly noticed that Sri Rama-krishna came in through the main gate and lay down on the cool earthen floor. Quickly I was about to spread the end of my sāri, and became dizzy. The women began to make a fuss. I told them there was nothing the matter with me."

The Udbodhan house, named after the Bengali monthly magazine conducted by the Ramakrishna Math, is appropri-ately called the Māyerbāti, or "The Mother's Residence." Here she spent the longest period of her life (1909–1920) outside Jayrambati and here she breathed her last. Devotees who could not go to Jayrambati or Koalpara, because those places were rather inaccessible, visited the Mother at the Udbodhan and many received initiation there.

The house was built by Swami Saradananda in 1908 with the help of a heavy loan. Later, rooms were added by acquiring the adjacent house. The remodelled house provided living quarters for the permanent inmates, and also for Holy Mother and her relatives when they were in Calcutta. The ground floor was used for the publication of the magazine *Udbodhan*. Holy Mother and her party used the upper floor. Swami Saradananda at first used the small room on the left of the entrance as his office, workroom, and bedroom. Later, in the remodelled house, he slept on the second floor, in the room east of the shrine. The Swami stationed himself in his office as the Mother's door-keeper, keeping a close watch on everyone who entered the house.

Holy Mother first entered her Calcutta house on May 23, 1909, and was delighted with its location. There was, at that time, an open space in front of the house where cows and goats grazed and roamed freely. The near-by Ganges could be seen from the terrace, as well as the tops of the pine trees of the Kāli temple at Dakshineswar.

The picture of Sri Ramakrishna was installed in the shrine room on the second floor. Sister Nivedita made a silk canopy for the altar with her own hands. At first two beds were placed in the adjacent room for the Mother and Radhu. But since she objected to living away from the Master, she slept with Radhu in the shrine. From the very beginning, Golap-Mā was a permanent resident. Yogin-Mā came to the Udbodhan twice a day to help with the storeroom and in preparing the vegetables. Some of the other women devotees, too, waited on the Mother from time to time and spent nights there.

The Mother's daily life followed more or less the same pattern at the Udbodhan as at Jayrambati. At the Udbodhan she got up at three in the morning; she used to say that at that time she heard, as it were, someone playing on a flute. She repeated the Lord's name as she got up and cast her eyes on the picture of Sri Ramakrishna. After washing, she sat for meditation, never deviating from this routine even when she did not feel physically well. After meditation she made arrangements for the morning worship and at eight started the function, which she generally finished in an hour. Towards the end of her life some of the monks performed the worship. She did not approve of their prolonging it, thus delaying the prasād, which was breakfast for the inmates. The servants and the cooks, too, received their share in generous measure. The Mother often said: "They work hard and should eat well." She herself apportioned the prasād. After all the others were fed, she had her share. Next she took a bath. Generally she bathed in the Ganges every other day. Chronic rheumatism prevented her bathing daily in the river. A woman devotee accompanied her. On her way home she worshipped with water the sacred trees or images by the roadside. After her return she would find a crowd of devotees and other people, both men and women, awaiting her to receive initiation. It would be after noon when

THE UDBODHAN HOUSE

HOLY MOTHER AT WORSHIP IN THE UDBODHAN HOUSE

she finished her midday meal. Now was her time for rest. But at this hour many women devotees visited her. The Mother talked to them lying on her bed. At half past three she washed and then worshipped the Master for a short while. Afterwards she sat for her devotions with her rosary, and now and then talked to the women devotees who were present. At half past five, men devotees came in to pay their respects, when the women retired to another room. The Mother, wrapping her body with a sheet, sat on the edge of her bed, with her feet down, and received their salutations. On hot days a devotee fanned her. In answer to their queries regarding her health, she usually gave a short reply by a gentle nod or in a whisper. Those who had special questions to ask came after the others had gone. If they were personally known to her, she talked to them directly; otherwise an intermediary helped. At sunset she again sat for meditation and then lay down for a while before supper, when someone among the women devotees rubbed her legs and back with medicinal oil. Holy Mother constantly suffered, especially during the summer, from prickly heat. After the evening offering at the shrine, she took her supper and retired to bed shortly before midnight. As to her food, she usually ate simple things cooked without much seasoning.

All these varied and unceasing activities were carried on at the Udbodhan without any excitement or turmoil. There were several reasons for this. Holy Mother had complete control of her floor, while Swami Saradananda looked after affairs on the ground floor. The Swami maintained a firm discipline so that the Mother would not be disturbed. She, on her own part, would not put off any work and finished everything, big or small, with great care. Her gentle, loving, and modest nature imparted a spirit of serenity to every action. Inmates of the house and visitors as well felt its influence. They never dreamt of making a noise or commotion in her presence. Their activities were restrained and their voices subdued. Her attendants, male or female, understood the Mother's nature and tried hard not to create any complication. Whenever men devotees came to the second floor, the women disappeared into one of the rooms. The men returned downstairs as soon as possible. But she often had her worries regarding her relatives because of their unseemly conduct. As we have seen, they had been spoiled by her affection. Being brought up in the village, they often forgot the refinements or formalities of city life. Consequently she had to watch them closely and scolded them when they transgressed. They were not allowed to talk unnecessarily or to make a loud noise. One day Radhu rushed down the steps, her anklets rattling all the way. "Radhi," the Mother reprimanded her sharply, "you should be ashamed of yourself. The monks are downstairs and you are making a racket with your ornaments. Take them off quickly. What will my children think of you? Their minds are always indrawn, and you are disturbing their peace." Angry at these words, Radhu took off the anklets and threw them at the Mother. Some of the visitors present were horrified.

Disciples often made many demands upon her. Some wanted to worship her feet, some begged her to put on new clothes brought by them, some wanted the Mother to give them prasād when she was eating, and some wanted her to sit turning her head towards them so that they could have a better look at her face. Some wanted her to accept their personal service. To the best of her ability she fulfilled these desires. She asked some to help with the storeroom, some to stroke her feet, and some to rub her body with medicinal oil. One day a disciple felt the desire to see her at the auspicious hour of dawn, and the Mother fulfilled it. Another disciple said to her that he would feel blessed if she would touch his chest with her foot. With a laugh she satisfied that wish, too. When a monk living at the Udbodhan made fun of this excessive emotionalism of the devotees, the Mother said: "How will you understand the suffering of the afflicted? You are not a mother."

Three young disciples once visited Holy Mother at Jayrambati. Filled with the spirit of renunciation, they sought her blessings so that they might spend the rest of their lives as wandering monks, practising austerities. The Mother received them kindly, heard their story, and with great love fed them. Two days later she gave them the ochre robe of a monk and prayed to Sri Ramakrishna: "O Master, please see that they keep their monastic vows. Please also see that wherever they may be—in hills, jungles, or wildernesses—they may get something to eat." She did not very much like the idea of their leading the austere life of ascetics, and asked them to walk on foot as far as Benares and then reside at the āshrama there, practising disciplines under the guidance of Swami Shivananda. She shed tears as they took their leave.

Holy Mother was, as we have repeatedly seen, the mother of her disciples, but especially of the members of the Ramakrishna Order.[2] She was a source of unfailing inspiration to the members of the Ramakrishna Math and Mission and showered her blessings upon all who renounced the world, inspired by the Master's teachings. She had felt the need of a religious organization for the purpose of preaching the Master's teachings and giving them practical shape, and also of affording shelter to the monks where they could be assured of food, clothes, and other simple necessities of life. After the establishment of the Math and Mission she became its spiritual centre. During her lifetime she kept her eyes on the monks to see that they faithfully dis-

---

[2] The Ramakrishna Order of monks consists of those who have renounced the world for the purpose of realizing God and serving humanity. They follow the ideal and teaching of Sri Ramakrishna and receive their monastic vows from the head of the Order. The Order includes two organizations: the Ramakrishna Math and the Ramakrishna Mission. The members of the former devote themselves mainly to contemplation, study, and preaching, and those of the latter to such philanthropic activities as are necessary in times of famine, flood, epidemic, or other providential calamities. Further, the Mission generally maintains hospitals, dispensaries, and various educational institutions. Householders can also be members of the Ramakrishna Mission.

charged their duties. Like Swami Vivekananda, she looked on
the organization as the visible body of Sri Ramakrishna and its
every part as one of her own limbs. She gave freedom to the
monks to develop their inner potentialities in their own way,
but did not shrink from severity when such an attitude was
found necessary. At one time it was thought advisable to discharge the hired cook of the Udbodhan; but the head of the
place declined to do so on the plea that this would inconvenience Holy Mother. When the matter was reported to her
she said to him: "Why should you think so? After all, you are
all monks. Renunciation is your goal. Can't you renounce a
cook?" On another occasion a monk of the Belur Math slapped
a servant for his insubordination. When the Mother heard
about it, she said: "They are monks. A tree is their proper
shelter. Now they have monasteries, houses, and servants to
boot. They even go to the length of beating the servants." She
also warned the monks against inordinate attachment to the
monastery or entanglement in activities which might interfere
with their spiritual practices. One day she scolded a Swami
because he was showing undue love for the āshrama: "You
have renounced the world to repeat God's name. But now you
are involved in activities. The āshrama has become your second
world. People come to the monastery, giving up their families,
but they become so attached to the monastery that they do not
want to give it up." Quoting a Bengali proverb, she added: "A
man eager to keep away from acid food builds a home under a
tamarind tree!"

Holy Mother was keenly interested in the flood and relief
operations and other philanthropic activities of the Ramakrishna Mission and encouraged the monks to undertake them.
Whenever any monk returned from relief work, she asked in
detail about the people's suffering and the extent of the relief
given. She knew very well that an average person could not practise meditation and prayer all the twenty-four hours of the day,
and that work was a great discipline. In her opinion an idle

mind created much confusion and trouble. "That is why," she said, "my Naren started all these centres for work. Our organization will function this way. Those who cannot adjust will leave." She foresaw that in the course of time there would be temples and maths at Kamarpukur and Jayrambati, and made arrangements for them during her lifetime.

The members of the Ramakrishna Order came from various parts of India, and from different castes, social positions, and backgrounds. Holy Mother always emphasized friendly feeling and brotherly love as the cement to strengthen the organization. She disapproved of the undue exercise of authority on the part of the leader in maintaining discipline among the monks. The leader of the Koalpara āshrama at one time became a hard taskmaster and demanded strenuous labour from the inmates. He did not exhibit much friendship towards them and often was negligent in regard to giving them proper food. Gradually some of the members left the āshrama and took shelter under Holy Mother or Swami Saradananda. The leader complained to the Mother and said: "Mother, my workers formerly always obeyed me. Now it seems they have become smart. They don't always carry out my orders. They know they can find shelter with you or Swami Saradananda. You give them good food, too. If you and the Swami do not keep them with you but return them to me, with the proper advice, I shall be able to keep them under control." Stunned by these words, the Mother remarked: "What is the matter with you? What do you mean? Love alone is the essential thing. Our organization is growing only through love. I am their mother. How impudent you are to mention to me their food." On another occasion she said: "How can you run the āshrama through diplomacy? If you scold your own children too hard they will part with you." On still another occasion the leader of the Koalpara āshrama told the Mother that his workers were not obeying him and that they wanted to go elsewhere. He wanted her to persuade them to stay at his place and requested her to see that they did not find encouragement at any other āshrama. Angrily the Mother replied: "How dare you ask me to speak to the workers that way? Do you mean to say they should not get protection anywhere else? They are my children and have taken shelter with Sri Ramakrishna. Wherever they go the Master will look after them. And you want to extract a promise from me that they will not find shelter at any other place! I can never utter any such promise." Everybody became frightened at the look on her face, which was glowing with indignation. The leader at once fell at her feet and begged her forgiveness. Leader and workers alike she constantly asked to exercise patience and forbearance and to adjust themselves to all conditions.

In Holy Mother one finds the two elements which have given the Ramakrishna movement its religion and philosophy. The religious element centres around the life and personality of Sri Ramakrishna and expresses itself through worship and ritual. The philosophical element is derived from his teachings. The religious element, as in all major faiths, stimulates an aspirant's devotion to the ideal, helps him deepen his love for it, and ultimately enables him to commune with God. Philosophy broadens the mind, develops the understanding, satisfies the intellect, and gives the *rationale* of spiritual life. Further, it protects the devotee from bigotry and harmful sentimentalism. But philosophy, without religion, degenerates into a vague universalism, or shallow optimism, or lifeless syncretism. When combined properly with philosophy, devotion to personality gives health and vitality to a religious movement. In Buddhism one finds that the religious element has been derived from the personality of Buddha, whereas its philosophy springs from his teaching about the Four Noble Truths and the Eightfold Noble Path. Likewise, in Christianity the religious aspect is based upon the concept of the Sonship of Christ to the Father in Heaven, whereas the philosophy is based on the Sermon on the Mount and other teachings of Jesus and the Apostles. The philosophical aspect of Islam is derived from the concept of the

Unity of God and the religious aspect from the belief that Mohammed is His Prophet.

Both these aspects are present in the Ramakrishna movement as well. Sri Ramakrishna is recognized by his followers as the Divine Incarnation of modern times, embodying in himself the spiritual experiences of past prophets and the truths of all religions. His teachings, as presented in *The Gospel of Sri Ramakrishna*, have been taken down with almost stenographic precision. He is the only Incarnation of God who has been photographed. Thus he is a living reality with whom a devotee can commune through selfless love, philosophical knowledge, and non-attached action. His life and personality have opened a new way for the spiritual development of many modern minds. But he never claimed that he was the exclusive bestower of liberation and he admitted the validity of all the major faiths. The philosophical element of the Ramakrishna movement is based upon the perennial and universal doctrines of Vedānta, which teaches the reality of God, the divinity of the soul, the oneness of existence, and the harmony of religions. This element is demonstrated in the life and experiences of both Sri Ramakrishna and Holy Mother.

Swami Vivekananda emphasized this universal philosophical element of the Ramakrishna movement, because his mission was international. He had to satisfy the doubts and aspirations of modern thinkers. But his devotion to the personality of Sri Ramakrishna was in no way less strong than that of other zealous devotees of the Master. For the devotees he instituted the ritualistic worship of Sri Ramakrishna. The Master was the ideal and goal of the great Swami's life. As a preacher he did not mention the Master very much because, on account of his intense devotion, he felt unworthy of him. Holy Mother emphasized the personality of the Master because the average aspirant needs a concrete symbol of reality to worship and to pray to. Sri Ramakrishna was to her God Incarnate. She assured his devotees of salvation here or hereafter. On account of her direct and immediate experience, she did not need a philosophy with which to argue about the reality of God. In other religions, too, the companions of the prophets do not always reason about God. Being witnesses of the spiritual experiences of God-men, they develop an unshakeable faith in God's reality. They bask in the heat of the fire lighted by the prophets. Philosophy is generally formulated later for doubters. But Holy Mother was not indifferent to the philosophy of Hinduism, as is demonstrated by her life and teachings. Thus she became the Śakti, or Power, behind the Ramakrishna movement, and an unfailing source of inspiration to devotees of the Master everywhere. She has given the movement its vitality.

Holy Mother and Her Intimate Devotees   (I)

L IKE HOLY MOTHER's own disciples, Sri Ramakrishna's direct disciples² regarded her as the incarnation of the Divine Mother of the Universe. Though they were endowed with the deepest spirituality, and some of them with vast erudition, they sought her advice not only about their own personal life but also about the management of the Ramakrishna Math and Mission. They brought their complicated problems to her and accepted her decisions. Holy Mother, too, respected their spiritual stature. She said to the present writer, after giving him initiation: "Ask Rakhal and Sarat about details." Swami Vivekananda, before sailing for America, asked her permission for this great venture, and the Mother blessed him with the words: "Come back safely after conquering the world. May the Goddess of Wisdom dwell on your tongue." Holy Mother regarded the Master's disciples as treasures, precious beyond compare, and loved them with all her heart. She referred to Naren as

---

¹ The word *devotee*, throughout this book, generally refers to Holy Mother's disciples, those who were initiated by her. They include both monks and householders. A comparatively small number of people who were not her disciples also visited her now and then, as a holy person, to pay their respects to her. The devotees mentioned in this and the following chapter were for the most part disciples of either Sri Ramakrishna or Swami Vivekananda.

² For further information regarding the disciples of Sri Ramakrishna mentioned in this section, see *The Disciples of Sri Ramakrishna*, Calcutta: Advaita Ashrama, 1955, and *The Gospel of Sri Ramakrishna*, pp. 47 ff., New York: Ramakrishna-Vivekananda Center, 1953.

"my all," to Rakhal as "the visible Nārāyana" or "my son in a special sense," to Baburam as "my very inner soul," and to Yogen and Sarat as "members of my inner circle." By word and conduct they gave her an exalted position. One day a devotee came to the Udbodhan and asked Swami Premananda: "Where is the Mother?" "There," he replied at once, touching his head. Swami Brahmananda literally shook with emotion in her presence. They visited her only rarely, for fear of making a display of their spiritual fervour.

We have already mentioned, now and again, the relationship between the Mother and Swami Vivekananda. Sri Ramakrishna had assured her that Narendra and his other disciples would take care of her after his death just as they were then doing for him. Since Holy Mother had seen, in a vision, the Master's body melting in the Ganges, she concluded that Swami Vivekananda would be the bearer of his message to the world. She had no doubt whatever that the Swami was an instrument in the Master's hands. Swami Vivekananda once wrote a letter from America urging the monks of the Ramakrishna Order to renounce everything in the service of God and man. When the Mother heard this, she said: "Naren is an instrument of the Master. It is the Master who writes through Naren about the future duties of his children and devotees for the good of the world. What he has written is all correct. You will see it bearing fruit in course of time."

Swami Vivekananda also wrote from America to the Belur Math about establishing an organization for the training of women, with Holy Mother as its centre, to translate into action the ideal of Hindu womanhood. Such an organization was established only in 1954, long after her passing away. It may be noted here, however, that though the Mother was intimately associated with the Ramakrishna Math and Mission, she did not actively manage these organizations or supervise their day-to-day activities. She silently influenced the spiritual life of the monks, being fully aware that when one develops spirituality,

Swami Vivekananda in Meditation

Swami Brahmananda

Swami Saradananda

all other things take care of themselves. Until nearly the last day of her life she lived with her relatives, looking after their worldly welfare.

If anyone mentioned Swami Vivekananda to the Mother, she would say: "Why do you drag Naren into everything? He is in a class apart." The Swami regarded Holy Mother as Divinity Itself. Once he remarked at the Belur Math: "Mother is the incarnation of Bagalā in the guise of Sarasvati.[3] Outwardly she is all peace, but inwardly she is the destroyer of the power of evil." After his return from the West, whenever he visited her he purified himself with Ganges water, because he felt he had lost some of his spirituality by associating with all kinds of people there. Often he would be overwhelmed as he reached the door of the Mother's house and could move no farther. On one of these occasions the Mother herself brought him in, holding him by the hand. In the course of a letter he wrote from America to a brother disciple, the Swami said: "You have not yet realized how precious Mother is. People will not understand her now, but they will, gradually. Brother, there will be no salvation of the world without the help of the Divine Power. . . .[4] Why is it that our country is the weakest and most backward of all countries? Because Śakti is held in dishonour here.[5] Mother has been born to revive this wonderful Śakti here. . . . Without the grace of Śakti nothing will be accomplished. . . . What do I find in America and Europe? The worship of Śakti, the worship of Power. Yet they worship Her ignorantly, through sense gratification. Imagine then what a lot of good they will achieve when they worship Her with purity, looking upon Her as their Mother! I am coming to understand

---

[3] Bagalā represents one of the terrific aspects of the Divine Power, as the slayer of a fierce demon, and Sarasvati represents Wisdom.

[4] Swami Vivekananda regarded all women as manifestations of Śakti, or the Divine Power, and Holy Mother as Her special manifestation.

[5] Referring to the degraded condition of Indian womanhood.

things every day; my insight is opening out more and more. . . .
Let Ramakrishna disappear, that does not frighten me. But it
will be a calamity if people forget Mother. . . . Don't be angry
with me. None of you has understood Mother. Her grace upon
me is one hundred thousand times greater than that of the
Master. . . . About Mother I am a little fanatic. I can do anything if she gives the order. I shall give a sigh of relief when
you purchase a piece of land and install this living Durgā
there. . . . Brother, when I think of Mother, I say to myself:
'Who is this Ramakrishna?' I say this because of my fanaticism.
Whether Ramakrishna was God or man—you may say whatever you like. But, Brother, shame upon him who is not devoted
to Mother!"

When Swami Vivekananda died on July 4, 1902, Holy
Mother was at Jayrambati. There is no record of the Mother's
outward reaction to this tragic event, except the brief remark:
"Alas, my Naren is gone." She wept. In later years she treasured
in her box a cloth given her by the Swami and asked her attendants not to handle it too much when arranging the con-
tents of the box.

When Swami Brahmananda[6] first went to Sri Ramakrishna
at Dakshineswar, the Master at once recognized him as his
spiritual child whom he had seen earlier in a vision as an intimate companion of Krishna. From the very beginning the
Master and Holy Mother regarded the Swami, who was then
known as Rakhal, as their spiritual son and treated him as such.
As he grew in years he developed a unique spiritual stature, and
this Holy Mother knew. Whenever she saw him she felt exceedingly happy. But because of her usual bashfulness, she did not
talk to the Swami directly; it was only during the last period of
her life that now and then she exchanged a few words with
him in a whisper.

Swami Brahmananda's reverence for Holy Mother is too deep

---

[6] President of the Ramakrishna Math and Mission from 1901 to
1922.

for words. At the very sight of her he would be overwhelmed with spiritual emotion. President of the Ramakrishna Math and Mission, and spiritual preceptor of many monks and house-holders, Swami Brahmananda was a person of grave tempera-ment. He often remained absorbed in spiritual moods that made him practically unapproachable. But in the presence of Holy Mother he often acted like a child.

One morning the Swami came to the Udbodhan from Bala-ram's house to see the Mother. She covered herself with a shawl, sat on the edge of the bed with her feet down, and sent for the Swami. As he was about to enter the Mother's room his legs began to tremble. Somehow he prostrated himself before her and asked about Radhu, perhaps to force his mind into a normal mood. Holy Mother affectionately caressed him, touch-ing his chin, and gently stroked his head and chest. She told him about Radhu's illness and asked him about his own welfare and that of his attendants. Swami Brahmananda very briefly answered her queries and quickly left the room. In the mean-time his body was covered with perspiration. The Mother sent him a tray of sweets, which he and Swami Saradananda ac-cepted as her blessings and enjoyed immensely.

When Holy Mother visited the Belur Math, and on other occasions as well, Swami Brahmananda worshipped her as a veritable Goddess. Once he remarked: "It is very difficult to understand Mother. She moves about, veiling her face, like an ordinary woman, but in reality she is the Mother of the Uni-verse. Could we have recognized her if the Master himself had not revealed to us who she was?"

On another occasion he said: "Is it possible for an ordinary being to digest the worship of an Incarnation like Sri Rama-krishna?[7] From this one may understand what a great fountain of power Mother is. We have seen with our own eyes that Mother has been taking sins and afflictions of many people

---

[7] Referring to the worship of Sarada Devi by the Master at Dakshineswar.

upon herself and giving them liberation. Can anyone but the Divine Mother have this power? . . . . Inside, the great ocean of realization; outside, absolute calm. How ordinary and simple she appears! Even the Incarnations cannot keep divine moods under control. Sri Ramakrishna manifested them outwardly. But it is extremely difficult to understand Mother. How she has kept us all deluded by her motherly love!"

Swami Premananda's name was Baburam before he embraced the monastic life. The Swami was one of the youngest of Sri Ramakrishna's monastic disciples. His mother, the mother-in-law of Balaram Bose, was also a devotee of Sri Ramakrishna. We have already seen how sharply the Master spoke to Holy Mother, one day at Dakshineswar, for feeding the young disciple with a few more pieces of bread than was stipulated by him, and also how firmly she justified the exercise of her motherly prerogative towards her children. After the Master's death Holy Mother visited Baburam's village home, where some of the Master's disciples took their monastic vows.

Swami Premananda, the supervisor of the general activities of the Belur Math, never went anywhere without the permission of Holy Mother, if she was present in Calcutta. Once two devotees invited the Swami to visit their place outside Calcutta in connection with Sri Ramakrishna's birthday festival. The Swami came with the devotees to the Udbodhan to receive the Mother's permission, but she refused it because Swami Premananda had been sick only a fortnight before. When the devotees again importuned the Mother about the trip, she asked the Swami if he wanted to go. He replied with great emotion: "What do I know, Mother? I shall carry out your order. If you ask me to jump into fire, I will jump; if you ask me to plunge into water, I will plunge; if you ask me to enter into hell, I will enter. What do I know? Your word is final." At last Holy Mother gave him permission, but she asked him to return soon. To the devotees she said: "You see, they are all great souls. Their bodies are channels for doing good to the world. Look after their physical comforts and ease."

The Swami's face actually glowed when he spoke about Holy Mother. He once said that those who differentiated between her and the Master would never make any spiritual progress; she and the Master were like the two sides of one and the same coin. In the course of a talk at the Belur Math he said to the devotees: "We have seen that she had a much greater capacity than the Master. She was the embodiment of Power, and how well she controlled it! Sri Ramakrishna could not do so, though he tried. His power became manifest through his frequent ecstasies, which were seen by all. The Mother repeatedly experienced samādhi, but others did not know of it. What wonderful self-control she exercised! She covered herself with a veil, like a young bride in her husband's home. The people of Jayrambati thought she was busy day and night looking after her nephews and nieces." He wrote to one of her disciples: "Those who have received Mother's grace are eternally free—very pure and righteous."

The death of Swami Premananda on July 30, 1918, bruised Holy Mother's heart deeply. She wept the whole day. "Baburam," she said, "was my very soul. When he walked on the bank of the Ganges at the Belur Math, the power, love, reason, and everything else of the Math shone through his body." In the evening she placed her head at the foot of a large picture of the Master hanging on the wall and said piteously: "O Master, so you have taken him away!" An eyewitness remarked: "How soul-piercing her words were! We, too, felt like crying."

Like the other disciples of Sri Ramakrishna, Swami Shivananda[8] regarded Holy Mother's view on every matter as final. At one time he was acting as a sort of manager of the Belur Math when a young brahmachāri did something foolish. The brahmachāri was told by some of his friends that he might be expelled from the monastery by Swami Shivananda, who was a strict disciplinarian. Frightened, he stole away and walked the

---

[8] President of the Ramakrishna Math and Mission from 1922 to 1934.

entire distance to Jayrambati. When he arrived there he looked haggard and his clothes were in rags. Holy Mother gave him proper garments. Then she wrote to Swami Shivananda: "The brahmachāri must have offended you. Afraid of being thrown out of the monastery, he has come to me, walking on foot all the way. How can a mother look at her child's fault? I want you to be kind to him." In reply the Swami said that he would be welcome at the Belur Math. When he returned to the Math, Swami Shivananda embraced him and said with a laugh: "So you went to the Supreme Court to file an appeal against me, you rogue!"

In a letter, Swami Shivananda wrote: "Holy Mother is not an ordinary woman, not a spiritual aspirant, not just a perfect person. She is eternally perfect, a partial manifestation of the Primordial Energy. If that Mother of the Universe, through her love that knows no reason, has touched a devotee with her blessed hand, his spiritual consciousness has either been awakened or will be so; this is my unshakeable conviction.

"Holy Mother assumed a human body to awaken the womanhood of the entire world. Don't you see, since her advent, what an amazing awakening has set in among the women of the world? They are now resolved to build up their lives gracefully and advance in all directions. A very surprising renaissance is swaying women in the fields of spirituality, politics, science, literature, etc. And more will come. This is the play of the Divine Power. Ordinary mortals cannot understand this mystery."

Swami Adbhutananda, an intimate disciple of Sri Ramakrishna, was called Latu before he became a monk. He was born of humble parents and was totally uneducated. Of all the monastic disciples of the Master, he was one of the few who were permitted to speak directly to the Mother. The Master asked him to knead flour for her, wash her dishes, do her marketing, and run other errands for her. She loved Latu as her own child, and he, too, acted like a baby in her presence. But with all this he held her in the highest respect and said of her: "She is none other than Lakshmi[9] and knows the past and future of all. To appreciate her grace one needs hard austerities." He always cherished this opinion of her.

In 1907 Holy Mother spent a few days at Balaram's house in Calcutta. Latu lived in a room downstairs next to the passage from the street. One day when the Mother had left her carriage and was walking into the house, she stopped for a minute at the door of Latu's room and said: "How are you, Latu, my child?" He always remembered the days at the Dakshineswar garden, when he had rendered her menial service. "Go away," he said. "You are a lady. Why have you come to the outer apartment to speak to me? Please go upstairs right away. I will not speak to you here. You could have sent for me, and I would have gone up to see you. I am your servant, you know." Holy Mother laughed. Daily she sent a little prasād for Latu, who visited her infrequently. When Holy Mother was leaving for Jayrambati, the devotees went upstairs to take the dust of her feet. Latu remained in his room. He began to pace up and down and muttered: "Who is mother or father to a monk? He is free from all māyā." The Mother stopped in front of his room and heard him still repeating those words. She said: "My child, you don't have to accept me." Latu sprang from his room and fell at her feet. He was weeping without restraint. The Mother's eyes, too, became moist. Then Latu began to wipe her tears with his cloth. He said: "You are going to your father's house, Mother; don't weep. Sarat will bring you back. Is it proper for one to cry when one departs?" Latu's childlike simplicity and naturalness deeply moved all those who were present. "Is Latu an ordinary person?" she said to a monk. "It will do you good if you live with him." Latu once remarked to a devotee: "I write to many people, but why do I not write to Mother? Mother knows my past, my future, my everything. What is the point of writing to her just for a public show? I do

[9] The Goddess of Fortune.

not speak about Mother to all and sundry, because all won't understand or they will misunderstand. I generally talk about Sri Ramakrishna and Swami Vivekananda."

Sarada, who later assumed the monastic name of Swami Trigunatitananda, visited Sri Ramakrishna during his lifetime and later was initiated by Holy Mother. After Swami Yogananda's death, he took charge of looking after her physical needs besides editing the *Udbodhan* magazine. His zeal for her service appeared to be almost an eccentricity. One day Holy Mother was coming to Jayrambati in a bullock cart. It was past midnight. Sarada was walking in front of the carriage as bodyguard, with a heavy stick on his shoulder. Suddenly he saw a wide breach in the road made by a flood. At once he realized that when the carriage came to it, it would either be overturned or receive a terrific jolt, not only disturbing the Mother's sleep but hurting her physically. Immediately he laid his large body in the breach and asked the driver to drive the vehicle over him. The Mother awoke, took in the situation, and rebuked the disciple for his rashness. On another occasion Yogin-Mā asked Sarada to buy some hot chillies for the Mother. In his eagerness to get the hottest he could, he walked from one end of the chilli market to the other and tasted all the hot chillies by chewing one of each till his tongue became swollen. When Holy Mother heard about it she said: "What devotion to the guru!"

Yogen, later known as Swami Yogananda, was, as we have seen, Holy Mother's first disciple. He was initiated by her at Vrindavan at the behest of Sri Ramakrishna himself. Even at Dakshineswar he had attended to her needs in various ways, and after the Master's death he accompanied her during her visits to Benares, Vrindavan, Hardwar, Puri, Kamarpukur, and other places. He often went with her to Jayrambati to look after her comfort. For the last twelve years of his life he was her chief attendant. The Mother was unstinting in her praise of Yogen's

Swami Ramakrishnananda

Swami Premananda

Swami Yogananda

Swami Adbhutananda

service. He lived in a room at the entrance of her rented house in Calcutta, did all the outdoor work connected with her establishment, received gifts for her from the devotees, regulated the visits of the devotees, and, in short, did everything to make her stay in Calcutta comfortable. Whenever someone gave him a little money he would save it for the Mother's future needs. He once presented Holy Mother with a quilt which eventually became worn out from constant use. At first she thought of changing the cover and having it stuffed with fresh cotton, but then she gave up the idea since, she thought, it would change the look of the gift from her beloved disciple. After Sri Ramakrishna's death he had subjected himself to intense austerities in Benares: he possessed no money and went without sleep except for two or three hours in a day. His meagre food consisted of powdered dry bread, which he got by begging every three or four days. As a result he suffered a severe attack of dysentery and had to be taken to the Belur Math. Thence he moved to Balaram's house in Calcutta. Whenever the Mother came to Calcutta, he attended her. Gradually his illness took a serious turn. Various physicians looked after him. At Holy Mother's insistence his wife was brought to his sick-bed. On his last day, an attendant found Holy Mother seated with outstretched legs, tears streaming from her eyes. When he tried to console her, she said: "What will happen to Yogen, my child?" He again tried to assure her that the Swami would be cured. "But," the Mother replied, "I saw early in the morning that the Master came to take him away," and she began to weep. Controlling her emotion a little, she said to the attendant: "Don't tell this to anyone; it would not be proper."

On March 28, 1899, Swami Yogananda breathed his last. The Mother, in her upstairs room, wept loudly and said: "I know my Yogen has gone to the Master. But he surely has snatched away my child from me." When an attendant tried to soothe her, she said: "Go away. My Yogen has departed, leaving me here. Who will look after me now?" The next day she remarked sadly: "A brick has fallen from the house. This is the beginning."[10]

Even before Swami Yogananda's death his successor to look after Holy Mother was, in a way, selected. One day Swami Saradananda[11] said to Swami Yogananda: "Yogen, I do not always understand what Naren means. He talks about many things. Whenever he speaks about something he does it with such emphasis that all his other statements become practically meaningless." Swami Yogananda replied: "Let me tell you something, Sarat. You stick to Mother. Whatever she says is right."

Some time after Swami Yogananda's death, Swami Saradananda took over the care of Holy Mother. She once said: "I shall be able to live at the Udbodhan so long as Sarat is there. I do not see anyone who can be responsible for me after that. Sarat can, in every respect. He is the man to bear my burden." In answer to the query if Swami Brahmananda could not assume responsibility for her, she said: "No, that is not in his line. He cannot put up with difficulties. He can look after me mentally or through someone else. He is cast in a different mould."

"What about Swami Premananda?"

"No, he can't either."

"But he is running the Belur Math."

"That may be; but looking after women is a bother. He can keep an eye on me from a distance."

Sri Ramakrishna once spoke of Swami Saradananda and his cousin Sashi, also a monastic disciple of the Master and known as Swami Ramakrishnananda, as having been companions of Jesus Christ. Physically well built and stout, Swami Sarada-

---

[10] Swami Yogananda was among the first of the Master's devotees. They were, as it were, the strong bricks of the edifice of the Ramakrishna Order.

[11] Secretary of the Ramakrishna Math and Mission from 1898 to 1927.

nanda was a cool-headed, serious, and introspective scholar. Swami Vivekananda had great faith in his spiritual integrity and sent him to America in 1896 as a Vedāntic preacher, bringing him back to India in 1898 to work as the Secretary of the Ramakrishna Mission. He became a strong pillar of the Mission and remained its Secretary till his death in 1927. On the eve of his departure for America, Holy Mother blessed him with the words: "My child, the Master is always protecting you. Don't be afraid."

From 1904 to 1920, in spite of his multifarious and heavy duties associated with the Secretaryship of the Ramakrishna Math and Mission and the management of the *Udbodhan* magazine, Swami Saradananda poured heart and soul into the service of Holy Mother. He also looked after the welfare of her relatives, nursed her youngest brother Abhay during his last illness, and made provision for Radhu's future financial security. He accompanied the Mother on her several pilgrimages and often visited her at Jayrambati and Koalpara, especially when she was ill. When the Mother was in Calcutta he personally looked after her; when she was away he kept in touch with her by mail, and looked after her finances. His devotion to her has become a legend among the members of the Ramakrishna Order. Holy Mother used to speak of him as her Vāsuki[12] who protected her with his thousand hoods. "Whenever water pours, he spreads his umbrella to protect me," she said. To attend Holy Mother, with her eccentric relatives, was a delicate and difficult task. As she herself put it: "I shall have no difficulty as long as Sarat lives. I do not see anybody else who can shoulder my burden." If anyone spoke of her going to Calcutta when the Swami was not there, she would say: "I simply cannot think of going to Calcutta when Sarat is not there. While I am in Calcutta, if he says that he wants to go elsewhere for a few days, I tell him: 'Wait awhile, my child. First let me leave the place and then you may go.'" The Swami sometimes sang to

---

[12] A mythical snake.

entertain her, and when her body burnt with a high fever he placed her tender hands on his bare body and this cooled her. Her confidence in the Swami was total. About the disciples of the Master, she once said: "Sarat, Rakhal, and others have come out of my body."

As we have already said, Swami Saradananda called himself the Mother's "doorkeeper," and he felt proud of the position. From his small room at the left of the entrance to the Mother's house in Calcutta he kept an eye on the devotees who went upstairs to salute her. It was not an easy task. One day a devotee walked a great distance to come to the Udbodhan and was very hot. It was about three in the afternoon. Holy Mother had just returned from a devotee's house and was resting. Swami Saradananda said to the devotee: "I won't allow you to go up now; Mother is tired." With the words "Is she just your mother?" the visitor practically pushed him aside and went to the Mother. Very soon he felt repentant for his rash act and prayed that he might avoid the Swami while going out. He also told the Mother about his improper conduct but was reassured by her. Sheepishly he came down the stairs and found Swami Saradananda seated in the same place. He asked his forgiveness for the offence. Swami Saradananda embraced him and said: "Why do you talk about offending me? Can one see Mother without such yearning?"

On another occasion, when the Mother was ill, a devotee came to her and prayed for initiation. She asked him to come a few days later. But as he insisted she asked him to speak to Swami Saradananda about it. "I do not know anybody else," he insisted again. "I have come to you; please initiate me." "What do you mean?" the Mother replied. "Sarat is the jewel of my head. What he says will be done." The devotee went to the Swami, who fixed a day for his initiation.

Soon after the present writer's release from internment camp in 1918, he went to the Udbodhan to salute the Mother and was told that no visitor was allowed to go in as she was ill.

Through Swami Saradananda's kindness he was allowed to see her for a few minutes.

In spite of all Holy Mother's affection and confidence in him, Swami Saradananda was the very image of humility. A disciple of the Mother on one occasion took the dust of his feet, perhaps with a little show, as the Swami was about to begin his daily duties. The Swami said: "Why such a big salutation? What is the idea?" "Sir, why do you say that?" the disciple replied. "Whom else should I salute but you?" The Swami said: "I am seated here awaiting her grace by whom you have been blessed. If she wishes, she can this very moment seat you in my place." When Swami Saradananda prostrated himself before the Mother, as a witness observed, it was an unusual sight. He melted, as it were, on the ground before her. He showed that with his salutation he offered at her feet his body, soul, and everything.

For over fifteen years Swami Saradananda had the unique privilege of being close to Holy Mother and looking after her needs. How small he felt in her presence! Once he remarked: "What can we understand of Mother? This, however, I can say: I have never seen such a great mind and I do not hope to see one. It is not within our capacity to comprehend the extent of Mother's glory and power. I have never seen in anyone else such attachment; nor have I seen such detachment. She was so deeply attached to Radhu. But before her death she said: 'Please send her away.' Radhu lost all attraction for her."

A devotee once said to Swami Saradananda that he could easily believe in the divinity of Sri Ramakrishna; at least he cherished that faith. But he could not comprehend Holy Mother as the Divine Mother. The Swami replied: "Do you mean to say that God married the daughter of a woman who maintained herself by gathering cow dung?"[13]

As we shall see, before her death Holy Mother left her dev-

---

[13] Poor women in rural Bengal often support themselves by picking up cow dung, which when dried is used as fuel.

otees in Swami Saradananda's care. It was through her grace that the divinity of women was revealed to him. One of his books, *Mother Worship in India,* he dedicated to her with the words: "By whose gracious glance the author has been able to realize the revelation of Divine Motherhood in every woman— to her lotus feet the work is dedicated in all humility and devotion."

Holy Mother and Her Intimate Devotees (II)

THREE OF SRI RAMAKRISHNA's most prominent householder disciples were Girish Chandra Ghosh, Nag Mahāsaya, and Mahendranath Gupta, widely known as Master Mahāsay or M, the chronicler of Sri Ramakrishna's conversations.

Girish was a disciple of the heroic type. A poet, playwright, actor, and brilliant conversationalist, Girish was an outstanding member of Calcutta society. Prior to his meeting with the Master he used to drink heavily and lived a fast life. But his contact with Sri Ramakrishna gradually weaned him from his habit of drinking and completely transformed his character. Before, he had been a vehement atheist; now he became a religious zealot. Just as, formerly, he had not concealed from anyone his Bohemian mode of life, now he did not hide his love of God. The depth of his faith no one could fathom. He had given the Master his "power of attorney" and was convinced that the Master would do everything for him. Sri Ramakrishna highly praised his intellectual powers, his reasoning faculty, and his faith. He was one of the few disciples of the Master who proclaimed him fearlessly in public, during his lifetime, as a Divine Incarnation.

At first Girish simply regarded Holy Mother as the wife of his guru and cherished a high respect for her. One day he was pacing up and down the terrace of his house with his second wife, when the Mother was on the terrace of Balaram's residence near by. Girish's wife noticed her and said to him: "Look, there is the Mother walking on that terrace." Girish at once turned his face away and replied: "No, no. I have sinful eyes. I won't look at her that way. I cannot be a sneak." Forthwith he went down from the terrace.

Girish was the father of three children by his second wife: two girls, and a boy, after whose birth his wife died. He occupied himself with the study of arithmetic and the care of his son. Somehow he believed that Sri Ramakrishna himself was born as his son. In 1890 Girish, at the insistence of Swami Niranjananda,[1] paid his first visit to Holy Mother at the Udbodhan in the company of his three-year-old son. The little boy could not speak at that time and expressed himself through inarticulate sounds and gestures. He had seen the Mother before. Anxiously he pointed at the upper floor where the Mother lived and simply said: "Ooh! Ooh!" An attendant of the Mother took him upstairs and he rolled on the ground before her. Presently he came down and began to pull at his father's hand. Girish burst out crying and said: "How can I go to Mother? I am a great sinner." The boy would not leave him alone. Finally he took his son in his arms and climbed the stairs, his body trembling and his eyes streaming. Falling flat at the Mother's feet, he said: "It is through him that I have seen your sacred feet." Very soon the child died.

At the earnest request of Swami Niranjananda, Girish went to Jayrambati with a servant and a cook. Three young Swamis accompanied him. After bathing, Girish went to the Mother, his body quaking with emotion. Casting his eyes upon her, he exclaimed with surprise: "Ah, you are that Mother!" He suddenly recalled a vivid dream of many years before, when he had been bedridden with a serious illness. A goddess appeared to him and offered sacred prasād, which immediately cured him. He now recognized Holy Mother as that deity and felt that she had always been looking after him as his guardian angel. He asked the Mother: "What sort of mother are you?" At once Holy Mother replied: "Your real Mother, not just the wife of

---

[1] A monastic disciple of Sri Ramakrishna.

your guru, nor an adopted mother, nor a vague mother. Your real Mother."

Girish spent a happy and carefree time at Jayrambati, roaming freely with the villagers in the meadows and drinking in the beauty of the sunset in the open fields. Soon his fame spread over the locality and he sang now and then to entertain the simple folk. Holy Mother learnt from him the following song:

> Gopāla crawls off from the queen[2]
> Lest she should catch hold of him.
> He casts at her a furtive glance.
> As she eagerly cries, "Stop, stop!"
> Gopāla crawls farther off.

We have already described a heated discussion of Girish with one of the Mother's brothers regarding her divinity. Girish was soon completely tamed by the Mother's tender care for his comfort. Together they visited Sri Ramakrishna's birthplace. He asked her permission to embrace the monastic life and gave convincing reasons for doing so. But she persuaded him to live as a householder, devoting himself to writing plays depicting the Master's life and teachings. Girish returned to Calcutta a new man.

During one of his visits to her in Calcutta, Girish said to her: "Mother, whenever I visit you I feel like a small child in the presence of his mother. If I were your real son, I could have rendered you personal service. Here everything is contrary to law. You are taking care of us, and not we of you. At Jayrambati you cook for us, sitting by the rustic stove. How can we serve you? What do we know about serving the Mother of the Universe?" His voice became choked and his eyes red. Looking at the devotees Girish said: "It is very hard to believe that God is born as a human being—just like one of us. Can you even dream that the Divine Mother of the Universe is standing be-

---

[2] Refers to Yashodā, the Mother of Gopāla, the Baby Krishna.

fore you in the form of a simple village woman? Can you imagine that Mahāmāyā, like an ordinary woman, is performing household chores and other duties? Nonetheless she is the great Māyā, the great Śakti, the Mother of the Universe. She is incarnated to establish the ideal of God's Motherhood and assure liberation for all."

On one occasion when Holy Mother arrived in Calcutta from Jayrambati, the train was three hours late and she was very tired. Swami Brahmananda, Swami Premananda, and some other devotees were at the railway station. As Yogin-Mā and Golap-Mā helped her out of the train, the two Swamis rushed to take the dust of her feet. Golap-Mā in her high-pitched voice said to Swami Brahmananda: "Mahārāj,[3] have you no sense whatsoever? The Mother has just got off the train, tired and worn out by the burning sun; if you make such a fuss about prostrating, how can I restrain the others?" The venerable Swamis felt like culprits and stepped back. The Mother drove to her residence in a carriage and went upstairs. Girish had been waiting on the ground floor. Hearing his voice, Golap-Mā, the redoubtable *gendarme* of the Mother's household, came down and said to him: "My words beat a retreat, Girish Babu,[4] before your grotesque devotion. Say, Girish Babu, you have come here to see the Mother. And she is so tired! Without giving her a chance to rest you are here to torture her." Girish, equally bold, and looking straight at her, said: "She is surely a boisterous woman! I had thought that the Mother would soothe her heart by looking at her children's faces after such a long time, and this woman is teaching me devotion to the Mother! Phew!" When Golap-Mā complained to Holy Mother about Girish's rude words, she replied: "I have warned you many a time about criticizing my children."

During one of the annual festivals of the worship of Durgā,

---

[3] The affectionate and respectful term by which Swami Brahmananda was addressed by the devotees of Sri Ramakrishna.

[4] The word *Babu* is a term of respect used when addressing a man, like "Mr." in English.

Holy Mother went to Calcutta especially to participate in the religious ceremonies at Girish's house. She stayed with Balaram. Girish felt highly blessed when she attended the worship, the most auspicious hour of which happened to fall that year at midnight of the second day. Holy Mother was not feeling well; besides, she had attended the worship in the morning; so it was decided that she would not be present at the midnight worship. Girish felt completely crushed. Late that night, just before the worship was to begin, the Mother changed her mind, walked to Girish's house, knocked at the back door, and said: "Here, I have come." Girish's joy knew no bounds. He felt that Mother Durgā had graciously accepted his worship. When Girish died the Mother said sadly: "A veritable Indra has fallen."[5]

In striking contrast to Girish is Nag Mahāsaya, the personification of humility, lowliness, and self-effacement. A disciple of the Master, he hailed from Dacca, in East Bengal. Sri Ramakrishna once said of him: "He is like fire—a live coal." Swami Vivekananda said: "I have travelled in many parts of the world, but nowhere have I seen another soul as great as Nag Mahāsaya. He is greater than us in renunciation and self-control." Nag Mahāsaya regarded the Mother as Bhagavati Herself. Whenever he returned to Dacca from his visits to the Mother, he used to say to his devotees: "I have seen the Goddess Herself; I have received Her grace."

Nag Mahāsaya came several times from Dacca to visit Holy Mother. He first met her in 1893 when she was residing at Nilambar Babu's house on the Ganges at the village of Belur. At that time no male devotee was allowed in her presence. If any such came, a maidservant announced him and the Mother sent her blessings. When Nag Mahāsaya arrived, the maid said to her: "Mother, who is this Nag Mahāsaya? He is saluting you, but he is striking his head so hard against the floor that it is going to bleed. One of the Swamis is trying to restrain him,

---

[5] Indra is the king of the gods. The expression is used to denote the death of a great person.

but he says not a word and seems to be unconscious. Is he a madman?" The Mother was deeply moved to hear of his devotion and told her to ask an attendant Swami to bring him upstairs. The Swami brought him to her, holding him by the hand. His forehead was swollen and his steps were unsteady. Blinded by tears, he was not even able to see the Mother. He was in another world, as it were. Holy Mother, putting aside her usual bashfulness, made him sit by her side. Nag Mahāsaya was repeating only the word "Mother," as if insane, but otherwise he was quiet and peaceful. She wiped away his tears. Her meal of bread, fruits, and sweets was in front of her. She touched some of it to her tongue and gave him the prasād. She tried to feed him herself. But he could not swallow anything. He sat touching the Mother's feet and repeating the word "Mother." As she stroked his head and body for some time and repeated the Master's name, he gradually regained consciousness. Then Holy Mother began to eat and also to feed the devotee. Afterwards, when he was taken downstairs, he said again and again: "Not I, but Thou!" He left with the remark: "Mother is more compassionate than Father."[6]

On another occasion the Mother gave Nag Mahāsaya prasād on a leaf-plate. He ate both the food and the leaf, because he felt that the latter, too, was sanctified by the touch of the prasād. On a third occasion she gave him a new cloth. Instead of wearing the cloth, he always wrapped his head with it to show respect to the Mother's gift.

Nag Mahāsaya wanted to present Holy Mother with mangoes from his own trees. Once he carried a basket of mangoes on his head and thus came to the Mother. As a sign of his lowliness he wore a tattered cloth. Some of the best mangoes he had marked with white spots. At the Mother's residence he began to walk around with the basket on his head and would not give it to anybody. He inwardly desired to feed the Mother with his own hands. The Mother sent for him. When he came upstairs,

---

[6] Meaning Sri Ramakrishna.

she noticed that he was unconscious, as on other occasions, only repeating the name of the Master and the word "Mother." Some of the fruits were offered at the shrine. She ate a little, gave Nag Mahāsaya the prasād on a leaf, and asked him to eat. But how could he eat? He had no body-consciousness and his hands were paralysed, as it were. The Mother took hold of his hand and pressed him to eat, but he could not. At last he took a piece of mango and began to rub it on his head. Finally Swami Saradananda had him brought down.

Holy Mother showed Nag Mahāsaya tender affection even after his death. There hung on the walls of her room some pictures of the Master's disciples. Nag Mahāsaya's also was there. One day a devotee noticed the Mother wiping the glass of the photographs and kissing them, touching the chins. Looking at the picture of Nag Mahāsaya, she said: "How many devotees come here, but I see no one like him."

Mahendranath Gupta, a beloved disciple of Sri Ramakrishna, was headmaster of a school. He was versed in English literature and Western philosophy and culture. Many devotees of Sri Ramakrishna used to visit him. No matter how the conversation started, within several minutes he turned it to the teachings of the Master. Serene and soft-voiced, he was a man of few words and seldom expressed his inner feelings. He held the monks of the Ramakrishna Order in high respect and treated them with sweets whenever they visited him. The present writer, on the eve of his departure for America, was fed by M's own hands. In his presence the writer felt as if he was with a prophet of the Old Testament. M had a tall, well-built body, with fair complexion and flowing beard. He advised householder devotees to cultivate the company of monks.

Holy Mother cherished a special affection for M's family. From time to time M's wife spent a few days with her at Dakshineswar, and after the Master's death she accompanied her on her pilgrimages. M, too, visited several places with her and saw her at Jayrambati. Prior to the building of the Udbodhan, Holy Mother stayed at his house many times when she went to Calcutta. After the Master's death he gave her a small monthly allowance and made a substantial contribution to the building of the Mother's new house at Jayrambati.

We do not have any record that M was effusive in the expression of his emotion, but his devotion to her was very deep. One day a disciple of the Mother said to her at the Udbodhan: "Mother, I don't have any inner peace; my mind is restless. I am troubled by carnal cravings." Silently she looked at him for a while. The disciple repented having given her trouble and forthwith went to M, to whom he said: "Many a time you stroked the Master's feet. Please pass your hand over my head. My brain is heated." "What do you mean?" M said. "You are Mother's child and she loves you dearly. Why should you act like a beggar? Didn't she cast her glance upon you?"

"Yes. She kept looking at me for a long time."

"Then what should you worry about?"

Quoting from a Bengali song, he said: "A man swims in bliss if the Divine Mother casts Her benign look upon him." As he repeated the line thrice with great fervour, the devotee felt peace of mind and realized that the Mother herself had sent him to M to explain the meaning of her kind look.

Among the women disciples of Sri Ramakrishna, Golap-Mā and Yogin-Mā had known her intimately since the Dakshineswar days. They were her companions on her travels and pilgrimages, and visited her often at Jayrambati; Golap-Mā later lived with her at the Udbodhan. They were her friends and confidantes. Gopāler-Mā, who looked upon Sri Ramakrishna as Gopāla, her child, accepted Holy Mother as her daughter-in-law. Sister Nivedita became devoted to her, kept her in a room at her girls' school in her old age, and nursed her when she fell ill. Holy Mother visited her every now and then and often sent her meals. During the last days of Gopāler-Mā's life she remained practically unconscious of the world, but was extremely alert about her rosary. Without it she would be very

YOGIN-MĀ

GOLAP-MĀ

GOPALER-MĀ

GAURI-MĀ

LAKSHMI-DIDI

restless. She did not recognize anybody, but whenever Holy Mother came near she would say in a whisper: "Is it my daughter? Come!" Shortly before her death, one day the Mother went to her bedside and the saintly lady said feebly: "Is it you, Gopāla, who have come?" and stretched out her hand. Holy Mother could not understand what she meant. Then an attendant explained to her that the old lady was looking upon her as Gopāla and wanted to take the dust of her feet. The Mother let Gopāler-Mā touch her feet and gave her her blessings. Shortly after, Gopāler-Mā left the world.

Gauri-Mā, as we have already seen, was of masculine type. She was devoted to the Mother. The founder of the Sāradesvari Āshrama, a girls' school named after Holy Mother, she lived independently but visited her often alone or with her students when the Mother was in Calcutta. The present author first met her at Jayrambati in 1916, and the moving scene when they took leave of the Mother has been described. The writer recalls a rather amusing incident in this connection. At the time of departure the Mother told him several times to look after Gauri-Mā during the journey by bullock cart to Vishnupur and by train from Vishnupur to Calcutta. The train arrived at Howrah Station in the morning. As they came out of the station, the writer found to his dismay that the middle part of the bridge over the Ganges connecting Howrah with Calcutta was not there. Being a stranger to Calcutta and rather young, he became frightened and asked Gauri-Mā how they would cross the river. He did not know that the middle part of the bridge was opened during high tide for the passage of steamers. Gauri-Mā grabbed his hand with a laugh and took him to the ferryboat. Reaching the other side, she took him to the steamer station, helped him to purchase his ticket, put him on the boat, and gave him detailed directions about reaching the Belur Math, where he was going. She also asked him to visit her at her school, which he later did.

Holy Mother also had some Western women devotees who

visited her from time to time. These devotees first came to know about the Master and the Mother from Swami Vivekananda. Though the Mother lived as an orthodox Hindu widow, she associated with them freely. When she met Mrs. Ole Bull, the widow of the famous Norwegian violinist, she recalled a vision Sri Ramakrishna had of his future devotees with white skin. One day at Dakshineswar Sri Ramakrishna was absorbed in deep meditation when Sarada Devi entered the room. A slight noise made by her brought his mind down abruptly to the physical plane. The Master told her that a sudden disturbance of meditation might be injurious to him. Sarada Devi was distressed. In order to console her he said: "Do you know what I was seeing in meditation when you came in? I felt I was in a far-off country where people were of fair complexion. They were different from us and spoke a language I could not understand. As I was wondering about the vision, the Divine Mother revealed to me that they too would follow my teachings. How sincere their devotion was!" Narrating this incident, Sarada Devi said that the Master must have referred to devotees in the West.

Miss Josephine MacLeod, an American devotee of Swami Vivekananda, visited the Mother many, many times. One day she paid her respects to her at the Udbodhan and returned to the Belur Math at dusk. After attending the evening worship at the shrine of the Math and spending a little while in meditation, she was going back to her quarters at the guest house, accompanied by a brahmachāri with a lantern. She was walking slowly, absorbed in thought, when he heard her say to herself: "I have seen her! I have seen her!" Then she said to him in a whisper: "The Holy Mother! I have seen her." She walked all the way muttering the word "Mother" and adding some other words which her companion did not understand.

On another occasion Miss MacLeod went to Calcutta to pay her respects to Holy Mother. Many women devotees were coming into the Mother's room. As they entered they saluted her in Hindu fashion, kneeling on the ground and touching the Mother's feet with their foreheads. Miss MacLeod stood there for a few moments unable to decide how she should pay her respects. Holy Mother caught her eye and with a slight movement of the hand indicated that Western devotees need not imitate the Hindus. Miss MacLeod was impressed with the Mother's common sense, which she later spoke of as one of the Mother's most impressive characteristics.

Sister Christine Greenstidel, an American disciple of Swami Vivekananda, was a close companion of Sister Nivedita in the management of the girls' school started by Nivedita, and received many blessings from the Mother. As far as we know, she has not left behind any reminiscences of Holy Mother. But both Sister Nivedita and Sister Devamata have left their impression of her in their books.

Miss Laura F. Glenn, who later took the name of Devamata, was a member of the Vedanta Centre of Boston. She visited Holy Mother many times in Calcutta. When the Mother first blessed her, as the devotee recounts, "a spring of new life seemed to bubble up from my innermost heart and flood my being." A desire flashed in her mind that she might be allowed to render the Mother personal service by gently stroking her body. Immediately Holy Mother motioned Devamata to come near her. The Sister wrote in *Days in an Indian Monastery:* "It was a benediction to pass my hand over her delicate shapely body, but the marble paving grew hard as I knelt beside her. Again she divined the unspoken thought and made me sit instead of kneel. We had no common language, but when there was none to interpret for us, she spoke that deeper wordless language and we never failed to understand each other."

One day Holy Mother wanted Devamata to take two choice mangoes which a devotee had offered her. Devamata said that she would feel greater pleasure if Holy Mother kept them. The Mother's response came quickly: "Don't you think it will give me greater pleasure to have you take them?" Devamata's spontaneous answer seemed to please her: "It must give you greater pleasure because you have a larger heart to feel it."

"Hers was an all-embracing Mother's heart," Devamata wrote in her book, "which wrapped itself in love about every child born of woman, and her family was the human race. . . . Those who had the rare blessing of living with Holy Mother learned that religion was a sweet, natural, joyous thing; that purity and holiness were tangible realities; that the odour of sanctity was literally a sweet perfume overlaying and destroying the foulness of material selfishness. Compassion, devotion, and God-union were her very nature; one scarcely knew that she possessed them. It was through the sweet benediction of a word or touch that one sensed her presence.

"She lived like a lake or river. The sun may dry up its waters, but they fall again to refresh the earth. So these saintly ones in body may be lifted from our sight, but their holy influence falls back upon us to revive our fainting hearts and give us new spiritual life, new strength of purpose."

Sister Devamata said that Holy Mother could enjoy a joke and lose herself in play with as much zest as a little child. Once she brought a jack-in-the-box for Radhu from an English shop and the Mother greatly enjoyed the toy. Each time it sprang out with the familiar squeak, she repeated the sound and laughed heartily.

Sister Nivedita's name has already been mentioned several times. Margaret E. Noble, born of Irish parents, met Swami Vivekananda in London in 1895 at the house of Lady Isabel Margesson. She was then acting as the secretary of the Sesame Club, where Bernard Shaw, T. H. Huxley, and other men of literature and science discussed highly intellectual subjects. At once she came under the spell of the Swami's personality and gradually made up her mind to dedicate herself to the cause of the education of Hindu women. She became a disciple of the Swami, who gave her her Hindu name[7] and moulded her spirit-

---

[7] The word *Nivedita* means the Dedicated One.

ual life. Completely identified with Hindu thought, she inspired many Indian leaders in their love for their country and became an interpreter of its cultural ideals. She associated with Holy Mother intimately, even sometimes sharing her bed.

Nivedita arrived in India from England on January 28, 1898. At first she had her own living quarters. She met Holy Mother for the first time with Mrs. Ole Bull and Miss Mac-Leod on March 17. It was St. Patrick's Day and she mentioned it in her diary as "A Day of days." At the request of Miss Mac-Leod, Holy Mother ate with the Western devotees. In general she was very punctilious about observing orthodox Hindu habits, especially in the matter of food, and avoided eating with people outside her own caste. This partaking of food with the foreign ladies was, as it were, a sanction given by her to Hindu society to accept and absorb them into its fold. Swami Vivekananda mentioned this event in a letter to a brother disciple. He wrote: "Mother is here, and the European and American ladies went the other day to see her. And what do you think? Mother even ate with them! Isn't that grand?" Sister Nivedita, in the course of a letter to a friend in London, wrote: "She is the very soul of sweetness—so gentle and loving—and merry as a girl. She has always been terribly orthodox, but all this melted away the instant she saw the first Westerners. Fruit is always presented by visitors, and this was naturally offered to her by us. And she, to the surprise of everyone, accepted it. This gave us all a dignity and made my future work possible in a way nothing else could have done." After a while she was given a separate room near Holy Mother's house at Baghbazar, in the northern section of Calcutta. Gradually, through the kindness of Holy Mother, she was accepted as a member of the household. This paved the way to her being accepted by orthodox Hindu society.

Sister Nivedita has left reminiscences of Holy Mother's life of this period. Swami Yogananda lived in a small room on the ground floor of the house and acted as the Mother's guardian.

Among the women devotees who associated with her intimately were Golap-Mā, Yogin-Mā, Gopāler-Mā, and Lakshmi—all widows. Long before dawn they awoke and sat for meditation. On special days one of them accompanied the Mother when she went to the Ganges to bathe. The Mother herself performed the daily worship in the shrine. In the afternoon many women devotees from Calcutta visited her. Men devotees—mostly her own disciples—came to her twice a week. She talked to them through an elderly lady. The Mother often indulged in light talk with the women devotees. In the evening, after the worship, they sang hymns together and again meditated. The Mother showed a special affection for Nivedita and often asked her to sit near her when she meditated. Nivedita always called this time the "hour of peace," and wrote: "A tremendous dynamic power emanated from Sarada Devi while she remained completely absorbed within herself. She touched upon the very heart of life." One evening, as the Mother was about to get up, Nivedita came and laid her head at the Mother's feet. Holy Mother placed her hand on her head and for a long time stroked it as she blessed her. "Now," she said, "your work is about to begin."

On November 12, 1898, Holy Mother graced with her presence the dedication of the girls' school started by Nivedita, later known as the Sister Nivedita Girls' School. She gave the following blessing in a low voice: "May the Divine Mother of the Universe bless the school. May the girls trained here be ideals for society." Nivedita said afterwards that she could not dream of a better omen for the future education of Indian womanhood than these words. The Mother visited the school many times.

Holy Mother loved Nivedita dearly and addressed her as Khooki.[8] Once Nivedita gave her a small silver box, in which she preserved some of Sri Ramakrishna's hair. It was her habit to cherish even insignificant gifts from her devotees. She used

----

[8] Meaning "Baby."

to say: "Things may be cheap, but the memories associated with them are precious." Regarding the silver box she often remarked: "Whenever I look at the box at the time of worship, I am reminded of Nivedita. One day she said to me: 'Mother, I was a Hindu in my previous birth. I was born this time in Great Britain to spread the Master's teaching there.' " In one of her trunks Holy Mother kept an old tattered silk cloth, which her attendant wanted to throw away. "No, child," she said. "Nivedita gave it to me with great love. Let us preserve it." She carefully folded the cloth, put it back in the box, and said: "The sight of it brings back Nivedita's memory. How wonderful she was! At first she could not speak to me directly. Someone had to interpret her words into Bengali. Afterwards she learnt our language. She loved my mother very much." One day Nivedita said to Shyamasundari: "Grandmother, I shall go to your village and cook in your kitchen." The old lady said at once: "No, child, you must not do that. Our people will ostracize me if you enter my kitchen."

It was by Mrs. Ole Bull's arrangement that the photograph of Holy Mother which is generally worshipped by devotees was taken in 1898. Sister Nivedita fixed her hair and clothes when the picture was taken.

Nivedita's deep feeling for Holy Mother was expressed in the following letter written from Cambridge, Massachusetts, on December 11, 1910, at the time of Sara Bull's illness:

"Beloved Mother,

"This morning early, I went to church—to pray for Sara. All the people there were thinking of Mary, the Mother of Jesus, and suddenly I thought of you. Your dear face, and your loving look, and your white sāri and your bracelets. It was all there. And it seemed to me that yours was the presence that was to soothe and bless poor Sara's sickroom. And—do you know?—I thought I had been very foolish to sit in your room, at the evening service to Sri Ramakrishna, trying to meditate. Why did I not understand that it was quite enough to be a little child at your dear feet? Dear Mother! You are full of love! And it is not a flushed and violent love like ours, and like the world's, but a gentle peace that brings good to everyone and wishes ill to none. It is a golden radiance, full of play. What a blessed Sunday that was, a few months ago, when I ran in to you, the last thing before I went on the Ganges, and ran back to you for a moment, as soon as I came back! I felt such a wonderful freedom in the blessing you gave me, and in your welcome home! Dearest Mother, I wish we could send you a wonderful hymn, or a prayer. But somehow even that would seem too loud, too full of noise! Surely you are the most wonderful thing of God— Sri Ramakrishna's own chalice of his Love for the world—a token left with his children, in these lonely days, and we should be very still and quiet before you—except indeed for a little fun! Surely the 'wonderful things of God' are all quiet—stealing unnoticed into our lives—the air and the sunlight and the sweetness of gardens and of the Ganges. These are the silent things that are like you!

"Do send to poor Sara the mantle of your peace. Isn't your thought, now and then, of the high calm that neither loves nor hates? Isn't that a sweet benediction that trembles in God, like the dewdrop on the lotus leaf, and touches not the world?

"Ever, my darling Mother, your foolish Khooki

Nivedita"

When Nivedita died, in 1911, Holy Mother shed tears and said: "What sincere devotion Nivedita had! She never considered anything too much that she might do for me. She often came to me at night. Seeing that light struck my eyes, she put a shade of paper around the lamp. She would prostrate herself before me with great tenderness and take the dust of my feet with her handkerchief. I felt that she hesitated even to touch my feet." As the women devotees present expressed their sorrow at Nivedita's death, Holy Mother said: "All creatures weep for a great soul."

Holy Mother and Sister Nivedita

Holy Mother

Further Glimpses

HOLY MOTHER WAS WELL BUILT for a Hindu woman of Bengal. She had a fair complexion and was of medium height, though in several of her photographs she gives the impression of being rather tall. The soles of her feet were ruddy. Her thick black hair, which Yogin-Mā used to braid, almost reached her knees. Before Sri Ramakrishna's death she usually wore a white sāri with a wide red border. She also wore a few gold ornaments which the Master had given her: two for her upper arms, bracelets for her wrists, a necklace, and rings for her nose and ears. When the Master gave her these ornaments he said to Hriday, jokingly: "I suppose that's all there is to my relationship with her." As already mentioned, after wearing them a short while she discarded most of them. After the Master's death she wore a single gold bracelet on each wrist. Speaking of her own appearance, she once remarked: "I was rather pretty in my youth. Later I became a little stout." Women often were struck by her physical beauty. As Golap-Mā said, she looked like a goddess. While meditating she appeared radiant. Swami Premananda's mother once asked her: "Mother, where did you get such celestial beauty and charm?" Once Sri Ramakrishna compared her to Sarasvati, a goddess of exquisite beauty and grace. Her fair complexion later became somewhat dark. By the time she was fifty, when most of her disciples saw her, she had again become slim from repeated attacks of malaria at Jayrambati, and she appeared pale. Towards the end of her life she developed a slight stoop and often limped because of rheumatism.

Holy Mother's immaculate purity, her unceasing meditation and prayer, her all-embracing compassion and utter selflessness, endowed her with the delicacy and tenderness of a maiden, a subtle grace and quiet dignity, and withal guilelessnesss and simplicity. Her innate motherliness put visitors at ease. To a person coming to her for the first time, she conveyed the feeling that she had been eagerly waiting for him. Holy Mother always inspired reverence but never a feeling of remoteness. During her later years, on rare occasions, a superficial observer would be deceived by her unassuming manner. During her last visit to Benares Holy Mother was one day seated with Golap-Mā and several other companions, when a woman who had never before seen her came in and wanted to show her respect. Her eyes first fell upon the dignified figure of Golap-Mā. As she moved towards her to take the dust of her feet, Golap-Mā at once pointed out Holy Mother. Now she approached the Mother, but the latter, out of innocent mischief, indicated by her finger that Golap-Mā was the one she was looking for. Golap-Mā again directed her attention to Holy Mother, but the Mother again pointed at Golap-Mā. This teasing game continued for some time. Then Golap-Mā said to the stranger, rather sharply: "Can't you distinguish a divine face from a human one?" The woman at last discovered the elusive grace and charm of the Mother's face.

Holy Mother, unlike any other orthodox Hindu widow, wore, after the Master's death, a sāri with a narrow red border, using it as skirt, blouse, and veil. Before strangers she covered herself practically from head to foot with an additional white cotton cloth. Once, during the cold season, she was given a thin woollen undershirt. She expressed pleasure at this gift and used it for three days. On the fourth day she took it off and said to the devotees: "Is it proper for a woman to wear a shirt? I put it on for three days just to please you."

Sri Ramakrishna used to speak of two kinds of illumined persons. One consists of ordinary human beings who through the practice of spiritual disciplines attain the knowledge of Brahman and merge in the Supreme Spirit. They are no longer concerned with the activities of the transitory phenomenal world. The others are God-men, born perfect, who have a special message for humanity. After the realization of their true nature, they remain at the phenomenal level, working for the spiritual regeneration of their fellow creatures. God becomes manifest through God-men. The Infinite sings its melody through their finite minds and bodies. Hence the sport of God as man, the Naralila, is so appealing. Reason cannot unravel this mystery, but the heart may enjoy it.

It is extremely difficult for ordinary men to recognize God when He is embodied as man. An apparent victim of hunger and thirst, pain and pleasure, hope and despair, sickness and fear, he weeps, laughs, and suffers without really losing awareness of his divine nature. In the God-man humanity blends with Divinity. When living at the phenomenal level, the God-man is alert about human affairs, possesses practical knowledge and realism, and observes the conventions of society. Side by side with divine ecstasies, he cultivates humility, magnanimity, ethical sensitivity, love, the spirit of service, modesty, and other similar traits in order to set a model for others. He also shows how one living in the world can rise above it and enjoy inner peace in the midst of life's turmoil and worry.

The life of Holy Mother is a demonstration of these facts. Though an embodiment of Divinity, she identified herself of her own accord with the lives of her relatives, the people of her village, and her devotees. She rejoiced at the happiness of others and wept at their suffering. Purposely she often suppressed her true nature, because, as she said, "the excessive manifestation of Divinity creates fear in the minds of devotees; they cannot feel intimate." Once a disciple spoke of her being the Divine Mother and she said: "You always harp on that one theme. I say that I am your mother, and that does not satisfy you." Her language was simple and natural, and her conduct spontaneous and unostentatious. She never lost these characteristics, even while giving initiation or spiritual instruction. In her conduct she was always alert, remembering that in the future people would regard her as an ideal to follow. She never forgot that she was a woman.

Her brothers regarded her as their affectionate big sister, her nieces and nephews as their indulgent aunt, and her disciples as their mother. Many ladies, after visiting her, said that she was just like one of them. Yet she said to a disciple that, even in the midst of all her activities, by a mere wish she could remember her divine nature in a flash, and realize the world to be the playground of māyā. If she was constantly conscious of her true self, how could she fulfil her mission?

How humble she was! Once when she was ill an ordinary priest was called in to perform some special worship for her recovery. After the ceremony she took the dust of his feet. When someone told her of his having a loose character, she remarked: "That may be. One must show respect for the brāhminical garb. The Master was not born to break traditions." Often she said to her disciples that she constantly prayed for the total effacement of her ego. And yet she once said openly: "I am the Primordial Power, the Mother of the Universe. I have assumed this body out of compassion for the world. I have been born in every epoch in the past; I shall be born, too, in the future."

She respected the traditions and norms of society. One notices here a difference between Holy Mother and Buddha and Śankarāchārya. Buddha repudiated the gods, religious rituals, the scriptures, and the caste system as obstacles to attaining the freedom of Nirvāna. Śankarāchārya accepted all these as preparatory disciplines for the knowledge of Brahman, which he said could be attained only by monks who renounced the world and went beyond rituals, worship, and social conven-

tion. Holy Mother, however, though practising true renunciation, remained a householder and till the end of her life
respected the gods, rituals, and social proprieties. She performed religious rites and showed veneration even to a minor
deity such as the village goddess Simhavāhini. Someone said to
her: "Mother, why do you do that? Everything happens by your
will alone." The Mother replied: "If you vow to worship gods
and goddesses at the time of illness, you can be cured by their
grace. Besides, everyone should get his due." Before she started
on a trip she consulted the almanac for the auspicious day, according to the Hindu belief. She enjoyed listening to the reading of Hindu religious books.

Generally Holy Mother obeyed caste rules; but she often
made exceptions in the case of her disciples, especially about
food restrictions. In her opinion devotees of God belonged to a
single caste, a spiritual family. About other social matters she
used her discrimination and common sense and did not wan-
tonly violate social standards. In most respects Holy Mother
lived as a Hindu widow of the brāhmin caste, though Sri
Ramakrishna had assured her that he was not really dead. An
orthodox Hindu widow is not permitted to remarry and thus
leads the austere life of a nun. This austerity is all the more
rigorous in the case of a brāhmin widow. She avoids such food,
clothes, and ornaments as may stimulate her physical desires.
Thus she is permitted to eat a full vegetarian meal at midday,
but takes only fruit and milk at night. She cannot eat certain
foods, such as onions or garlic. A widow in Bengal uses a white
sāri without a border, cuts her hair short, and gives up all ornaments. Through these strict disciplines imposed on widows, the
Hindu lawgivers constantly reminded them of the ideal of
chastity, which is deeply ingrained in the Indian mind. They
wanted widows to be living examples of simplicity, renunciation, purity, non-attachment, and the spirit of unselfish service.
A Hindu widow, who is free from many ordinary worldly en-
tanglements, has an opportunity to devote her time to worship

and prayer, visit shrines and holy places, and minister to the needs of the other members of the family. If she remarried, the Hindu lawgivers contended, some of her sisters would not have a chance to get husbands. It is said that in any highly developed society the number of women eligible for marriage is usually higher than that of men. A widow, it is argued, has had her opportunity to lead a happy married life, but on account of her past karma, or for some other reason, she has lost it. To be sure, not all Hindu widows accept this situation cheerfully. But they are not really as unhappy as many non-Hindus believe, because in general they are conditioned from birth by the spiritual ideals and disciplines of the race.

Holy Mother observed some of these rules. Like a Hindu widow, she was a vegetarian, but again, unlike a Hindu widow, she did not cut her hair, wore gold bracelets, put on a sāri with a narrow red border, and ate a light supper at night. On many occasions she did not observe the pollution of food by touch, especially when some of her non-brāhmin women disciples touched her plate. She regarded all her disciples as her own children. But during her last illness she refused to eat bread from a Moslem bakery. For some young widows who were her disciples she relaxed the strict rules about food, saying to one of them: "What good will it do to torture the soul?" To another she said: "If the soul's craving for food is not satisfied, one commits an offence."

Holy Mother condemned the morbid passion for purity, especially regarding pollution by touch, that people show in the name of religious orthodoxy. But she never encouraged or condoned carelessness, and she disapproved of vanity.

Holy Mother was practical and realistic about mundane affairs. She learned to be so from Sri Ramakrishna at Kamarpukur after her marriage, and later at Dakshineswar. For example, she scolded some of her disciples for going on foot to Jayrambati from Koalpara on a stormy night and said: "This kind of rashness is not right." She advised a young widowed disciple to entrust a competent person with the management of her property. The Mother asked a monastic disciple to go home and quickly arrange for the support of his mother, remarking: "A woman does not generally know how to make proper use of money. You had better arrange it yourself. But finish the job quickly; if you delay you may feel an attraction for money. Money raises difficult problems. You may think that you are not interested in it and that, once having renounced it, you will never again be attached to it. But never cherish such foolish ideas. Through some loophole money will strangle you before you know it." The Mother reprimanded an elderly lady for being over-strict about her daughter-in-law. A brahmachāri who attended the Mother at Jayrambati offered the milkman an excessive price for milk if the man did not adulterate it with water. Coming to learn about it, the Mother said to him sharply: "What have you done? Don't you know that you are raising the price of milk and making it hard for the villagers to buy it? It is the milkman's nature to mix water with milk. If the price is raised, he will add more of it to earn a higher profit." After the construction of the Mother's new house, the village headman put a high tax on it and obtained the amount from her attendant. The Mother was then in Calcutta. After her return she learnt about it and said: "Why should we pay such a high tax? Try to cut it down. I may be able to pay it, but how can the monks and brahmachāris who will live here after my death do so? They may have to get their food by begging." One day Swami Vivekananda dismissed a servant for stealing money. The servant went to Holy Mother at the Udbodhan and said to her with tears in his eyes: "Mother, I am very poor and cannot manage my expenses with my small salary. I have a big family. That is why I acted that way." In the afternoon Swami Premananda came to her house and the Mother said to him: "Look here, Baburam, this man is very poor. Being harassed by want he stole the money. But why should Naren scold him and send him away? You are all monks and do not realize the afflictions of householders. Take this servant back." When told that this might annoy Swami Vivekananda, she said with firmness: "Take him back; I am asking you to do so." When Swami Premananda returned to the Belur. Math with the servant, Swami Vivekananda said: "See what Baburam has done; he has brought back that fellow." But when he heard what the Mother had said, the Swami did not utter another word and took him back.

Holy Mother highly disapproved of carelessness and waste. Once, after sweeping the courtyard at Jayrambati, someone threw the broom aside carelessly. She reprimanded the person, saying that the broom could have been treated a little more gently. Everything should be shown proper respect. On another occasion, at the Udbodhan, she expressed her displeasure because an empty basket was thrown away by one of the inmates. She said to the monks that, being world-renouncers, they might not care for a trivial thing like a basket, but nonetheless it could have been preserved for some other useful purpose. One day she gave a disciple a special dish of food that she had prepared. The quantity was too great. He ate what he could and was about to throw away the rest when the Mother asked him to give it to a poor neighbour. Afterwards she said to the disciple: "We should give everyone his due. What is not edible for man, give to a cow; what is not edible for a cow, give to a dog; what is not edible for a dog, throw into a lake for fishes to eat. But never waste."

In her attitude towards money or ornaments, Holy Mother showed an outward contrast with Sri Ramakrishna. The Master, an embodiment of renunciation, could not bear any contact with money or gold. The Mother, on the other hand, respected them. She often touched an ornament to her head out of respect. When someone reminded her of the Master's extreme dislike of gold, she replied guilelessly: "Why do you compare me with him? I am a woman. He had gold ornaments made for me." Though she respected money, she was unattached to it;

she put it away in a box and never kept an account. An attendant looked after it, and she was an indifferent witness of her income and expenses. Though outwardly involved in the world, she was inwardly unattached.

Though the serious side of Holy Mother's life has been emphasized, it should not be overlooked that now and then she acted like a simple, guileless girl. When she first came to Calcutta, as she turned on the water tap—something she had never seen in her village—the air pressure made a hiss, and she quickly ran away. She told people there was a snake in the pipe. Everybody laughed and she too enjoyed the fun. In her village home there was a hurricane lantern whose chimney was protected by a wire net. She did not know how to take it out and once said: "The lantern is a complicated piece of machinery. I do not know how to remove the glass." She envied a girl who could wind a clock. She was nervous about crossing the Ganges in a country boat and was afraid of ghosts. When a monk died at the Belur Math, all the inmates of the Udbodhan, except one, went to the monastery. He was asked to sleep on the porch outside the Mother's bedroom. After putting Radhu to sleep she came out, sat near him, and asked: "Are you afraid of ghosts?" "We are the children of the Divine Mother," he replied. "What can they do to us?"

Mother: "But I am afraid of ghosts."

Disciple: "Yes, I know it. You are frightened by your goblins and imps."[1]

Mother (with a laugh): "You are right, my child. They are terrible; they shrivel up my innards and make them stick to my belly."

Holy Mother urged the monks to shun idleness, and she herself was intensely active both in Calcutta and at Jayrambati. Her life in both places generally followed the same pattern. She always got up at three in the morning, as was her habit during the Dakshineswar days, and did not retire before eleven o'clock

[1] Referring to her troublesome relatives.

at night. We have already given a routine of her daily life at the Udbodhan. At Jayrambati, where she was mistress of the house, she busied herself with various household activities and at the same time talked to her intimate attendants. When she was in good health she also took part in the more strenuous household duties, like scouring utensils, carrying water from the tank, or husking paddy. The Mother herself made the arrangements for the daily worship, such as gathering flowers, at which she was sometimes assisted by her nieces or devotees. After the worship she went into the kitchen and relieved the cook, who would then go out for her refreshment or to attend to any other personal needs. She herself cooked most of the food to be offered to the Master in the shrine. In the afternoon many villagers visited her with their children and grandchildren to show her their respect, and they always got something to eat. She generally gave initiation in the morning, and had mail read to her either in the morning or in the evening, according to her leisure, and dictated replies. In earlier days Holy Mother with her own hands served all the devotees their meals, and she herself ate only after they had finished eating. Sometimes she worked in the kitchen in the evening in order to relieve the cook from over-work. The rest of the routine was about the same as in Calcutta.

One evening an attendant was reading her a letter from a disciple. It was full of eulogy and adoration. After listening to it she remarked: "Often I say to myself, I am but the daughter of Ram Mukherjee. Many of my contemporaries are still alive at Jayrambati. In what respect do I differ from them? Devotees come from unknown places and prostrate themselves before me. I am told that some of them are judges and some lawyers. Why should they come to me in this way?" The answer to her query was given by herself. She once said: "People call me the Divine Mother. I think, maybe they are right. How otherwise can one explain the strange things that have happened in my life? Yogin and Golap know much about them. If I say to myself that a certain thing should happen, the wish is always fulfilled."

Holy Mother, in a unique way, fulfilled the duties of wife, mother, and nun. There have been before in the world the ideal wife, the ideal mother, and the ideal nun, but a combination of the three in one person is rare indeed. Holy Mother was wedded to Sri Ramakrishna at the age of five, lived with him as long as he lived, and ministered to his physical needs in the best tradition of a Hindu wife. She was his companion in spiritual life. She demonstrated that wifely devotion and love are possible without demanding physical satisfaction from one's mate. In spite of her marriage she remained a nun, pure in body and mind, and in uninterrupted communion with God. Though she had no children of the flesh, she had many of the spirit. Like an earthly mother she looked after her disciples' physical comfort. But unlike an earthly mother she was totally unattached in her love and expected no return from it. Truly Sister Nivedita declared that Holy Mother was Sri Ramakrishna's last word on the ideal of Indian womanhood. But why of Indian womanhood alone? She can very well represent the universal ideal of womanhood.

There existed an extraordinary relationship between Sri Ramakrishna and Holy Mother. She often spoke of herself as his handmaid and instrument, as one of the many seekers who found refuge at his feet. When a devotee asked her advice she said: "I do not know anything. I repeat only what I have heard from the Master. Read *The Gospel of Sri Ramakrishna* and you will know all you need." To another who asked her blessing she said: "The Master will bless you." How often she asked her disciples to pray for her so that she might not have a trace of vanity. She repeatedly asked the devotees to cling to Sri Ramakrishna in order to avoid the pitfalls of life. One day a disciple, asked about his welfare, said that through her blessing he was well. "You all make the same mistake," she rebuked him. "Why do you bring me into everything? Can't you speak of the Master? Don't you see that everything happens by his will?" Regarding the Master she stated: "He is the Supreme God and the Supreme Goddess. He is the essence of all mantras and the embodiment of all deities. He is Purusha and Prakriti, and contains in himself all the deities." She carried Sri Ramakrishna's picture everywhere and worshipped it daily, seeing in it his living presence. Often she remarked that one should not make a distinction between the physical body and its shadow in a picture. It has already been said how intimately she talked with the Master and fed him in the picture. And yet she did not conceal the fact that she and the Master were identical and that there was no difference between them except in outer form.

Sri Ramakrishna, too, knew Holy Mother's nature. He spoke of her as the bestower of wisdom, as his own Śakti. Once, seeing Latu meditating in the Panchavati, he said to him: "You fool, the Deity whom you are contemplating is working herself to death by scouring pots and pans." Here are a few other statements of his about her: "The Mother who is in the temple is the same as the mother who dwells in the Nahabat." "If she is displeased with a person, it is beyond even my power to protect him." "If she is angry she can destroy everything." "If anybody gives me an offering, I send it to the Nahabat; otherwise how will the giver attain liberation?" We have seen that as the culmination of his spiritual practices, the Master formally worshipped Holy Mother as the Divine Mother of the Universe.

In this book Holy Mother has been described by such epithets as the Divine Mother, the Mother of the Universe, Prakriti, Śakti or Power, Mahāśakti or the Great Power, and Mahāmāyā or the Great Deluder. These epithets are not sentimental expressions but have a noetic meaning. In the chapter entitled "Spiritual Practices" it has been explained why Hinduism worships God as the Mother. Like modern science, Hinduism describes Śakti or Energy as the creator of physical objects and the source of the universe. But according to science this inert and non-intelligent energy is a self-creating, self-preserving, and self-dissolving category. It does not need extraneous help to project phenomena. According to Hinduism, Śakti is the potency of Brahman and inseparable from It, like fire and its power to burn. The potency is unable to function by itself. Brahman, which is Existence, Consciousness, and Bliss, by Its mere presence impregnates Śakti, as it were. Thus names and forms are evolved. The why and wherefore of the infinite Brahman's becoming the manifold creation, or the One's becoming the many, or the Absolute's appearing as the relative, is a profound mystery which cannot be solved by the human mind. After projecting the universe, Śakti casts a spell on the creatures in order to perpetuate the creation. Hence She is called Mahāmāyā, the Great Deluder. The Creative Energy contains in Her womb the seeds of creation and nourishes the creatures after giving birth to them. Finally, at the end of a cosmic cycle, She withdraws the universe into Herself.

All women, in a sense, function as the Divine Energy. But Her fullest manifestation is seen through the body and the mind of a woman of unblemished character. Holy Mother was such a woman. Hence she is regarded as the Supreme Goddess or Great Power, a special manifestation of the Divine Energy. Once a devotee said to her that after her no one would worship the minor goddesses of the Hindu religion. She replied: "Why, they too are parts of me." Conscious of her divine nature, she kindled the sparks of spirituality in her disciples, accepted their worship, and gave them assurance of liberation.

Final Years

BEFORE RESUMING the chronological account of Holy Mother's life, which we interrupted at 1898, the year of the dedication of the Belur Math, we shall briefly recapitulate its principal events up to 1909, when she moved to her permanent residence at the Udbodhan.

The death of Swami Yogananda, her beloved disciple, in 1899, moved the Mother deeply. Shortly thereafter Swami Vivekananda started on his second trip to America, with Holy Mother's blessings, accompanied by Swami Turiyananda and Sister Nivedita. That day, at noon, the Mother gave them and other Swamis of the Belur Math a sumptuous feast. The same year she suffered a bereavement in the death of her brother Abhay, who was dearest to her among her brothers. The following year Radhu was born. In 1902 Swami Vivekananda passed away when the Mother was at Jayrambati, and she silently bore this irreparable loss.

In 1904 Holy Mother came again to Calcutta, where she lived in a rented house, Swami Saradananda acting as caretaker. She was not well at this time. In a letter, Sister Nivedita wrote: "Holy Mother is here, so small, so thin, so dark—worn out physically, I should say, with village hardship and village life— but the same clear mind, the same stateliness, the same womanhood as before. O how many comforts I would like to give her! She needs a soft pillow, a shelf, and so many things. She is so crowded. People are about her, always."

About this time Holy Mother visited the retreat at Kankurgachi, in the suburbs of Calcutta, established by Ramchandra Dutta, a householder disciple of Sri Ramakrishna, and was received with great respect. A new cloth was spread over the pathway, and her coming was announced by the blowing of conch shells. The Mother's face was veiled and her body covered by a shawl. Numerous devotees prostrated themselves before her and she had to spend many hours in one position in the hot and humid weather.

During her stay in Calcutta, Holy Mother was often taken out in the carriage of the Nivedita Girls' School for visits to the Municipal Market, the Zoological Garden, the Botanical Garden, and other places of interest, all of which she enjoyed immensely. During this same year the Mother made her second pilgrimage to Puri in the company of some relatives and devotees. A few days after her arrival, she developed a painful abscess on one foot, but she refused to see a doctor. Swami Premananda had to play a trick. He invited a young doctor and sent him to the Mother to take the dust of her feet. While prostrating himself before her, the doctor took out his knife, opened the abscess, and quickly left the room, saying: "Mother, please forgive me for my offence." The Mother was wrapped in a shawl and did not notice anything. Immediately a disciple squeezed the pus from the abscess. Though she at first scolded him for hurting her, she felt relieved. In Puri she visited the different shrines and improved in health. She made jokes with her women companions. One of them, M's wife, said to her: "We never knew that you were such fun!" The Mother replied: "How few my jokes are! You have seen the Master; he knew so many. His joking knew no end."

In 1905 Holy Mother lost her uncle Nilmadhav and in 1906 her own mother and Gopāler-Mā. In the meantime the flow of devotees continued, both in Calcutta and in Jayrambati. In 1907 Swami Arupananda, the chronicler of Holy Mother's conversations, paid her his first visit. The same year, in the autumn, she went to Calcutta to witness the worship of Durgā at

Girish's house. From that time her name became widely known and devotees began to stream in. This tide went on unchecked till the day of her death, thirteen years later.

In 1909 Swami Saradananda went to Jayrambati to settle the division of the ancestral property among Holy Mother's brothers. In the meantime her permanent residence at the Udbodhan was built and she moved into it on May 23. In this house Holy Mother's spiritual ministry continued unabated till her death.

In June 1909 the Mother was laid up at the Udbodhan with an attack of chicken-pox; after her recovery she returned to Jayrambati. In January 1910 she came to Calcutta, still in indifferent health. Balaram's wife earnestly requested her, for a change, to visit Kothar in Orissa where her family owned an estate. Holy Mother agreed and left Calcutta on December 5, 1910, accompanied by several members of the Ramakrishna Order, men devotees, and relatives, including Radhu. At Kothar she spent about two months and initiated a number of disciples. The local postmaster, a brāhmin, had in his youth become a convert to Christianity in order to marry a Christian girl. The marriage was not a success and the repentant man was converted again to Hinduism with Holy Mother's permission, and finally initiated by her. One of her disciples, having noticed that she was a vegetarian, gave up eating fish and flesh. When she pressed him to resume his old food habit, the disciple referred to her own vegetarianism. The Mother replied: "Do you think that I eat only through one mouth? Don't be foolish. I am asking you to eat fish and flesh."[1] The disciple

---

[1] A similar incident is recorded in the life of Sri Ramakrishna. The Master was then suffering from cancer of the throat. It was very painful for him to swallow even liquid food. A pundit one day told him that a yogi like himself could easily get rid of his ailment by concentrating his mind on the affected part. But the Master replied that he could not divert to his body the mind which he had given to God. Though the pundit was silenced, young Narendra begged the Master to concentrate his mind on his throat. Sri Ramakrishna told him that he could not do anything of his own will and that everything depended upon the Divine Mother. There-

obeyed her. At Kothar she experienced many spiritual moods. Among them was the startling one, which we have already described, in which she declared herself as the Power of Sri Ramakrishna, embodied from time to time out of compassion for humanity.

About this time someone proposed a pilgrimage to Rameswar, at the southern tip of India, an important sacred place where, according to the *Rāmāyana*, Rāma and Sitā, on their return from Ceylon after the destruction of Rāvana, first touched the soil of India and where Sitā made an image of Śiva and worshipped it. Holy Mother cheerfully said: "Yes, I shall go to Rameswar. My father-in-law, too, visited the place." Swami Saradananda heartily approved of the idea and Swami Ramakrishnananda, the head of the Ramakrishna Math at Madras, undertook the entire responsibility for the trip. The party of several devotees and relatives, including Radhu, left for Madras during the early part of 1911. At dawn the railway train passed by Chilka Lake, which is studded with small islands. With the sunrise, vapours of various forms arose from the water and birds began to sing melodiously. Holy Mother enjoyed the natural scene. After spending the night at Berhampore, in the district of Ganjam, the pilgrims arrived in Madras at noon of the second day and received a hearty welcome from Swami Ramakrishnananda and the local devotees.

In Madras Holy Mother stayed about a month in a two-storey house rented for her. There she visited the Aquarium, the Fort, and the important temples and also had her first rickshaw ride. Many men and women of Madras received initiation from her. An American brahmachāri, too, was initiated

---

upon Narendra asked him to pray to the Divine Mother about it. The Master said that he would try. After a short while the disciple entered the Master's room and found him in a melancholy mood. He said to Narendra that he had asked the Divine Mother about curing his throat so that he could swallow some food, but Her reply crushed him. The Mother had said to him: "Are you not eating through many mouths? Must you eat through only one mouth?"

there. Neither the Mother nor the new disciples understood one another's language, and yet the disciples followed her instructions regarding japa and meditation without the help of an interpreter. But in general conversation an interpreter was needed. Several of these disciples had already seen Sri Ramakrishna and Holy Mother in dreams. She said later: "When asking for initiation they all just repeated the word 'dream.'"

From Madras Holy Mother and her companions went to Rameswar, halting on the way at Madura to worship the well-known Sundareśvar Śiva and His Consort Minākshi. Rameswar was situated in the territory of the Rājā of Ramnad, a disciple of Swami Vivekananda, who referred the Mother to his local officials as the "guru of my guru, the Supreme Guru." Arrangements were made by the Rājā for her comfort. Every day she worshipped Śiva in the main temple and witnessed the evening service. One day while worshipping the image, the Mother suddenly said: "I see it is just the same as when I placed it here." When asked by the devotees what she meant, she replied: "Never mind; I was absent-minded and it was a slip of the tongue." As already mentioned, it was Sītā, the Consort of Rāma, who had installed the image at Rameswar. On several occasions Holy Mother spoke of her identity with her.

The Rājā of Ramnad had given orders to his officers to open the royal treasures for Holy Mother and offer her anything she asked for. When informed about it, the Mother said that she felt no need of any gift, as Swami Ramakrishnananda had provided every comfort for her. In order to avoid hurting their feelings, however, she suggested that Radhu might ask for something if she felt like doing so. Though she said this out of politeness, yet her heart palpitated as she looked at the diamonds and other precious stones sparkling in their cases. She fervently prayed to the Master that Radhu might not ask for any of these. To everybody's surprise, Radhu looked at the treasures and said: "What shall I take from here? I don't require these things. I have lost my pencil; you may buy one for me." Holy Mother sighed with relief and bought a pencil for her niece at a neighbouring store.

After spending three days at Rameswar, Holy Mother returned to Madras, where she stayed for several days and took part in the birthday festival of Sri Ramakrishna. From Madras she went to Bangalore, where the Ramakrishna centre was situated in a quiet neighborhood. The grounds contained many fruit trees and flowering plants. Devotees, coming daily in large numbers to the monastery to pay their respects to her, offered flowers at her feet. At times these formed a mound. One afternoon as she was returning from a visit to a temple, her carriage stopped at the gate. When she had left the monastery, there was hardly a stranger there, but now the big compound was a sea of human heads. As the crowd heard the rumbling of the carriage, they prostrated themselves on the ground. Overwhelmed by their devotion, the Mother got out of the carriage. For five minutes she stood silently with her right hand lifted in the posture of bestowing her blessings on them. Slowly she went to the monastery building and sat in the hall in front of the shrine. The devotees also sat down. Everybody was silent. After a short while the Mother broke the silence and said to a young Swami who was seated near her: "What a pity I do not know their language! They would feel peace of mind if I could say a few words." As her words were translated to the devotees in English, they said: "No, no. This is very nice. Our hearts are filled with joy. There is no need of spoken words."

Another evening, Holy Mother and one or two companions climbed a hillock at the back of the monastery to look at the sunset. As soon as Swami Ramakrishnananda heard of this, he hurried to the place, prostrated himself before her, and recited a hymn to the Divine Mother. The Mother meditated there for a while at the request of the monk in charge of the place. This hillock is now regarded by devotees of the Mother with great veneration.

From Bangalore Holy Mother returned to Calcutta on

April 11, 1911, after spending a few days in Madras and Puri. The devotees in Calcutta were exceedingly pleased to have her back, and the inmates of the Belur Math gave her a grand welcome at the monastery.

The Mother spent about a month in Calcutta and then returned to Jayrambati to be present at the marriage of Radhu, which took place on June 10. On August 1, 1911, she suffered a grievous shock in the death of Swami Ramakrishnananda, who only a short while before had accompanied her on her pilgrimage to Rameswar. Before his death the Swami was brought to the Udbodhan while the Mother was at Jayrambati. He expressed an earnest desire to see her for the last time. But she did not come. Swami Ramakrishnananda, however, had a vision of her and exclaimed: "Ah, Mother has come." When informed of his death, Holy Mother said mournfully: "Alas, Sashi is gone. My back is broken." On October 13 of the same year Sister Nivedita died in Darjeeling. During the next nine years, death cruelly took further toll, as we shall see, of those who were dear to her.

In 1912 Holy Mother graced the Belur Math by her presence on the occasion of the worship of Mother Durgā. A few days later, on November 5, 1912, she left for Benares, where she lived for two and a half months in a two-storey house owned by a devotee. This time, too, as during her visit to South India, the Mother was accompanied by a number of devotees and relatives, including Radhu. She and the ladies lived on the second floor, and a monk, with some men devotees, on the ground floor. There were two Ramakrishna centres near by: the Advaita Āshrama, whose inmates devoted themselves mainly to scriptural study and meditation, and the Ramakrishna Mission Sevāshrama, which conducted a free hospital and dispensary for the poor. Holy Mother was taken in a palanquin around the different hospital wards donated by the generous public. She also saw the flower and kitchen gardens and the living quarters of the monastic workers. Swami Brahmananda, Swami Turiyananda, Swami Shivananda, and several other devotees were present when Holy Mother visited the Sevāshrama. Greatly pleased with the visit, she remarked: "Sri Ramakrishna is ever present in the place, and Mother Lakshmi always casts her benign glance upon it." She was told how the work had originally been started by a few young men who were inspired by letters of Swami Vivekananda, written from America, to dedicate their lives to the service of the sick and the needy, and who had only a few pennies to start the work with. She was also told that as their first patient they had picked up an old woman from the roadside and nursed her on the porch of a gentleman's house. The Mother was delighted to see how quickly the work had expanded in the course of a few years and drew the admiration of the whole country. "The place," she remarked, "is so beautiful that I feel like living here." After returning to her residence she sent a small donation for the Sevāshrama, which was accepted as her blessing.

The inmates of the Sevāshrama were talking about the Mother's appreciation of the institution when M arrived. He had often expressed the view that the Master did not approve of anyone's performing social service before the realization of God. One of the monks said to M: "Mother has just told us that the activities of the Home of Service were service to the Master himself and that he was tangibly present here. Now what do you say?" M replied, with a laugh: "How can I deny it any more?"

Swami Brahmananda used to visit Holy Mother's house every morning to inquire about her health. He would not go upstairs, where Holy Mother lived, for fear of being overwhelmed with emotion. Instead, he engaged in light talk with Golap-Mā or the servants. One morning he stood in the courtyard, in his usual place, and sent his respects upstairs to the Mother. Golap-Mā said: "Rakhal, the Mother asks why a devotee propitiates Śakti, the Divine Mother, at the beginning of worship." The Swami replied: "It is because the key to the knowledge of

Brahman is in the Divine Mother's keeping. There is no way of communing with Brahman unless the Mother graciously unlocks the door." Then he sang, like a God-intoxicated minstrel:

"O Mind, remain immersed in meditation on Śankari's[2] feet,
Remain immersed and escape the suffering of life.
All these three worlds are unreal and in vain you roam about them;
Meditate on the Divine Mother in your heart.
Kamalakanta[3] says: Sing the Mother's glory
And the world will become a river of bliss; in it paddle slowly."

As he sang, he danced in ecstasy and finally rushed out of the house crying: "Ho, ho, ho!" like one inebriated with God. The Mother, who was watching from the porch of the second floor, was delighted to see his fervour and his dancing.

Holy Mother paid her respects to the principal shrines of Benares. One day she visited Sarnath, about seven miles from the city, where Buddha preached his first sermon after attaining Nirvāna. Swami Brahmananda and three other devotees followed her in another carriage. The Mother went around the place looking at the various ruins associated with Buddha and his followers, and noticed that several European visitors, too, were doing so. Referring to the visitors, she said: "They built all this in a previous birth, and now they have come back again to see what they did centuries ago. They are speechless with wonder, admiring these amazing relics." While returning to Benares, Holy Mother, at the earnest request of Swami Brahmananda, exchanged carriages with him. On the road, the Swami's carriage had an accident, though nobody was seriously hurt. When the Mother heard about it she said: "I was fated for this mishap, but Rakhal, by force as it were, took it on his own

---

[2] The Consort of Śiva, an epithet of the Divine Mother.
[3] The writer of the song.

shoulders. I had several children with me; who knows what would have happened to them?"

In Benares Holy Mother was impressed by Chameli Puri, a very old monk. Golap-Mā asked him who provided him with his food. "Mother Durgā," the holy man answered in a strong voice. "Who else, do you think?" Holy Mother was delighted with his words and said later: "The face of that old man—I cannot forget it; it is just like a child's." After visiting him Holy Mother did not desire to visit any other holy man.

One day several women visitors called on Holy Mother and found her busy with her nephews and nieces. She asked Golap-Mā to mend her torn cloth. One of the visitors said: "Mother, we see you are terribly entangled in māyā." "What can I do?" she replied. "I myself am māyā." It is doubtful whether the visitor understood the meaning of the Mother's words.

Another day the inmates of the Mother's house were resting after their noonday meal when they heard someone crying sadly at a distance. The Mother looked outside and saw a beggar woman singing in a plaintive voice: "Where are You gone, my Mother?" The beggar came to her, saluted, and said: "My long-cherished hope has been fulfilled at last. I cannot tell you, Mother, how happy I am." When the Mother asked who she was, she replied that she was her beggar child and assured the Mother that she had no want. All she cared for was a little love for God. She further told the Mother that she had been hoping for a long time to see her, but was afraid that she, a mere beggar, would not be allowed in her presence. At the Mother's request she sang again, and was asked to visit her whenever she wished. A few days later the beggar woman arrived again, this time with a guava in her hand which she had received with her alms, and she offered it to the Mother. Holy Mother very graciously took the fruit, touched it to her head, and said: "The food one obtains by begging is very pure: the Master loved it. I will eat your fruit." "Mother, I am a mere beggar," the woman wept, "and you are so kind to me."

After her return from Benares, Holy Mother again plunged
into the activities of her spiritual ministry both in Calcutta and
in Jayrambati. She was now in her middle sixties and had never
been in robust health. The sun had crossed the meridian and
the time was not far off when it would sink below the horizon
and disappear from men's eyes. Perhaps she had a premonition
of this. In any case she poured her heart and soul into minister-
ing to the spiritual needs of those who sought her help. As we
have already seen, she made no distinction between high and
low, rich and poor, the sinner and the virtuous. All she expected from the aspirant was a longing to break the bonds of
the world and realize God. None was rejected who addressed
her as "Mother." Many came heavily laden with worldly afflictions. Many also came with yearning of soul to enjoy the bliss
of God. She bestowed upon all her guidance and blessing. She
treated them with kindness, patience, and forgiveness, and satisfied their demands. When disciples could not practise prayer
and meditation, she did it on their behalf. Willingly she suffered physical pain as a result of taking upon herself the burden
of their iniquity. Hers was a love that sought no tangible return
nor even a word of gratitude. Often she told the disciples that
she had assumed responsibility for them and would continue to
guide them, here and hereafter, till they attained liberation. It
was a spiritual relationship that knew no barrier of time or
place, caste or social position.

In 1918 Holy Mother was attacked with malarial fever at
Koalpara. It soon took a serious turn. Swami Saradananda and
Yogin-Mā arrived with a physician from Calcutta under whose
treatment she recovered within a short time.

On July 30, 1918, Swami Premananda died, and it took several days for the Mother to get over the shock. Shortly after,
Holy Mother returned to Jayrambati. There she began to follow
her usual routine: initiating new devotees, taking care of Radhu
and her child, and trying to meet the demands of her brothers,

her sisters-in-law, and her nephews and nieces. Everybody noticed she was losing physical strength and that she had to use a
cane while walking. To a disciple she said: "My child, I am
feeling more and more helpless every day. As my health is
breaking down, duties are multiplying." Very few, however,
realized that Holy Mother was turning the last pages of her life.

At Jayrambati she was frequently confined to her bed with
malaria. It was the time of the annual worship of Jagaddhātri.
In spite of her ill health she supervised the celebration for three
days, even to its minutest details. On the final day, before the
immersion, she whispered into the ear of the image: "Mother,
come again." A disciple, however, noticed that in the midst of
the worship the Mother was indrawn, her mind far away from
the excitement of the big celebration.

About this time Holy Mother made a permanent settlement
with her brothers about the site of her birth. She asked a
disciple to make plans for a building where, in future, the
monastic devotees would find shelter. Her attendants about this
time noticed a peculiarity in her conduct. She had never before
allowed anybody to partake of the food offering before the
worship. Now on several occasions she gave it to a boy or a
tame parrot before it was offered to the Master. When asked
about the reason she said that she saw the Master in them.
One day she gave her own pillow to a woman attendant for
her use with the remark: "The Master alone dwells in you all."
She was seeing Sri Ramakrishna in all creatures; her mind was
being lifted above physical appearances.

Every day, now, Holy Mother had a slight temperature. But
no one anticipated any serious trouble. December 13, 1919, was
her birthday. Several devotees came from outside for this auspicious occasion. She asked all to observe the day as quietly as
possible. In the morning she sponged her body with tepid water
and put on a new cloth sent by Swami Saradananda and accepted the offering of flowers from the devotees who were

present. In the evening her temperature rose again and she felt very tired. The fever persisted. But in spite of it all she did not stop initiating people.

As the Mother's condition worsened and local treatment produced no result, the attendants asked Swami Saradananda's advice. He decided to take her to Calcutta and sent several monks and householder devotees to accompany her. February 24, 1920, was fixed for her departure from Jayrambati, for good as it turned out.

In the morning Holy Mother finished the worship and made ready for the journey. A few of her relatives, including Radhu, and two devotees were in the party. Many villagers, men and women, came to see her and said: "Get well soon and come back. Please do not forget us long." "All depends on the Master's will," she replied. "Can I ever forget you?" She wrapped the Master's photograph in a cloth and saluted all the village deities. Slowly she walked through the village and got into a palanquin which was waiting outside. Turning her face towards the village she saluted Jayrambati.

As she passed through the villages on the road she bowed before the local deities. It was eleven o'clock when the party arrived at Koalpara. After spending the night there, early next morning she left for Vishnupur. Addressing a young disciple, she suddenly said: "My child, I am leaving Sarat behind." He could not understand the implication of her words. Another disciple accompanied the palanquin on his bicycle. About two in the afternoon she arrived in Vishnupur. On the road she had tried to eat some puffed rice; after taking a few grains she said: "I cannot chew any more." Evidently she was feeling very weak. The party spent two days at Vishnupur at the house of a disciple and reached Calcutta at nine o'clock on the evening of February 27.

Yogin-Mā and Golap-Mā looked at the Mother's emaciated body and said to her companions with a shudder: "What sort of Mother have you brought here? Her complexion has become almost black. She is nothing but skin and bones. We never thought she was in such a bad state." Next day Swami Saradananda took courage in both hands and began arrangements for the Mother's treatment. Various medicines were tried: homoeopathic, native, and allopathic. Noted physicians of Calcutta treated her. At last the illness was diagnosed as kala-azar, for which no treatment was then available. Swami Saradananda also arranged special religious rites; but her condition went from bad to worse. The temperature rose three or four times a day, and the Mother suffered from an excruciating sensation of burning. When the temperature was high she would become unconscious. Sometimes her attendants stroked her body after cooling their own hands with ice. Certain devotees asked the Mother to pray to Sri Ramakrishna for recovery. "How can I do that?" she replied. "Whatever he has ordained will happen. What can I say about it?" Another time she said: "When the Master takes me I shall go." On a third occasion, when a disciple begged her to ask Sri Ramakrishna for relief from her suffering, she said with a smile: "You have not seen how much he himself suffered from his illness. I saw it all with my own eyes."

But in the midst of all this suffering she never forgot the comfort and welfare of others. When in the morning a disciple would go to the physician to report her condition, she always asked him to eat something first, for it might be late before he returned. She always asked her attendants to serve the physicians with fruits and sweets after their visits. Whenever any devotee came from the direction of Jayrambati, she inquired about the rainfall there. There were many monks at the Udbodhan at that time to attend her, and they felt highly blessed if they could render her any personal service. But she was often reluctant to give anyone trouble on her account. One noon Holy Mother lay on her bed, half dozing, when an attendant began to fan her to put her to sleep. After a few minutes she said: "You may stop now; your hand must be aching." The attendant told her that he was quite all right and went on fanning. The Mother again asked him to stop. As he continued to fan, she said: "I cannot sleep at all; I am worried that your hand may be aching. If you do not fan me, I shall feel relieved and be able to sleep." Even in that state of health she initiated at least two disciples. A monastic disciple said: "When the Mother recovers from her illness we will stop this business of initiation. She suffers by taking others' sins upon herself." When the Mother heard this, she remarked: "Why should it be so? Was the Master born just to eat rasagollas?"[4]

On her sickbed she came to know about the death of Swami Adbhutananda on April 24, of Balaram Bose's son on May 14, and of her own brother Barada a week later. She wept at these sad pieces of news.

It was being noticed that Holy Mother was shaking off her attachments to the world, one by one. One day, when a disciple remarked about her suffering and her emaciated condition, she said: "Yes, my child, I am feeling very weak. It seems that what the Master wanted to be done through this body has been accomplished. My mind now wants him alone; it relishes nothing else. You know how much I loved Radhu and how much I have done for her comfort. Now my attitude has completely reversed. When she comes to me I feel annoyed and say to myself: 'Why is she here, trying to drag my mind down?' It was the Master who through all this kept my mind down to the world for his work; otherwise how could I possibly have lived after he was gone?"

Her displeasure at the sight of old friends gradually became manifest. Gauri-Mā, her companion of many years, used to visit her every morning with one of her disciples. One day, noticing them in her room, she said: "Don't touch me. Why do you come here daily and annoy me?" Gauri-Mā heard these words and was confounded. She said in a pained voice:

---

[4] A popular sweetmeat of Bengal.

"Mother, you are ill; we have no peace of mind. We want to be with you all the time, but we don't always find the leisure. So we come to see you in the morning." Holy Mother said: "What do you expect of me? I can't put up with any more botheration." "If you must come," she added a moment later, "do not enter my room. Just look at me from outside the door. Don't make me talk." Gauri-Mā burst into tears. From the following day she sat every morning for an hour outside the room. The Mother noticed this but did not relent.

Now came the turn of Radhu, the apple of her eye, her earthly support for the past twenty years, the companion of her daily life, whose prolonged absence she could not bear. Holy Mother wanted to snap the last bond of māyā. A few days before her death she said to Radhu: "Look here, Radhu, I want you to return to Jayrambati. Don't stay here any longer." Then she said to Sarala, a woman disciple attending her: "Tell Sarat to send her to Jayrambati." Sarala replied: "Why do you say that? Will you be able to live without Radhu?" The Mother said firmly: "Certainly, I have withdrawn my mind." The attendant reported the matter to Yogin-Mā and Swami Saradananda. Yogin-Mā went to the Mother and said: "Mother, why are you asking Radhu to go back?"

"Yogin, she shall have to live at Jayrambati afterwards. He [referring to a disciple] is going there. Send her with him. I have withdrawn my mind. I don't want her here any more."

"Mother, if you detach your mind, how shall we live?"

"Yogin, I have cut the chain of māyā. No more of this."

Yogin-Mā reported the whole thing to Swami Saradananda, who said with a deep sigh: "Now it will be impossible to keep Mother on earth any longer. As she has detached herself from Radhu, there is no hope whatsoever." Sarala was there. The Swami said to her: "See if you can direct her mind again to Radhu." But the effort was futile. The Mother said very clearly: "Know once for all that the mind which has been withdrawn will not come down again."

Holy Mother wanted her other nieces, Nalini and Maku, to return to Jayrambati too. Frightened by this new attitude, Nalini did not dare enter her room. Maku wept in a quiet corner. Nalini remarked: "If our presence hurts our aunt, we had better go away. But I don't know what people will say. They will criticize us for leaving her at this time." Swami Saradananda tried again to persuade the Mother and said: "Mother, these girls feel badly at the thought of going away when you are so ill. Let them stay awhile; they will go back to Jayrambati when you recover a little." "It would have been better," the Mother persisted, "if you had sent them away. All right, they must not come near me. I do not want to see even their shadow."

Now she was completely free of māyā and ready to depart. She showed the same detachment in all her actions. The Mother had been very fond of Radhu's child. One noon, ten days before her death, this child left his own mother asleep in the adjacent room, crawled to Holy Mother, and was about to climb on her body as was his wont, when the Mother noticed him and said: "Go away. Go. I have no attachment to any of you. You will not succeed any more." Then she said to an attendant: "Take him away. I do not relish this any longer."

The illness was becoming more and more serious every day. The Mother's body, thin and emaciated, almost blended with the bed. The physicians gave up all hope. Devotees began to flock to the Udbodhan from far and near. Holy Mother realized all this and made herself ready. During one of her previous illnesses she had remarked: "Maybe I shall have to suffer again like this." Now a favourite disciple said in an earnest voice: "Mother, you can live if you wish." "Who craves death?" came the quick reply. She had surrendered her will completely to the Divine Will and appeared to be awaiting the Master's final summons. Again and again she said: "I shall go when the call comes." Her last words to Radhu were: "I have cut the string. What can you do to me? Do you think I am a human being?" Radhu had always looked upon Holy Mother simply as her aunt; she could not grasp the import of these words.

A week before the final day, Holy Mother sent for Swami Saradananda at about half-past eight in the evening. The Swami came in, knelt on the left side of the Mother's feet, and was about to stroke her hands when Holy Mother caught the Swami's right hand under her left and said: "Sarat, I leave them all behind," and at once released his hand. Swami Saradananda controlled his tears with great effort, got up, tiptoed backward, and left the room.

Both men and women devotees attended the Mother. The men reported the Mother's condition to the physicians, procured the medicine, prepared her diet, and fanned her. The women cooked her rice, helped her to eat, washed her clothes, and fixed her bed. Holy Mother became like a child and often sulked. Once, at midnight, Sarala was about to feed her when the Mother said petulantly: "No, I will not eat. You always say the same thing: 'Mother, eat,' and put that stick[5] under my arm." The attendant asked if she should call Swami Saradananda. Still refusing to eat, she said: "Yes, bring Sarat, I will not eat from your hand." The Swami immediately came to the room. The Mother made him sit near her and asked him to stroke her body. Taking his two hands into her own she said: "See, my child, they give me no end of trouble. Always they say the same thing: 'Eat, eat.' And the only other thing they know is to put that stick under my arm. Please tell them not to annoy me any more." The Swami said very gently: "No, Mother, they won't annoy you again." A few minutes later Swami Saradananda asked: "Mother, will you eat a little now?" "Yes," she said. The Swami asked Sarala to bring the milk. The Mother said to him: "You feed me. I won't take it from her hand." The Swami took the feeding cup, poured a little of the liquid into her mouth, and said: "Mother, please rest a little and take your time." These gentle words pleased her and she said: "See

---

[5] Referring to the thermometer.

how sweet his words are—'Mother, take your time.' Can't they talk like that? How much trouble they give me! Now go to your room, child, and sleep." She stroked the Swami's body affectionately. The Swami put down the mosquito net and said he was leaving. The Mother again expressed her regret for the trouble he had had to take for her in the middle of the night. The Swami felt blessed that he could render her this last personal service. Until then he had served her only from a distance.

But Holy Mother's childish petulance went on. One day she said to Barada, her young attending disciple: "Don't go away from me. Always stay near. Sarala tortures me very much: always the same stick, and the same word 'eat.' I will not eat anything from her hand nor allow her to come near." She began to show this annoyance more and more. Swami Saradananda was worried. He came to the Mother, sat on her bed, took her hand in his lap, and said to her in a wheedling voice, as if she were a child: "Mother, Sarala is very much hurt. She will not put the stick under your arm again. This is your eating time. Who will feed you?" Turning to Barada, he said: "Bring the milk in the feeding cup. This time I shall feed her." The Mother said: "Why should you take the trouble? Barada will feed me. Bring the milk, Barada. I will drink it." As soon as the attendant poured the milk into her mouth, the Mother gave a start: the milk was a little too hot. Lest the Swami and the attendant should feel badly about it, she said: "Never mind, cool the milk a little. Barada can feed me very well."

Sarala easily assessed the whole situation and requested Swami Saradananda to change her duties. The Swami agreed. For the next two days she kept herself as far away from the Mother as possible while other attendants took on her duties. The Mother noticed her absence from the room and sent for her. When Sarala came in the Mother held her head, drew it to her bosom, and said: "My child, are you angry with me? If I have said anything that may have hurt you, forget it." Tears flowed from Sarala's eyes and she resumed her usual duties.

THE TEMPLE OF HOLY MOTHER AT THE BELUR MATH

THE BELUR MATH WITH THE TEMPLE OF SRI RAMAKRISHNA

The Temple of Holy Mother at Jayrambati

The rest is very simple, in keeping with the utter simplicity of the Mother's whole life. Her legs were swollen and she could not move from her bed. The girls of the Nivedita School began to nurse her by turns. It was only five days before the end.

A woman devotee who had known Sri Ramakrishna came. As no one was allowed to enter the sick-room, she stood at the door. When the Mother turned on her side, she saw the devotee and signed to her to come near. She came in, saluted the Mother, and said as she wept: "Mother, what will happen to us?" In a feeble voice Holy Mother said to her: "Why should you be afraid? You have seen the Master. What should frighten you?" Then she added very slowly: "Let me tell you something. My child, if you want peace, then do not look into anybody's faults. Look into your own faults. Learn to make the world your own. No one is a stranger, my child; the whole world is your own." This was Holy Mother's last message to suffering humanity.

For the last three days the Mother seldom uttered a word and always remained indrawn. She felt annoyed if anyone tried to draw her out. Gradually she lost the power of speech. Her last consoling words to a weeping attendant were: "Sarat is there; why should you be afraid?"

On Tuesday, July 21, 1920, about one o'clock in the morning, it became evident that Holy Mother's last moments were at hand. The attendants began to chant the Lord's name. Half an hour later the Mother breathed deeply several times and entered into deep samādhi. Peace-eyed slumber settled over her body, which, though ravaged by a long illness, suddenly relaxed and gave out a celestial light. Many of her devotees were deceived by this radiance and thought she was still with them.

Next morning, about half-past ten, the funeral procession was formed. Swami Saradananda and many devotees joined it. To the accompaniment of devotional music, the body was taken across the Ganges to the Belur Math. There the women devotees bathed it and dressed it in a new cloth. A funeral pyre of sandalwood was made on the bank of the river, to the north of Swami Vivekananda's memorial temple. About three o'clock the fire was lighted. Before the funeral was over it began to rain heavily on the other side of the Ganges and the devotees were afraid it might interfere with the cremation. But not a drop of rain fell on their side. At last the mournful ceremony was over and Swami Saradananda poured the first pitcher of water over the slow-burning fire. Then rain came in torrents and extinguished the last embers.

Three shrines now stand as memorials to Holy Mother, all erected by the loving care of her beloved child Swami Saradananda. One is the Udbodhan, where she spent the last eleven years of her active life. The second, a white temple, stands on the bank of the Ganges at the Belur Math where her body was consigned to fire. The third, another white temple, has been erected on the site of her birth at Jayrambati. From the top of this temple flutters a flag emblazoned with the simple word "Mā," reminding her devotees from far and near of her repeated assurance that she would stand by them till their hour of liberation, and recalling to them her words of benediction: "I am the Mother of the virtuous, I am the Mother of the wicked. Whenever you are in distress, say to yourself: 'I have a mother.'"

Glossary

Glossary

ADBHUTANANDA, SWAMI A monastic disciple of Sri Ramakrishna who at one time served Holy Mother at Dakshineswar; also known as Latu.

ARUPANANDA, SWAMI A monastic disciple of Holy Mother who served her for many years.

ĀSHRAMA A retreat for the practice of spiritual discipline.

ĀTMAN Self or Soul; denotes also the Supreme Soul, with which, according to non-dualistic Vedānta philosophy, the individual soul is identical in essence.

AVIDYĀ-MĀYĀ Māyā, or illusion causing duality, has two aspects, namely, avidyā-māyā and vidyā-māyā. Avidyā-māyā, or the "māyā of ignorance," consisting of anger, passion, and so on, entangles a man in worldliness. Vidyā-māyā, or the "māyā of knowledge," consisting of kindness, purity, unselfishness, and so on, leads him to liberation from the bondage of the world. Both belong to the relative world.

BABU A term of respect used when addressing a man, like "Mr." in English.

BABURAM A foremost monastic disciple of Sri Ramakrishna, who later was known as Swami Premananda.

BARADA A monastic disciple of Holy Mother who attended her for some years; also a brother of Holy Mother.

BEL A tree whose leaves are sacred to Śiva.

BELUR MATH The headquarters of the Ramakrishna Math and Mission, near Calcutta.

BETEL LEAF A leaf chewed with spices after meals as a digestive.

BHAGAVAD GITĀ A well-known Hindu scripture, comprising eighteen chapters of the epic *Mahābhārata*.

BHAGAVATI   An epithet of the Divine Mother.

BHAKTI   Love of God. It is one of the main spiritual disciplines of Hinduism. The devotee loves God with heart and soul, expecting no worldly return from Him.

BRAHMĀ   The Creator God; the First Person of the Hindu Trinity, of which the other two members are Vishnu and Śiva.

BRAHMACHĀRI   A religious student, or novice, devoted to the practice of spiritual discipline.

BRAHMAN   The Absolute; the Supreme Reality of Vedānta philosophy.

BRAHMANANDA, SWAMI   A foremost monastic disciple of Sri Ramakrishna, President of the Ramakrishna Math and Mission (1901–1922); formerly known as Rakhal.

BRIHADĀRANYAKA UPANISHAD   One of the principal Upanishads, or philosophical scriptures, of the Hindus.

CAR FESTIVAL   An important Hindu religious festival in which three deities—Krishna, His brother Balarāma, and His sister Subhadrā—are placed in a chariot and drawn by devotees.

CHĀPĀTIS   The Indian home-made bread. The making of this bread is a sort of chore. First flour is kneaded; then small balls are made, which are flattened on a board with a rolling-pin; finally it is baked over charcoal.

CHRISTINE, SISTER   An American disciple of Swami Vivekananda; her original name was Miss Christine Greenstidel.

COSMIC CYCLE   The chain of cosmic evolution and dissolution.

DAKSHINESWAR   A village near Calcutta where the temple of Kāli is located at which Sri Ramakrishna spent most of his life.

DEVAMATA, SISTER   An American disciple of Swami Paramananda; her original name was Miss Laura F. Glenn.

DEVI   (*Lit.*, Goddess.) A generic title for high-caste Hindu women.

DEVOTEE   The word is used in this book to denote one devoted to God, generally a follower of the path of love. A devotee of Holy Mother is one who is devoted to her and follows her teachings. The word *disciple*, when used in connection with Holy Mother, refers to one who has been initiated by her into spiritual life and regards her as his guru, or teacher.

DHARMA   Generally translated by such terms as "religion," "duty," "nature"; in Hinduism it denotes the law of inner growth determined by a man's actions in his past lives, which influences his present way of life.

DISCIPLE   See devotee.

DURGĀ   An aspect of the Divine Mother; Her worship is observed by Hindus, mostly in Bengal.

GADAI   Shortened from Gadadhar, the early name of Sri Ramakrishna.

GAURI-MĀ   A woman disciple of Sri Ramakrishna.

GIRISH GHOSH   A foremost householder disciple of Sri Ramakrishna, famous in Bengal as a playwright and actor.

GOLAP-MĀ   A woman disciple of Sri Ramakrishna, a member of Holy Mother's household in Calcutta; also called Golāp.

GOPĀLA   A name of the Baby Krishna.

GOPĀLER-MĀ   A foremost elderly woman disciple of Sri Ramakrishna. Mā means literally mother.

GURU   Spiritual teacher.

HARI   God; a name of Vishnu representing the preserving aspect of the Godhead.

HRIDAY   The son of Sri Ramakrishna's sister, and his attendant for many years.

INDRA   The king of the gods.

INITIATION   The imparting of a holy name or sacred formula to stimulate a disciple's spiritual consciousness.

ISHTA   The Chosen Ideal.

JAGADDHĀTRI   (Lit., The Support of the Universe.) An aspect of the Divine Mother.

JAPA   Repetition of God's name.

JAYRAMBATI   Holy Mother's birthplace.

KĀLI   A name of the Divine Mother; the presiding deity of the Dakshineswar temple.

KALIKRISHNA   A disciple of Holy Mother, later known as Swami Virajananda; he served as President of the Ramakrishna Math and Mission (1938–1951).

KALIYUGA   According to Hindu mythology, the last of the four cycles of the universe. In it there is a minimum of virtue and a preponderance of vice. The world is said to be now passing through the Kaliyuga.

KAMARPUKUR Sri Ramakrishna's birthplace.

KARMA Action in general; the law of karma signifies the law of cause and effect.

KARMA-YOGI A follower of the path of action, by which one seeks to realize God through action without attachment.

KAUŚALYĀ The mother of Rāma.

KRISHNA One of the ideal deities of the Vaishnavas, or worshippers of Vishnu, and the teacher of the Bhagavad Gitā.

LAKSHMI The Consort of Vishnu and Goddess of Fortune; also the name of Sri Ramakrishna's niece.

LATU A monastic disciple of Sri Ramakrishna; see Swami Adbhutananda.

LIBERATION Mukti, or freedom from the bondage of the world; the goal of spiritual practice.

LOTUS FEET An honorific expression.

M Mahendranath Gupta, a foremost householder disciple of Sri Ramakrishna, chronicler of The Gospel of Sri Ramakrishna.

MAHĀBHĀRATA The famous Indian epic which includes the Bhagavad Gitā.

MAHĀMĀYĀ The Great Enchantress; a name of the Divine Mother of the Universe. Mahāmāyā is the potency of Brahman; in one aspect She casts a veil over the eyes of creatures to perpetuate the creation; in another aspect She liberates them from the snares of the world.

MAKU One of Holy Mother's nieces.

MALLICK, SAMBHU A wealthy householder disciple of Sri Ramakrishna, one of the suppliers of his personal needs.

MANTRA A sacred word or formula associated with a name of God or of a deity. A mantra is used in japa.

MĀRHĀṬṬĀ An inhabitant of Mahārāshtra in Western India,

MATH Monastery.

MĀYĀ (Lit., illusion.) A term of Vedānta philosophy denoting ignorance obscuring the vision of Reality; the cosmic illusion on account of which the One appears as the many, the Absolute as the relative.

MIRĀBĀI A great mediaeval woman saint of the Vaishnava sect, who was a worshipper of Sri Krishna.

NAG MAHĀSAYA   An outstanding householder disciple of Sri Ramakrishna.

NAHABAT   A two-storey building near the northwest corner of the Dakshineswar temple, originally intended for the playing of religious music, where Sarada Devi mostly lived while at Dakshineswar. There is a similar structure at the southwest corner of the temple grounds.

NALINI   A niece of Holy Mother.

NĀRĀYANA   A name of Vishnu.

NAREN   Short for Narendranath Datta (1863–1902), the foremost monastic disciple of Sri Ramakrishna, subsequently world-famous as Swami Vivekananda.

NIRVIKALPA SAMĀDHI   The highest state of samādhi, in which the aspirant realizes his total oneness with Brahman or Ultimate Reality.

NIVEDITA, SISTER   (*Lit.*, the Dedicated One.) The name given by Swami Vivekananda to Margaret E. Noble, an Irish disciple.

PADDY   Unhusked rice.

PĀNDAVAS   The five sons of Pāndu: King Yudhisthira, Arjuna, Bhima, Nakula, and Sahadeva. They are among the chief heroes of the epic *Mahābhārata.*

PICE   An Indian copper coin, one fourth of an ānnā and one sixty-fourth of a rupee, under the old system.

PRAKRITI   Primordial Nature, which, in association with Purusha, the eternal Conscious Principle, creates the universe.

PRASĀD   Food or drink that has been offered to the Deity or a holy person. It is supposed to possess spiritual efficacy.

PREMANANDA, SWAMI   *See* Baburam.

PUJĀ   Ritualistic worship.

PURUSHA   The Eternal Conscious Principle, from the union of which with Prakriti, or Primordial Nature, the universe evolves. Also denotes the soul or the Absolute.

RĀDHĀ   Shortened form of Rādhikā; Sri Krishna's most intimate companion among the gopis or cowherd girls of Vrindavan.

RADHARANI   The daughter of Holy Mother's brother Abhay, who lived with her both in Jayrambati and in Calcutta. Also known as Radhu and Radhi.

RADHI   *See* Radharani.

RADHU　*See* Radharani.

RĀJĀ　King; a title of distinction.

RAKHAL　A foremost young disciple of Sri Ramakrishna, later known by the monastic name of Swami Brahmananda.

RĀMA　The hero of the epic *Rāmāyana*; regarded by the Hindus as a Divine Incarnation.

RĀMĀYANA　An important Hindu epic depicting the story of Rāma.

RAMESWAR　An elder brother of Sri Ramakrishna; also a sacred place situated at the southern tip of India.

RAMLAL　A son of Rameswar; nephew of Sri Ramakrishna and priest in the Kāli temple at Dakshineswar.

RĀNI　Queen.

RĀVANA　The monster-king of Lankā, or Ceylon, who forcibly abducted Sitā, the wife of Rāma.

RUDRA　A manifestation of Śiva.

SACRED THREAD　A cluster of threads worn over the left shoulder by men of the three upper castes of Hindu society after a special initiation ceremony during their boyhood.

SĀDHANĀ　Spiritual discipline.

SĀDHU　Holy man; a monk.

ŚAKTI　The Creative Power of Brahman; an epithet of the Divine Mother of the Universe.

SAMĀDHI　Ecstasy, trance, communion with God.

SARADANANDA, SWAMI　One of Sri Ramakrishna's monastic disciples formerly known as Sarat; he was Holy Mother's chief attendant for many years and Secretary of the Ramakrishna Math and Mission from 1898 to 1927.

SARAJUBALA　A woman disciple of Holy Mother.

SARALA　A woman disciple and attendant of Holy Mother.

SARASVATI　The Goddess of Wisdom and Music.

SARAT　*See* Saradananda, Swami.

SĀRI　The Indian woman's garment, which consists of a single length of cloth.

SIBU　Shortened form of Sivaram, *q.v.*

SIVARAM　Youngest son of Rameswar, and nephew of Sri Ramakrishna.

SHIVANANDA, SWAMI　A disciple of Sri Ramakrishna; second President of the Ramakrishna Math and Mission (1922–1934). His premonastic name was Tarak.

SHYAMASUNDARI   The mother of Holy Mother.

SIMHAVĀHINI   (*Lit.*, She whose bearer is the lion.) A name of the Divine Mother Durgā.

ŚISHYA   Disciple.

SITĀ   The wife of Rāma.

ŚIVA   (*Lit.*, the Good One.) God as the Destroyer, in Hindu mythology; the Third Person of the Hindu Trinity, which is composed of Brahmā, Vishnu, and Śiva. He is a symbol of renunciation and benignity.

SWAMI   (*Lit.*, Master.) A title of monks belonging to the Vedānta school.

TARAK   *See* Shivananda, Swami.

TOTAPURI   The monk who initiated Sri Ramakrishna into monastic life.

UDBODHAN   The house built in Calcutta for Holy Mother by Swami Saradananda, named after the Bengali monthly magazine *Udbodhan,* which is published there.

UPANISHADS   The philosophical scriptures of the Hindus.

VAISHNAVA   A worshipper of Vishnu.

VĀLMIKI   The author of the *Rāmāyana.*

VEDĀNTA   (*Lit.*, the conclusion or the essence of the Vedas.) A system of philosophy discussed in the Upanishads, the Brahma Sutras, and the Bhagavad Gitā.

VIDYĀ-MĀYĀ   The "māyā of knowledge." *See* Avidyā-māyā.

VINĀ   A stringed musical instrument.

VISHNU   God as the Preserver; the Second Person of the Hindu Trinity, which is composed of Brahmā, Vishnu, and Śiva; the Personal God of the Vaishnavas.

VIVEKANANDA, SWAMI   *See* Naren.

VRINDAVAN   A town in North India associated with Sri Krishna's childhood.

YOGA   Union of the individual soul and the Universal Soul; also the method by which to realize this union.

YOGAMĀYĀ   Śakti, or the Divine Power.

YOGANANDA, SWAMI   *See* Yogen.

YOGEN   An outstanding devotee of Sri Ramakrishna, initiated

by Holy Mother; he associated intimately with Sri Ramakrishna; later known as Swami Yogananda.

YOGIN *See* Yogin-Mā.

YOGIN-MĀ A woman disciple of Sri Ramakrishna and close associate of Holy Mother; also called Yogin.

INDEX

Index

Abhaycharan, 119
Adbhutananda, Swami, 262-64, 314.
 See also Latu
Ahalyābāi, 8
Amjad, 134-35
Andal, 6
Arupananda, Swami, 157, 206 ff.

Barada (Brother), 121
Belur Math, 114, 240-241. *See also*
 Ramakrishna Order
Bhairavi Brahmani, 31
Bhanu, 25, 53-54
Brahmananda, Swami, 258, 307-08
Bull, Mrs. Ole, 59

Chandra Devi, 26, 48

Devamata, 281-83

food, 223

Gāndhāri, 10
Gauri-Mā, 62, 157-59, 279, 314-15
Ghosh, Girish, 271-75
God, Motherhood of, 80
Golap-Mā, 59, 61, 67, 69-70, 86,
 181, 288
Gopāler-Mā, 64, 278-79
grace, 231-32
Greenstidel, Christine, 281
Gupta, Mahendranath, 277

Harish, 106
Hindu women: religious status of, 2;
 social status of, 3-4
Holy Mother: birth centenary of, 1;
 various visions, 91-92, 96, 104,
 107; visit to Puri, 108, 111; life at
 Jayrambati, 116 ff., 130, 132 ff.,

at Koalpara, 135-36; spiritual ministry of, 153 ff.; as mother, 153
ff.; as teacher, 166-67, 170 ff.; attitude towards India's freedom
movement, 167-70; attitude towards marriage, 178, 227; advice
to monks, 179 ff.; as divinity, 185
ff.; attitude towards Sri Ramakrishna, 214-15; relationship with
Ramakrishna Order, 243 ff.; advice to householders, 273; en-
couraging of work, 229; her
language, 234-35; her humour,
237-38; personal appearance of,
287-88; respect for tradition, 290-
292; life at Jayrambati, 296; as
mother, wife, and nun, 297-98;
visit to South India, 302 ff.; at
Rameswar, 304; last visit to Benares, 306-09; farewell to Jayrambati, 312; medical treatment in
Calcutta, 313; death of, 319. See
also *Sarada Devi*
Hriday, 27, 28, 32, 37

japa, 219 ff.

Kalikumar, 120-23, 192 ff.
Koalpara, 243-44

Lakshmi-Didi, 62
Latu, 65. *See also* Adbhutananda,
 Swami

M, *see* Gupta, Mahendranath
MacLeod, Josephine, 280-81
Maitreyi, 15
Maku, 124
meditation, 219 ff.
Mirā, 9